SOUS VIDE

COOKBOOK

Effortless Home-Cooked Meals
Made on Low Temperature

From Beginner to Master With
500+ Easy-to-Copy Delicious

MARK ROSS

Copyright @ 2021 All rights reserved

The content contained within this book may not be reproduced, duplicated or transmitted without direct written permission from the author or the publisher. Under no circumstances will any blame or legal responsability be held against the publisher, or author, for any damages, reparation, or monetary loss due to the information contained within this book, either directly or indirectly.

Legal Notice

This book is copyright protected. It is only for personal use. You cannot amend, distribute, sell, use, quote or paraphrase any part, or the content within this book, without the consent of the author or publisher.

Disclaimer Notice

Please note the information contained within this document is for educational and entertainment purposes only. All efforts have been executed to present accurate, up to date, reliable, complete information. No warranties of any kind are declared or implied. Readers acknowledge that the author is not engaged in the rendering of legal, finalcial, medical, or professional advice. The content within this book has been derived from various sources. Please consult a licensed professional before attempting any techniques outlined in this book . By reading this document, the reader agrees that under no circumnstances is the author responsible for any losses, direct or indirect, that are incurred as a result of the use of the information contained whithin this document , including, but not limited to, errors, omissions, or inaccuracies.

Designed by

MSHdesigns - mshdesignspk@gmail.com

CONTENTS

INTRODUCTION — 04

CHAPTER 1 SOUS VIDE COOKING — 06

CHAPTER 2 EGGS AND DIARY — 12

CHAPTER 3 VEGETABLES AND SIDES — 33

CHAPTER 4 POULTRY — 57

CHAPTER 5 PORK — 78

CHAPTER 6 BEEF AND LAMB — 104

CHAPTER 7 GOURMET RECIPES — 132

CHAPTER 8 DRINKS AND DESSERTS — 165

CHAPTER 9 RUBS, SAUCES AND DRESSINGS — 199

MEASUREMENT CONVERSIONS — 217

INTRODUCTION

Sous Vide is a French term that means "under vacuum," and it refers to a way of cooking a dish at a precise temperature and time. Your food should be cooked at the temperature at which it will be eaten. Essentially this method entails placing food in vacuum seal bags and boiling it for longer than ordinary cooking durations in a specially prepared water bath (usually 1 to 7 hours, up to 48 or more in some cases). Cooking at a precise temperature guarantees a flawless meal. You can effortlessly cook your steak, chicken, lamb, hog, and other meats exactly the way you like them.

It is simple to use and consistently produces excellent results. You'll have food that's more tender and juicier than anything else you've ever cooked. This method will boost your usual cooking to a higher level. Most of the time, you don't need fancy ingredients to make a great dish; it's just a matter of getting the most out of the ingredients you already have.

One of the advantages about sous vide cooking is that you don't need to stay in the kitchen all the time. When the meal is wrapped in a bag and placed in the water bath, it can be left to cook on its own at a low temperature without requiring your supervision. Sous Vide Cookers, which are now widely accessible, are capable of changing the ideal emperature for cooking food according to texture while keeping the minimum required temperature. As a result, while your meal is cooking, you may prepare some other foods or spend your time elsewhere. It's a useful skill to master, and it's well worth the effort. If this is your first time, don't be discouraged if you don't receive the desired outcomes. Gaining expertise with this cookbook can help you improve. And the best part of learning this cooking method is that it is a very tasty journey! Patience, the appropriate information, and consistency are the keys to success. Since this technique does not use extra fats during the preparation of your dish, the meals cooked with Sous Vide are both tasty and healthful. Using a low temperature also guarantees that the proper cooking point is attained.

When you cook sous vide, you don't have to guess whether the components are cooked or not. This method is suitable for all foods such; you will easily cook meals with pasta, meat, seafood, veggies, eggs, and much more. Without worrying about overcooking or undercooking your food, you may prepare meals ahead of time and cook them according to your lunch time. It enables you to get the most out of your dish by determining how long each component will take to cook. Despite the fact that your components will be packed in a bag for longer time than usual, you won't have to worry about bacteria contaminating them. When you utilize this method you know exactly what goes into and what comes out of your food.

For the modern cook, the Sous Vide cooker offers numerous advantages. In general Sous Vide Cooking at home will definitely change your culinary life.

1. SOUS VIDE COOKING

In general, the practice of vacuum sealing food to extend its shelf life has been around for quite some time. However, it was not widely used as a cooking method until the 1940s. Even after that, it took a lot of trial and error before people began to cook vacuum-sealed food in a pot of boiling water.

The origins of the Sous Vide technique as a cooking method may thus be traced back to the mid-1970s when Chef Georges Praulus attempted to design a cooking technology that would prevent costly shrinking while also assisting in the creation of an optimal cooking environment for cooking Foie Gras! The technology of Sous Vide cooking was not limited to him. Chef Bruno Goussault took up the technique soon after Praulus presented it to the world, refining it to the point where he could utilize Sous Vide to prepare meals for Air France's first-class passengers. Bruno worked tirelessly to promote this new approach to the broader market after recognizing its huge potential. Despite its widespread popularity, it remained an expensive technique for common people to afford, and it took two years of development until it completely broke through the barriers and became one of the "Best" cooking techniques ever created.

Contrary to common assumption, thanks to a huge number of economical Sous Vide circulators available in the market, anyone can pick up the device and start experimenting with Sous Vide cooking.

WHAT IS IT AND HOW DOES IT WORK?

Despite its current popularity, the Sous Vide cooking technique continues to stun newcomers. The term "Sous Vide" means "Under Vacuum" in French. The name itself is inspired by the procedure that is employed in Sous Vide cooking.

One of the most significant distinctions between Sous Vide and other traditional cooking methods is that with Sous Vide you will be required to place all your ingredients in a zip bag or a canning mason jar and seal them in such a way that a vacuum is generated within.

This sealed vessel is then immersed in water that is precisely heated to a specific temperature using a Sous Vide circulator resulting in perfect cooking every time.

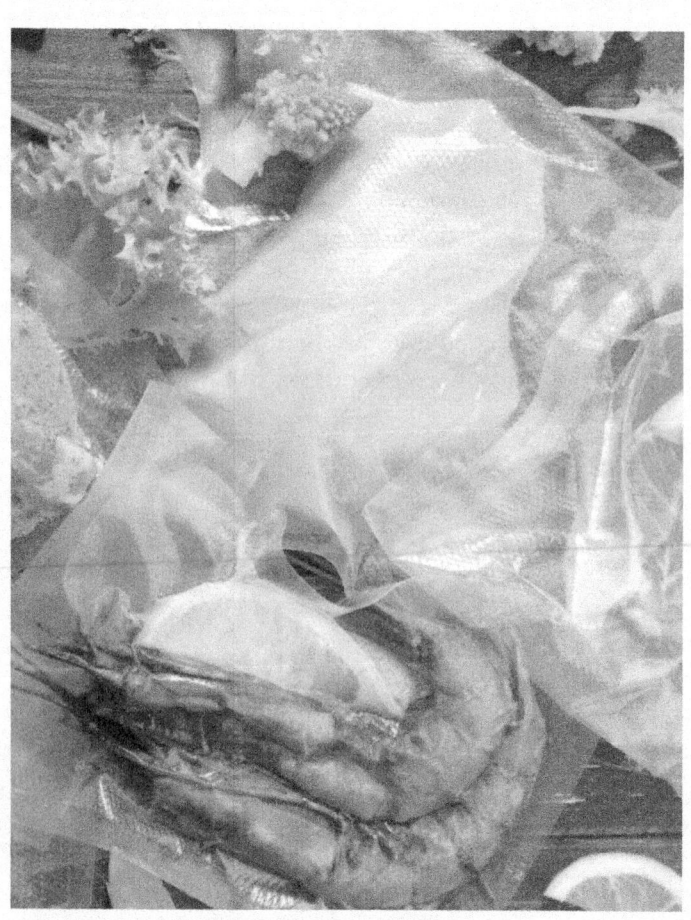

ESSENTIAL SOUS VIDE

There is a widespread misperception that Sous Vide cooking needs much of expensive equipment and tools to be successfully performed. While it is true that ultra-expensive equipment exists that allows you to prepare even more "luxury" meals, you can still obtain very good results without blowing your budget.

Sous Vide circulators have become incredibly cheap and affordable thanks to technical improvements (you can acquire some nice ones for as little as $60), making it easier for the broader public to get into Sous Vide cooking.

Aside from the circulator, you'll only need a few other parts of equipment, all of which can be acquired at a low cost in the supermarket or online.

The Circulator for Sous Vide Cooking is the heart of Sous Vide cooking.

The main functions of these gadgets is to precisely heat your water bath to a set temperature and keep it during the cooking procedure.

The water is additionally circulated by the circulator to ensure that the heat is equally distributed.

However, if you're looking for a Sous Vide circulator for the first time, the following are the greatest options right now.

Anova Wi-Fi Precision Cooker: When it first came out, the Anova Wi-Fi Circulator was the top in the Sous Vide market, and it took the globe by storm. Aside from the obvious cooking capabilities, other features such as Bluetooth or Wi-Fi connectivity, which allows for wireless control, round out the package, making it ideal for novices.

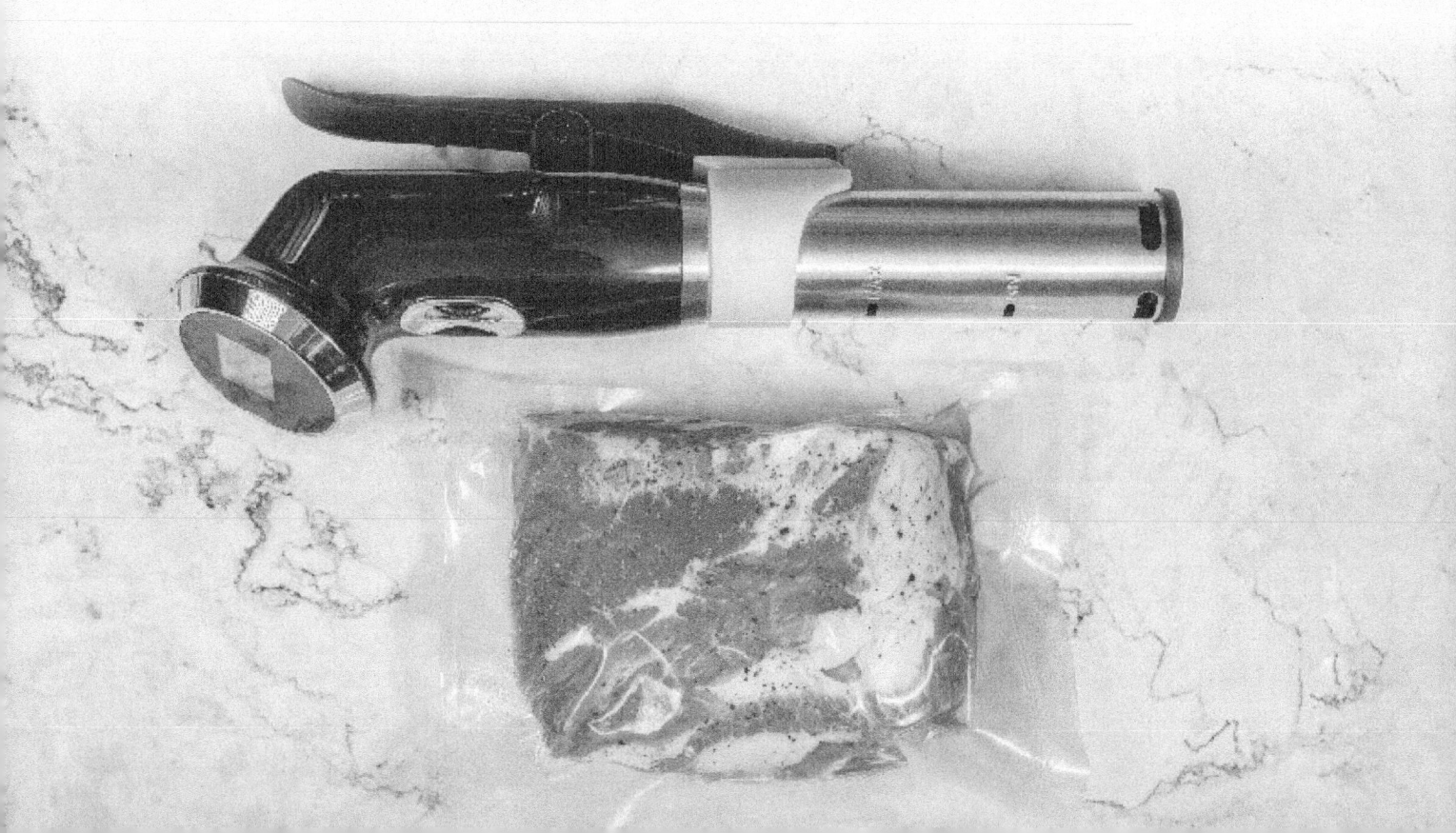

Chef Steps Joule: While the Anova is the most popular device, the Chef Steps Joule is the first in the "Smart Kitchen" scene! Aficionados fell in love with this device as soon as it was released, because of its small size and extensive set of capabilities.

Gourmia Sous Vide Pod: If you're on a budget, the Gourmia is the best option. This Sous Vide circulator includes all of the fundamental features you'd expect without sacrificing the "Cool" appearance!

Apart from the circulator, the following are some of the other key materials you will require.

A large container: you'll need a good quality container to make your water bath and submerge your vacuum-sealed bag or jar and cook the contents. As a result, a good quality 8-12-quart stockpot is recommended. Another option is a 12-quart square polycarbonate food storage container. In any case, be sure you get a container that can hold water that's been heated up to 203º Fahrenheit. Preferably use a container with lid as the water evaporates.

Resealable bags and jars: Once you've decided on a container, the resealable bags and sealing jars are the next goods you'll need.

When it comes to bags, you should choose heavy-duty, resealable bags that can withstand temperatures up to 195º Fahrenheit. If at all feasible, purchase bags that are labeled "Freezer Safe" and have a double seal. You can choose between different kind of plastic bags but they have to be BPA FREE.

There is also the chance to buy vacuum sealed bags but in that case you should have also a vacuum sealer!

Concerning jars simply choose mason jars or canning jars with a tight cap for the jars.

Cast Iron Pan: Because some recipes call for searing your dish after Sous Vide cooking, having a Cast Iron Pan on hand is optional but very useful.

Alternatively, a blowtorch can be used to create a brown texture.

THE BASICS OF SOUS VIDE COOKING

While some recipes will require you to deviate from the technique, the following are the basic steps to follow when using the Sous Vide Device to cook.

- Prepare the container and fill with water. Check with the Circulator you choose and make sure the water level is only 1 inch higher than the circulator's minimum watermark.

- Sous Vide cooking can be done in a Dutch oven, plastic storage containers, stockpot, or large saucepan.

- Select a temperature: Set the temperature of your circulator to the temperature specified in your recipe.

- Turn on the device and wait for the water bath to achieve the proper temperature; this should take 20-30 minutes, depending on your device.

- Season and vacuum seal the meal: Season the food according to the recipe, then vacuum seal it in zip bags or canning jars.

- Submerge the food underwater and cover the container with plastic wrap once the necessary water level has been attained and your bags have been sealed.

- Wait as indicated in the Directionss. Once the time has passed take your bag out and add some finishing touches.

Learning About Sealing Techniques

While you can certainly utilize stylish systems to automatically seal your zip bags, you can also vacuum seal bags using the method described below.

Water Immersion Procedure called also Archimedes Principle Method. The procedure is as follows:

- Start by putting the ingredients in your bag.
- Begin gently submerging the bag in water, keeping the upper segment (the enclosure) above water.
- As you continue to submerge the bag underwater, the water's pressure will gradually drive out any air that may be present in the zip bag.
- Only submerge it up to the zipper, then swiftly close it, ensuring that no water has entered the bag.
- That's all you need to do. It is as simple as that.

When it comes to canning jars, you'll need to know how to use the Finger Tip Tight Technique.

Finger Tip Tight: To tighten jars, use the Finger Tip method.

To use this approach, simply tighten the lid of your jar slowly and carefully, stopping just as you begin to feel the tiniest amount of resistance.

This is to ensure that the air inside the jar can leak after it is submerged.

BENEFITS OF SOUS VIDE

The sous vide cooker provides many benefits for the modern cook. The sous vide method is suited to cook at temperatures between 0 and 122° Fahrenheit. You will have perfectly cooked food every time.

When you use the sous vide method you seal your food in a vacuum-sealed bag. This will not only make your food safe from air, but it will also help with consistent cooking times and temperatures. The sous vide method lets you cook foods without the fear of overcooking. If you are cooking something that comes out unevenly, you can simply adjust your temperature to get back to the desired temperature range.

Principles Benefits of Cooking Sous Vide:

1. Promotes healthy eating habits because the food can be cooked slowly with gentle heat. At higher temperatures there is an increasing loss of vitamins and nutrients in foods such as meats, fish, and vegetables.
2. Perfect way to cook for busy families because you don't need to check the process.
3. Allows to prepare different types of foods in the same cooking session.
4. Easy to prepare even for beginners because provides with a larger variety of recipes than other cooking methods such as grilling or frying food
5. Affordable way to create gourmet meals.
6. Proven method to get better taste and texture to meat
7. Allows to cook even in the winter, or when it's hot outside because sous vide is not affected by changes in the humidity of the kitchen.
8. Recipes can be tailored perfectly to your taste. Certain parts of a recipe can be added or removed to get

exactly the results you want.

9. Incredibly versatile tool that can be used for many different kinds of cooking. It's perfect for braises, stews, and even bread-based recipes, to name a few.

10. Allows to use cuts of meat you may not have otherwise considered.

11. Allows to put food in straight from the freezer.

When it comes to cooking, the sous-vide method offers several advantages over other techniques that are commonly used. If you've never used a sous vide device before, be prepared for some initial bumps in the road – but once you've come up with a few simple recipes, you'll find that your time spent preparing meals is much shorter and more efficient.

One of the biggest advantages of sous-vide cooking is that it allows for precise control. Because the dish is sealed in an airtight bag or container, you're able to orchestrate the cooking curve precisely.

You can adjust the temperature and time to ensure that the food is cooked through completely without overcooking or undercooking any part of your dish.

It will also let you cook in a controlled environment that's inaccessible to bacteria and other microorganisms. This allows you to prepare dishes safely without having to use unusual cleaners or techniques that might damage your food.

THE HEALTH BENEFITS OF SOUS VIDE COOKING

While the above-mentioned advantages focused on the general aspects of Sous Vide, the following will provide you an elaborate outline of the health benefits of accompanying Sous Vide.

- While cooking with Sous Vide devices, you won't need to add any kind of additional fats needed in other methods. This immediately eliminates the need for using harmful oils that increase the cholesterol levels of the food, making Sous Vide meals much healthier.

- Exposing ingredients to heat, oxygen, and water causes them to lose a lot of vital nutrients, leading to over-carbonization of meats and vitamin/antioxidant loss in vegetables. The vacuum sealing technique that is implemented while cooking with Sous Vide prevents this from happening, as the food is not exposed to any water or oxygen. As a result, the nutritional contents are preserved to near-perfect levels.

- Sous Vide cooked meals are easier to digest, as it helps to break down the collagen proteins into gelatin, which is easier for our body to digest and absorb.

- Undercooking is very harmful, as it not only leads to unpleasant tasting food but also causes the foods to be overrun by bacteria and viruses. The vacuum seal of Sous Vide prevents this from happening, and the oxygen that is required for the pathogens to live is sucked out. The precise cooking technique ensures that you are getting perfectly cooked meals every single time.

TIPS TO SEAR MEAT STEAKS

Once you have cooked STEAK MEAT as indicated, do not forget to sear the meat. It is necassary to dry up the meat before searing it and then proceed. To sear the steak you can choose between:

- A torch
- A cast-iron oan
- A BBQ

Searing is not made for the look but especially for the flavor so DO NOT SKIP STEP and you steak will be EXCELLENT!

2. EGGS AND DAIRY

1. EGGS CHEESY MIX

 1 HOUR   5 MIN   4

NUTRITION:
CAL: 229 | FAT: 17 | PROTEIN: 10

INGREDIENTS
- 4 eggs, whisked
- 1 tbsp chives, chopped
- salt and black pepper to the taste
- ½ cup heavy cream
- ½ cup mozzarella, shredded

DIRECTIONS
1. Combine the cream, eggs, and other ingredients in a mixing dish, whisk well, and pour into a sous vide bag.
2. Seal the bag, cook for 1 hour at 170 °F, and serve for breakfast.

2. EGG OMELETTE WITH CHERRY TOMATOES

 40 MIN   15 MIN   6

NUTRITION:
CAL: 152 | FAT: 10 | PROTEIN: 16

INGREDIENTS
- 1 cup cherry tomatoes
- 10 eggs
- ½ cup milk
- 1 tsp salt
- 1 tsp ground black pepper
- ½ tsp nutmeg
- 1 tsp butter
- 1 tbsp chives
- 2 tbsp sour cream

DIRECTIONS
1. Wash the cherry tomatoes and cut them into the halves.
2. Then crack the eggs into the mixing bowl and whisk them.
3. Add milk, salt, ground black pepper, nutmeg, and sour cream.
4. Mix the mixture up.
5. Add the cherry tomatoes halves.
6. Then add the chives and butter.
7. Pour the egg mixture into the zipper lock bag.
8. Then preheat the Sous Vide to 170ºF.
9. When the water is preheated put the bag with the egg mixture there and cook it for 30 minutes.
10. When the omelet is cooked remove it from the sous vide and chill for 5 minutes.
11. Then discard the dish from the bag, cut it into the serving pieces.
12. Serve it!

3. SHALLOT SCRAMBLE

 1 HOUR   5 MIN   4

NUTRITION:
CAL: 145 | FAT: 13 | PROTEIN: 14

INGREDIENTS
- 4 eggs, whisked
- ½ cup shallots, chopped
- salt and black pepper to the taste
- ½ cup mozzarella, shredded
- 2 tbsps heavy cream
- 1 tbsp chives, chopped

DIRECTIONS
1. Combine the eggs, shallots, and remaining ingredients in a mixing dish, whisk well, and pour into a sous vide bag.
2. Seal the bag, cook for 1 hour at 160ºF, and serve for breakfast.

4. EGGS MIX WITH CRAB

 25 MIN   5 MIN   2

NUTRITION:
CAL: 162 | FAT: 13 | PROTEIN: 15

INGREDIENTS
- 2 eggs, whisked
- salt and black pepper to the taste
- 1 tbsp chives, chopped
- 2 tbsps cream cheese
- 1 tbsp crabmeat
- 1 tbsp butter, melted

DIRECTIONS
1. In 2 sous vide bags, whisk together the eggs, butter, crabmeat, and remaining ingredients.
2. Dip in your sous vide bath and cook for 25 minutes at 167ºF.
3. Serve by dividing the mixture across plates.

5. LIME COCONUT JARS

 3 HOURS   5 MIN   2

NUTRITION:
CAL: 144 | FAT: 14 | PROTEIN: 6

INGREDIENTS
- ½ cup coconut cream
- 1 tbsp brown sugar
- ½ tbsp heavy cream
- ½ tbsp lime juice
- 1-quart almond milk, heated
- ½ tbsp lime zest, grated

DIRECTIONS
1. Combine the milk, cream, and remaining ingredients in a mixing bowl, whisk well, pour into canning jars, cover, and place in your sous vide bath to cook for 3 hours at 120 ºF.
2. Serve warm.

6. PARMESAN EGGS

 35 MIN   5 MIN   4

NUTRITION:
CAL: 128 | FAT: 13 | PROTEIN: 10

INGREDIENTS
- 4 eggs
- ½ cup parmesan, grated
- salt and black pepper to the taste
- 2 scallions, chopped
- 2 tbsps chives, chopped
- ½ tsp sweet paprika
- ½ tsp cumin, ground

DIRECTIONS
1. In a sous vide bag, crack each egg and season with the chives, paprika, and other seasonings. Seal the bags and submerge in the water bath, and cook for 35 minutes at 150ºF.
2. Serve for breakfast by dividing the mixture between plates.

7. SCRAMBLED EGGS

 30 MIN   10 MIN   2

NUTRITION:
CAL: 150 | FAT: 10 | PROTEIN: 11

INGREDIENTS

- 4 eggs, whisked
- 1 tsp cumin, ground
- salt and black pepper to the taste
- 1 tbsp chives, chopped
- ½ tsp rosemary, dried
- ½ tsp sweet paprika
- ½ tsp chili powder

DIRECTIONS

1. In a bowl, whisk together eggs, paprika, rosemary, and the remaining ingredients. Transfer to a sous vide bag, seal it, place it in a water bath and cook for 30 minutes at 160 ºF.
2. Serve for breakfast by dividing the mixture between plates.

8. PESTO EGGS

 30 MIN   5 MIN   2

NUTRITION:
CAL: 227 | FAT: 17 | PROTEIN: 14

INGREDIENTS

- 1 tomato, cubed
- 2 tbsps basil pesto
- 4 eggs
- salt and black pepper to the taste
- ½ tsp hot paprika

DIRECTIONS

1. Place the eggs in your sous vide water bath and cook for 30 minutes at 150 ºF before cracking them on plates.
2. For breakfast, divide the pesto, tomato, and paprika among the eggs and serve.

9. SPINACH AND EGGS MIX WITH ASPARAGUS

 50 MIN   10 MIN   4

NUTRITION:
CAL: 201 | FAT: 17 | PROTEIN: 10

INGREDIENTS

- 4 eggs whisked
- Cooking spray
- 1 tsp smoked paprika
- salt and black pepper to the taste
- 1 tsp chives, chopped
- 2 asparagus spears, chopped
- ¼ cup parmesan, grated
- ½ cup heavy cream

DIRECTIONS

1. Spray four ramekins with cooking spray and divide the eggs, asparagus, and other ingredients among them.
2. Preheat your water bath to 180ºF, then place the ramekins inside, cover them with tin foil, and bake for 50 minutes.
3. Breakfast is an excellent option.

10. COCONUT EGGS

 40 MIN   10 MIN   4

NUTRITION:
CAL: 195 | FAT: 17 | PROTEIN: 8

INGREDIENTS

- ½ tsp nutmeg, ground
- 3 tbsps sugar
- 2 tbsps coconut milk
- 4 eggs, whisked
- 1 cup coconut cream

DIRECTIONS

1. In a mixing bowl, whisk together the eggs, cream, and remaining ingredients, then distribute among four ramekins.
2. Place the ramekins in the water bath, fill halfway with water, cover and bake for 40 minutes at 140 ºF. Serve immediately for breakfast.

12. CINNAMON EGGS

 30 MIN   5 MIN   2

NUTRITION:
CAL: 290 | FAT: 22 | PROTEIN: 14

INGREDIENTS

- 1/3 cup heavy cream
- ½ tsp cinnamon powder
- 4 eggs, whisked
- 1 tsp ginger powder
- 2 tbsps sugar

DIRECTIONS

1. Combine the eggs, sugar, and other ingredients in a sous vide bag, seal, and place in your sous vide water bath preheated to 167 ºF for 30 minutes.
2. Serve by dividing the mixture into bowls.

13. CHICKEN AND EGGS

 30 MIN   10 MIN   2

NUTRITION:
CAL: 522 | FAT: 36 | PROTEIN: 35

INGREDIENTS

- 4 eggs, whisked
- 1 avocado, peeled, pitted and cubed
- salt and black pepper to the taste
- 1 cup rotisserie chicken, cooked and shredded
- ½ cup black olives, pitted and halved
- 1 tomato, chopped

DIRECTIONS

1. Combine the meat, eggs, and other ingredients in a sous vide bag, toss, seal, and place in your sous vide water bath preheated to 170 ºF for 30 minutes.
2. Serve by dividing the mixture across plates.

14. CHIA EGGS AND LIME

 20 MIN   10 MIN   2

NUTRITION:
CAL: 350 | FAT: 32 | PROTEIN: 14

INGREDIENTS

- 4 eggs, whisked
- 1 tbsp lime juice
- ½ cup heavy cream
- 1 tsp sweet paprika
- salt and black pepper to the taste
- 1 tbsp chia seeds

DIRECTIONS

1. Combine eggs, chia seeds, and other ingredients in a sous vide bag, toss, seal, and place in your sous vide water bath. Cook for 20 minutes at 167 ºF.
2. Serve warm.

15. BROCCOLI EGGS

 30 MIN   10 MIN   4

NUTRITION:
CAL: 170 | FAT: 16 | PROTEIN: 7

INGREDIENTS

- 4 eggs, whisked
- salt and black pepper to the taste
- 2 garlic cloves, minced
- 1 tbsp chives, chopped
- ½ cup heavy cream
- 1 cup broccoli florets
- ½ tsp sweet paprika
- ½ tsp coriander, ground

DIRECTIONS

1. Combine eggs, broccoli, paprika, and other ingredients in a sous vide bag, toss, seal, and place in your sous vide water bath to cook at 175ºF for 30 minutes.
2. Serve for breakfast by dividing everything between plates.

16. GINGER TOMATOES EGGS

 30 MIN   15 MIN   4

NUTRITION:
CAL: 100 | FAT: 8 | PROTEIN: 12

INGREDIENTS

- 4 eggs, whisked
- A drizzle of olive oil
- 1 red onion, chopped
- salt and black pepper to the taste
- A pinch of red pepper, crushed
- 1 garlic clove, minced
- 1 tbsp chives, chopped
- 1 cup cherry tomatoes, cubed
- 1 tbsp ginger, grated

DIRECTIONS

1. Heat the oil in a skillet over medium heat, then add the ginger, onion, and remaining ingredients (except the eggs), stirring constantly, for 10 minutes.
2. In a mixing bowl, whisk together the eggs and ginger mixture. Pour into a sous vide bag, seal, and place in the water bath to cook for 30 minutes at 170 ºF.
3. Arrange the ingredients on plates and serve for breakfast.

17. BOK CHOY AND EGGS

 20 MIN   10 MIN   2

NUTRITION:
CAL: 170 | FAT: 12 | PROTEIN: 14

INGREDIENTS
- 4 eggs, whisked
- ½ tsp chili powder
- 2 bunches bok choy, chopped
- 2 bacon slices, chopped
- salt and black pepper to the taste
- A drizzle of avocado oil
- 2 garlic cloves, minced
- ½ tsp turmeric powder

DIRECTIONS
1. Combine eggs, bok choy, and other ingredients in a sous vide bag, toss, seal, submerge in the water bath, and cook at 170 °F for 20 minutes.
2. Serve for breakfast by dividing the mixture between plates.

18. GREENS AND EGGS

 20 MIN   10 MIN   4

NUTRITION:
CAL: 160 | FAT: 10 | PROTEIN: 12

INGREDIENTS
- 8 eggs, whisked
- 1 tbsp lime juice
- ½ tsp chili powder
- salt and black pepper to the taste
- 1 cup baby spinach
- 1 cup collard greens, chopped
- ¼ cup spring onions, chopped

DIRECTIONS
1. Combine greens, eggs, and other ingredients in a sous vide bag, seal the bag, and cook at 170 °F for 20 minutes in your sous vide water bath preheated.
2. Serve for breakfast by dividing the mixture between plates.

19. EGGS AND ASPARAGUS

 20 MIN   10 MIN   4

NUTRITION:
CAL: 190 | FAT: 14 | PROTEIN: 14

INGREDIENTS
- 4 eggs, whisked
- ½ tsp sweet paprika
- ½ tsp chili powder
- 1 cup cheddar cheese, grated
- ¼ cup red onion, chopped
- 1 lb asparagus spears, chopped

DIRECTIONS
1. Toss the eggs with the remaining ingredients in a sous vide bag, toss, seal, and place in your sous vide water bath to cook at 168 °F for 20 minutes.
2. Serve for breakfast by dividing the mixture amongst dishes.

20. ZUCCHINI BOWLS

 25 MIN   15 MIN   4

NUTRITION:
CAL: 164 | FAT: 14 | PROTEIN: 8

INGREDIENTS

- 4 eggs, whisked
- 1 tbsp butter, melted
- 1 tsp oregano, dried
- 2 spring onions, chopped
- 1 ounce parmesan, grated
- ¼ cup heavy cream
- 2 zucchinis, cubed
- salt and black pepper to the taste

DIRECTIONS

1. Over medium-high heat melt the butter in a pan, then add the spring onions and zucchinis and cook for 5 minutes.
2. Combine eggs, zucchinis, and other ingredients in a sous vide bag and close it. Place the bag in your sous vide water bath preheated and cook for 25 minutes at 180 ºF.
3. Serve for breakfast by dividing the mixture into bowls.

21. KALE, EGGS AND SAUSAGE

 35 MIN   15 MIN   4

NUTRITION:
CAL: 230 | FAT: 17 | PROTEIN: 14

INGREDIENTS

- 4 eggs, whisked
- ½ cup red bell pepper, chopped
- salt and black pepper to the taste
- ½ cup kale, chopped
- 1 tsp garlic, minced
- ¼ cup red hot chili pepper, chopped
- 1 tbsp chives, chopped
- 1 red onion, chopped
- A drizzle of olive oil
- 1 cup Italian pork sausage, sliced
- 1 cup kale, torn

DIRECTIONS

1. Heat the oil in a pan over medium-high heat, then add the onion, kale, and sausage, toss to combine, and cook for 10 minutes.
2. Transfer to a sous vide bag, add the remaining ingredients, swirl to combine, seal the bag, submerge in the wa-ter bath, and cook for 35 minutes at 180 ºF.
3. Serve by dividing everything amongst plates.

22. PERFECT EGG TOSTADA

 16 MIN   10 MIN   4

NUTRITION:
CAL: 234 | FAT: 15 | PROTEIN: 10

INGREDIENTS

- 4 large eggs, at room temperature
- ¼ cup cooked or canned black beans, heated
- 4 sprigs cilantro, chopped
- 4 corn tostadas
- 4 tsps salsa taquera or salsa Verde or chili de arbol
- 4 tsps Queso fresco, crumbled

DIRECTIONS

1. Preheat your sous vide water bath to 162ºF.
2. Place the eggs on a spoon, one at a time, and gently lower them into the water bath and place on the rack. Set the timer for 15 minutes.
3. When the timer goes off, immediately remove the eggs from the water bath. Place the eggs in a bowl of cold water for a few minutes.
4. To assemble: Place the tostadas on 4 serving plates. Spread a tbsp of beans over it, then salsa, then sprinkle cheese on top and serve.

23. OVERNIGHT OATMEAL

 10 HOUR   11 MIN   4

NUTRITION:
CAL: 224 | FAT: 6 | PROTEIN: 9

INGREDIENTS

- 2/3 cup rolled oats
- 2/3 cup pinhead oatmeal
- 1 1/3 cups milk or cream
- 4 tsps raisins
- 2 cups water
- 2 tsps maple syrup or honey

DIRECTIONS

1. Preheat your sous vide water bath to 140ºF.
2. Take 4 Mason jars or glass jam jars with lids. Divide the oats and pinhead oatmeal (you can also use quick-cook steel-cut oats) among the jars. Divide the milk and pour over the oats. Pour ½ cup water in each jar.
3. Add a tsp of raisins to each jar. Fasten the lids lightly, not tight.
4. Immerse the filled jars in the water bath. The lids of the jars should be above the level of water in the cooker. This is important.
5. Set the timer for 9 to 10 hours.
6. Once done, stir and serve with some butter, if desired.

24. OVERNIGHT OATMEAL WITH STEWED FRUIT COMPOTE

 6 HOUR   10 MIN   4

NUTRITION:
CAL: 364 | FAT: 12 | PROTEIN: 11

INGREDIENTS

For oatmeal:

- 2 cups quick-cooking rolled oats
- ¼ tsp ground cinnamon
- 6 cups water
- A pinch salt

For Stewed Fruit Compote:

- 1½ cups mixed dried fruit of your choice—cherries, apricots, cranberries, etc.
- 1 cup water
- Zest of an orange and a lemon, finely grated
- ¼ cup white sugar

DIRECTIONS

1. Preheat your sous vide water bath to 155ºF.
2. Place oatmeal, water, salt, and cinnamon in a vacuum-seal pouch or Ziploc bag.
3. Place all the ingredients of the fruit compote in another similar pouch, and vacuum seal both.
4. Submerge both pouches in the water bath and set the timer for 6 to 7 hours.
5. Remove the pouches and shake them well.
6. Divide the oatmeal into 4 bowls. Top with fruit compote and serve.

25. FRENCH TOAST

 1 HOUR   10 MIN   8

NUTRITION:
CAL: 244 | FAT: 29 | PROTEIN: 4

INGREDIENTS

- 8 slices bread
- 1 cup heavy cream
- 1 tsp ground cinnamon
- 4 eggs
- 2 tsps vanilla extract

For Finishing:

- ½ cup butter
- Oil, as required

DIRECTIONS

1. Preheat your sous vide water bath to 147°F.
2. Add eggs, vanilla, cream, and cinnamon into a bowl and whisk well.
3. Dip the bread slices in the egg mixture, one by one, and place in a large vacuum-seal pouch or Ziploc bag. Use 2 bags, if desired. Place in a single layer.
4. Vacuum seal the pouch.
5. Submerge the pouch in the water bath. Set the timer for 60 minutes.
6. Remove the pouch from the water bath and remove the bread slices from the pouch.
7. For finishing: Place a large skillet over medium heat.
8. Add 1 or 2 tbsps butter. When butter melts, place 2 or 3 bread slices on the pan and cook as desired.

26. POACHED EGGS IN HASH BROWN NESTS

 1 HOUR   11 MIN   3

NUTRITION:
CAL: 474 | FAT: 30 | PROTEIN: 19

INGREDIENTS

- 6 large eggs, at room temperature
- 3 cups frozen shredded hash brown, thawed completely
- 1 tsp fresh rosemary, chopped, or ¼ tsp dried rosemary
- Freshly ground pepper to taste
- Salt to taste
- 2 tbsps chopped fresh chives
- 1 ½ tbsps olive oil
- ¼ tsp paprika
- 3 thin slices prosciutto, halved crosswise
- Cooking spray

DIRECTIONS

1. Preheat your sous vide water bath to 147°F.
2. Place the eggs on a spoon, one by one, and gently lower them into the water bath and place on the lower rack. Set the timer for 60 minutes.
3. Meanwhile, grease a 6-count muffin pan with cooking spray.
4. Place hash browns on a kitchen towel. Squeeze out as much moisture as possible.
5. Place the hash browns in a bowl. Add oil, rosemary, pepper, paprika, and salt. Mix well.
6. Divide this mixture among the muffin cups. Press down at the bottom and sides of the muffin cups. Spray cooking spray over it.
7. Preheat oven to 375°F.
8. Place the muffin tin in the oven and bake for about 30 minutes or until nearly golden brown.
9. Place half slice of prosciutto over each hash brown. Let it hang from the edges of the hash brown nests. Bake for 5 minutes.
10. Remove from the oven and cool for 4 or 5 minutes. Run a knife around the edges of the hash brown nest and gently lift it out from the muffin tin.
11. When the timer of the sous vide cooker goes off, immediately remove the eggs. Break 2 cooked eggs in each nest. Garnish with chives and serve immediately.

27. EGG WITH SUNCHOKES VELOUTÉ, CRISPY PROSCIUTTO AND HAZELNUT

 50 MIN   20 MIN   3

NUTRITION:
CAL: 193 | FAT: 15 | PROTEIN: 11

INGREDIENTS

For Sunchokes Velouté:

- 2 tbsps butter
- 1 small leek, only white part, thinly sliced
- 1 lb Jerusalem artichokes (sunchokes), peeled
- ½ quart milk
- ¼ cup heavy cream (optional)
- 1 medium onion, thinly sliced
- 1 clove garlic, sliced
- ½ quart chicken stock
- ¼ vanilla bean, scraped

For bouquet garni:

- 2 or 3 thyme sprigs
- 2 or 3 fresh sage leaves
- 1 bay leaf
- Leek greens, to wrap

For sous vide eggs:

- 3 eggs, at room temperature

For finishing:

- 3 thin slices prosciutto
- Few strips fried Jerusalem artichokes (sunchokes)
- A handful baby watercress
- 6 hazelnuts, toasted, chopped

DIRECTIONS

1. Preheat your sous vide water bath to 145ºF.
2. Place the eggs on a spoon and gently lower them into the water bath. Place on the lower rack. Set the timer for 47 minutes.
3. Meanwhile, make the sunchoke velouté as follows: Place a casserole dish over medium flame. Add butter. When butter melts, add onion, garlic, leeks, salt and pepper.
4. To make bouquet garni, place together thyme, sage, and bay leaf and wrap it with leek greens.
5. Place bouquet garni in the casserole dish. Cook for a few minutes.
6. Stir in the artichokes and cook until slightly tender. Stir occasionally.
7. Add rest of the ingredients and stir. Once it boils, reduce the flame and let it simmer until tender. Turn off the heat and remove the bouquet garni.
8. Blend the mixture in a blender. Strain the mixture through a wire mesh strainer placed over a saucepan.
9. To finish: Smear oil over the prosciutto slices and lay them on a lined baking sheet.
10. Bake in a preheated oven at 300ºF until crisp. Remove from the oven and cool.
11. Place a few strips of sunchoke on a nonstick pan. Add a bit of oil.
12. Add sunchoke and cook until crisp. Sprinkle salt.
13. Crack a cooked egg into each of 3 bowls.
14. Spoon the sunchoke velouté over the eggs in each bowl.
15. Serve topped with prosciutto, hazelnuts, watercress, and fried sunchoke strips.

28. SAUSAGE SCRAMBLE

 20 MIN   10 MIN   5

NUTRITION:
CAL: 429 | FAT: 134 | PROTEIN: 100

INGREDIENTS

- 10 large eggs, well beaten
- 8 oz breakfast sausages, crumbled
- 4 tbsps butter
- Salt and pepper, as per taste
- ½ cup Mexican cheese, grated

DIRECTIONS

1. Preheat your sous vide water bath to 165°F.
2. Place a skillet over medium heat and cook the sausages until they are browned.
3. Transfer the cooked sausages in a bowl lined with paper towels and allow them to cool. Once the sausages are cool, place them in a Ziploc bag. Add the eggs, butter, cheese, salt and pepper and vacuum seal the bag.
4. Submerge and cook in the sous vide water bath for around 20 minutes. Take the pouch out occasionally and shake the contents well before submerging again. Cook the eggs to your liking.
5. Remove from the water bath and serve.

29. EGGS BENEDICT

 1 HOUR   15 MIN   4

NUTRITION:
CAL: 434 | FAT: 32 | PROTEIN: 15

INGREDIENTS

- 4 English muffins, halved, toasted
- 8 slices Canadian bacon
- A handful fresh parsley, chopped
- 8 eggs
- butter, as required

For hollandaise sauce:

- 8 tbsps butter
- 2 tsps lemon juice
- 1 shallot, diced
- Salt to taste
- Cayenne pepper to taste
- 2 egg yolks
- 2 tsps water

DIRECTIONS

1. Preheat your sous vide water bath to 148°F.
2. Place the eggs in a vacuum-seal pouch or Ziploc bag. Place all the ingredients for hollandaise sauce into another bag. Vacuum seal the pouches.
3. Submerge both pouches in the water bath and set the timer for 1 hour.
4. Meanwhile, cook the bacon in a pan to the desired doneness. Keep warm in an oven along with muffins if desired.
5. Remove the pouches from the water bath. Transfer the contents of the sauce into a blender and blend until smooth.
6. Place muffins on individual serving plates. Crack an egg on each muffin and place on the bottom half of the muffins.
7. Spoon hollandaise over the eggs and garnish with parsley. Cover with the top half of the muffins and serve.

30. SMOKED FISH AND POACHED EGG

 35 MIN   14 MIN   4

NUTRITION:
CAL: 177 | FAT: 14 | PROTEIN: 10

INGREDIENTS

- 4 fillets smoked fish
- 2 lemons, cut into slices
- Seasonings of your choice
- 4 large eggs
- 4 tbsps olive oil

DIRECTIONS

1. Preheat your sous vide water bath to 140ºF.
2. Divide all the ingredients except eggs into 4 vacuum-seal pouches or Ziploc bags.
3. Seal the pouches, but do not remove the air completely.
4. Submerge both pouches in the water bath and set the timer for 20 minutes.
5. When the timer goes off, remove the pouches and set aside.
6. Increase the temperature to 167ºF.
7. Place the eggs on a spoon, one at a time, and gently lower them into the water bath and place on the lower rack. Set the timer for 15 minutes.
8. Empty each pouch onto individual serving plates. Break an egg over each fillet and serve.

31. BRIOCHE AND EGGS

 45 MIN   15 MIN   6

NUTRITION:
CAL: 288 | FAT: 14 | PROTEIN: 19

INGREDIENTS

- 6 brioche buns
- 6 large eggs
- 2 scallions, sliced (optional)
- 1 ½ cups grated cheese

DIRECTIONS

1. Preheat your sous vide water bath to 149ºF.
2. Place the eggs on a spoon, one at a time, and gently lower them into the water bath and place on the rack. Set the timer for 45 minutes.
3. When the timer goes off, immediately remove the eggs from the water bath. Place the eggs in a bowl of cold water for a few minutes.
4. Place brioche buns on a baking sheet and break a cooked egg on each bun. Sprinkle cheese on top.

32. EGGS AND OREGANO

 30 MIN   5 MIN   2

NUTRITION:
CAL: 141 | FAT: 10 | PROTEIN: 12

INGREDIENTS

- 4 eggs, whisked
- 1 red bell pepper, chopped
- 2 shallots, chopped
- A pinch of salt and black pepper
- 1 tbsp oregano, chopped
- ½ tsp chili powder
- ½ tsp sweet paprika

DIRECTIONS

1. Preheat your sous vide water bath to 170º F.
2. Pour the whisked egg into a cooking pouch and add the other ingredients.
3. Immerse the pouch into the water bath and cook for 30 minutes.
4. Once done, remove the pouch from the water bath and transfer the contents to a serving plate.
5. Serve and enjoy!

33. EGG BITES

 1 HOUR   9 MIN   4

NUTRITION:
CAL: 120 | FAT: 9 | PROTEIN: 10

INGREDIENTS

- 5 eggs
- ¼ cup shredded Colby Jack cheese
- 3 tbsps unsweetened almond milk
- Salt to taste
- Pepper to taste

DIRECTIONS

1. Preheat your sous vide water bath to 172ºF.
2. Add a tbsp of cheese into each of 4 canning jars or Mason jars.
3. Whisk together eggs and milk in a bowl. Divide the egg mixture among the jars. Season with salt and pepper.
4. Fasten the lid lightly, not very tight.
5. Submerge the canning jars in water bath and adjust the timer for 1 hour or until eggs are set.
6. Remove the jars from the water bath. Serve directly from the jars.

34. SOUS VIDE SCRAMBLED EGGS

 22 MIN   5 MIN   4

NUTRITION:
CAL: 199 | FAT: 18 | PROTEIN: 13

INGREDIENTS

- 8 large eggs
- Freshly ground pepper to taste
- Salt to taste
- Aleppo pepper to taste (optional)
- 2 tbsps butter

DIRECTIONS

1. Preheat your sous vide water bath to 165ºF.
2. Add eggs, salt, and pepper into a bowl and whisk well. Pour into a large silicone bag and vacuum seal the pouch.
3. Submerge the pouch in the water bath and adjust the timer for 10 minutes.
4. Remove the pouch from the water bath and place the pouch between your palms. Press it and shake it.
5. Place it back in the water bath. Set the timer for 12 minutes.
6. When the timer goes off, remove the pouch from the water bath.
7. Open the pouch and divide onto 4 plates.
8. Garnish with Aleppo pepper. Serve immediately.

35. COCONUT & ALMOND PORRIDGE

 3 HOURS   5 MIN   2

NUTRITION:
CAL: 336 | FAT: 32 | PROTEIN: 8

INGREDIENTS

- ½ cup ground almonds
- ¾ cup coconut cream
- 1 tsp Cinnamon powder
- 1 tsp Stevia
- 1 pinch ground cardamom
- 1 pinch ground cloves
- 1 pinch Nutmeg

DIRECTIONS

1. Combine all the fixings in a vacuum-sealed bag.
2. Introduce the bag to the preheated water bath for 3 hours at 180ºF.
3. Remove from the bag and serve.

36. HUEVOS RANCHEROS

 2.5 HOURS   10 MIN   3

NUTRITION:
CAL: 275 | FAT: 16 | PROTEIN: 20

INGREDIENTS

- 6 eggs
- 6 corn tortillas
- ½ can (7 oz) crushed tomatoes
- ½ small yellow onion, minced
- 2 cloves garlic, minced
- ¼ tsp dried oregano
- ¼ tsp ground cumin
- ½ lime juice
- 1 canned chipotle adobo chili, minced
- ½ can refried beans
- ¼ cup fresh cilantro, chopped
- ½ cup crumbled cotija cheese or grated Monterey Jack

DIRECTIONS

1. Preheat the water bath to 147° F.
2. Combine tomatoes, onion, garlic, oregano, cumin, lime, and chili in a bag. Seal using the water method.
3. Pour refried beans into a second bag and seal using the water method. Place eggs in a third bag and seal using the water method.
4. Place all three bags into the water bath. Cook for 2 hours.
5. When the other components have 20 minutes left to cook, heat tortillas in a pan. Place 2 on each plate.
6. Top the tortillas with salsa, followed by the shelled eggs, cheese, and cilantro. Serve with refried beans.

37. SAUSAGE TOMATO

 40 MIN   5 MIN   2

NUTRITION:
CAL: 135 | FAT: 8 | PROTEIN: 14

INGREDIENTS

- 1 cup baby spinach
- 1 tbsp avocado oil
- 2 pork sausage links, sliced
- 1 cup cherry tomatoes, halved
- 1 cup kalamata olives, pitted and halved
- 2 tbsps lemon juice
- 2 tbsps basil pesto
- Salt and black pepper to the taste

DIRECTIONS

1. Prepare your sous vide water bath to 180° F.
2. Get a cooking pouch and add all the listed ingredients.
3. Immerse the pouch into the water bath and let it cook for 40 minutes.
4. Once done, remove the pouch from the water bath.
5. Transfer the contents into two serving bowls.
6. Serve and enjoy!

38. HARD-BOILED EGGS

 1 HOUR   3 MIN   3

NUTRITION:
CAL: 78 | FAT: 5 | PROTEIN: 6

INGREDIENTS

- 1 ice bath
- 3 large eggs

DIRECTIONS

1. Set the temperature of your Sous Vide machine at 165°F.
2. Arrange the eggs in the water bath and cook for 1 hour.
3. Once the time is elapsed, place the eggs into an ice bath.
4. When cool, peel and enjoy salads as a meal or just a snack anytime.

39. PORRIDGE WITH CHIA AND FLAX SEEDS

 3 HOURS   10 MIN   2

NUTRITION:
CAL: 115 | FAT: 9 | PROTEIN: 4

INGREDIENTS

- 2 tbsps flax seeds
- 1 cup almond milk
- 1 tbsp Stevia
- 1 tbsp Chia seeds
- ½ cup hemp hearts
- ½ tsp cinnamon powder
- ¾ tsp vanilla extract
- ¼ cup almond flour

DIRECTIONS

1. Preheat your sous vide water bath to 180º F.
2. Combine all the fixings in a mixing container.
3. Pour into a vacuum-sealable baggie and cook for 3 hours.
4. Add to your plate and enjoy it.

40. BAR-STYLE PINK PICKLED EGGS

 2 HOURS   6 MIN   6

NUTRITION:
CAL: 106 | FAT: 5 | PROTEIN: 6.5

INGREDIENTS

- 6 eggs
- 1 cup white vinegar
- 1 can beets Juice
- ¼ cup sugar
- ½ tbsp salt
- 2 cloves garlic
- 1 tbsp whole peppercorn
- 1 bay leaf

DIRECTIONS

1. Preheat the water bath to 170ºF.
2. Place the eggs in the bag. Seal the bag and place it in the bath. Cook 1 hour.
3. After 1 hour, place the eggs in the bowl of cold water to cool and carefully peel. In the bag in which you cooked the eggs, combine vinegar, beet juice, sugar, salt, garlic, and bay leaf.
4. Replace eggs in the bag with pickling liquid. Replace in the water bath and cook 1 additional hour.
5. After 1 hour, move eggs with pickling liquid to the refrigerator. Allow cooling completely before eating.

41. SHRIMP AND MUSHROOMS

 30 MIN   11 MIN   4

NUTRITION:
CAL: 216 | FAT: 14 | PROTEIN: 19

INGREDIENTS

- 1 cup shrimp, peeled and deveined
- 3 spring onions, chopped
- 1 cup mushrooms, sliced
- 4 eggs, whisked
- ½ tsp coriander, ground
- Salt and black pepper to the taste
- ½ cup coconut cream
- ½ tsp turmeric powder
- 4 bacon slices, chopped

DIRECTIONS

1. Prepare your sous vide water bath to 140º F.
2. Vacuum seal all the listed ingredients and lower the pouch in the water bath.
3. Cook for 30 minutes.
4. Serve and enjoy!

42. OLIVES SQUASH

 3 HOURS   10 MIN   2

NUTRITION:
CAL: 207 | FAT: 18 | PROTEIN: 15

INGREDIENTS

- 1 tbsp butter, melted
- 1 butternut squash, peeled and cubed
- 4 eggs, whisked
- 1 cup black olives, pitted and cubed
- Salt and black pepper to the taste
- ½ cup tomatoes, chopped
- 2 garlic cloves, minced
- ½ tsp Italian seasoning
- 3 oz Italian salami, chopped
- 1 tbsp oregano, chopped

DIRECTIONS

1. Prepare your sous vide water bath to 170º F.
2. Get a cooking pouch and add eggs and other ingredients listed above.
3. Shake the pouch to combine thoroughly, then vacuum seal it.
4. Immerse the pouch in the water bath and cook for 40 minutes.
5. Remove the pouch once done and transfer the contents to a serving platter.
6. Serve and enjoy!

43. SMOKED SALMON EGGS BENEDICT

 3 HOURS   10 MIN   2

NUTRITION:
CAL: 144 | FAT: 9 | PROTEIN: 18

INGREDIENTS

- 4 eggs
- 8 oz smoked salmon
- 2 English muffins, split
- Sous Vide Hollandaise sauce, bagged and uncooked

DIRECTIONS

1. Preheat the sous vide bath to 147º F.
2. Seal the eggs in a bag. Place the bag of eggs, and the bag of hollandaise into the sous vide bath. Cook for 2 hours.
3. 30 minutes before the end of cooking time, toast and butter the English muffins.
4. Remove eggs and sauce from the bath.
5. Pour sauce into a blender and blend until smooth and meanwhile, cold eggs in a bowl of cold water.
6. Arrange 2 oz of smoked salmon on each English muffin half to form a cup that will hold the poached egg.
7. Carefully crack each egg over a slotted spoon held over a bowl to allow the excess white to drip away.
8. Place one egg in each smoked salmon cup.
9. Top with hollandaise sauce.

44. BREAKFAST YOGURT

 3 HOURS   11 MIN   4

NUTRITION:
CAL: 50 | FAT: 3 | PROTEIN: 1

INGREDIENTS

- 1 cup almond milk
- ½ cup coconut yogurt
- ½ tbsp lime —zest and grated
- ½ tbsp orange —zest and grated
- ½ tbsp lemon —zest and grated

DIRECTIONS

1. Warm up the milk and mix with the yogurt in a bowl.
2. Whisk and add the rest of the fixings.
3. Pour the mixture into canning jars. Immerse the jars into the water bath and cover the tops with some foil.
4. Cook for 3 hours at 113ºF.
5. Serve and enjoy.

45. EGG AND CHOPPED SCALLION

 1 HOUR   11 MIN   6

NUTRITION:
CAL: 62 | FAT: 4 | PROTEIN: 9

INGREDIENTS

- 6 egg whites
- ½ of finely chopped roasted red bell pepper
- 2 tbsp finely chopped scallions
- Salt and black pepper, to taste
- ¼ cup shredded Monterrey Jack cheese
- 1 tsp arrowroot starch
- ¼ cup chopped fresh spinach
- ¼ cup shredded cottage cheese
- 1 tbsp unsalted butter

DIRECTIONS

1. Prepare your sous vide water bath to 173ºF.
2. Set up a rack in sous vide bath.
3. Grease 6 of 4oz mason jars.
4. Add egg whites in a deep bowl and beat thoroughly and add all the other ingredients.
5. Distribute mixture in equal proportion over the 6 mason jars. Seal the jars.
6. Cook underwater for 1 hour.
7. Remove the sous vide bag from the bath.
8. Remove food from the sous bag and serve warm!

46. TURKEY WITH ARUGULA AND EGGS

 16 MIN   11 MIN   6

NUTRITION:
CAL: 231 | FAT: 14 | PROTEIN: 24

INGREDIENTS

- 2 large eggs
- 1½ tbsp melted butter
- 1 lb cooked and shredded turkey
- Salt and freshly ground black pepper, to taste
- 3 tsp butter
- ¼ cup heavy cream
- 2 cups fresh baby arugula

DIRECTIONS

1. Fill water in 6 ramekins
2. Fill water in the sous vide half way up the height of the ramekins.
3. Apply butter to your clean ramekins.
4. Preheat the water in the sous vide to 168ºF
5. Whisk 1 egg over each ramekin and add cream, butter, black pepper and salt.
6. Place the ramekins on the baking rack and cook for 14 minutes. Serve with cooked turkey.

47. CLASSIC TOAST

 70 MIN   7 MIN   4

NUTRITION:
CAL: 227 | FAT: 16 | PROTEIN: 14

INGREDIENTS

- 8 large eggs
- 2 tbsp unsalted butter
- 2 large day-old challah pieces
- Pinch salt
- ¾ cup milk
- 1/8 tsp vanilla extract

DIRECTIONS

1. Prepare your sous vide water bath to a temperature of 148ºF.
2. In a deep bowl, whisk the eggs together with the vanilla extract, salt and milk.
3. Beat thoroughly until the mixture is well combined.
4. Transfer the mixture to zip lock bag and add the challah pieces.
5. Remove the excess air from the bag and seal the bag.
6. Place the bag in the sous vide water bath container.
7. Let it cook for 70 minutes.
8. When ready, remove the zip lock bag from the water bath.
9. Add butter to a skillet placed over high heat.
10. Transfer the food content from the bag to the skillet and cook until it turns golden brown.
11. Divide each piece into halve and serve immediately.

48. SWEET EGG BITES

 56 MIN   14 MIN   4

NUTRITION:
CAL: 202 | FAT: 17 | PROTEIN: 12

INGREDIENTS

- 4 large eggs
- 3 tbsp softened cream cheese
- 1/3 cup grated Gruyere cheese
- 2 cooked and halved pancetta slices
- Salt and freshly ground black pepper, to taste

DIRECTIONS

1. Prepare your sous vide water bath to 173ºF
2. Set up a rack inside the container.
3. Apply grease to 4oz of mason glass jars.
4. Add all the ingredients in a food processor except the pancetta.
5. Press and hold the pulse until mixture becomes smooth.
6. Place halve sliced pancetta into each jar and carefully pour egg mixture. Seal the jars.
7. Place the jars in the sous vide water bath and cook for 56 minutes.
8. Remove content from the jars and serve.

49. SOFT-POACHED EGGS

 12 MIN   2 MIN   2

NUTRITION:
CAL: 133 | FAT: 13 | PROTEIN: 8

INGREDIENTS

- 6 large eggs
- 2g Basil
- A pinch of salt and pepper

DIRECTIONS

1. Preheat a water bath to 167ºF.
2. With a slotted spoon, lower the eggs into the bath. Be careful not to break them. Cook for 12 minutes straight – no more, no less.
3. In the meantime, grab a large bowl and fill it with the water and ice. When the eggs are done, transfer them to an ice bowl. Let them cool for 2 minutes.
4. Serve with the salad of your choice or with toasts.

50. COCONUT CONGEE

 1.5 HOUR   10 MIN   3

NUTRITION:
CAL: 430 | FAT: 32 | PROTEIN: 6

INGREDIENTS

- 2 cups coconut milk
- 1/2 cup short grain rice
- 2 cups water
- Salt
- 1/2 tbsp pumpkin pie spice
- 1/2 cup sugar

DIRECTIONS

1. Prepare your sous vide water bath to 191ºF
2. In a large zip-lock bag, add the coconut milk, pumpkin, water, and rice and seal tightly. Ensure the excess air is properly removed from bag, then seal.
3. Immerse the bag into the water bath and cook for 1 hour 25 minutes.
4. Remove bag from the water bath and transfer the content to a platter
5. Sprinkle with salt. Serve and enjoy!

51. OMELET WITH PARMESAN

 20 MIN   3 MIN   1

NUTRITION:
CAL: 153 | FAT: 15 | PROTEIN: 12

INGREDIENTS

- 2 large eggs
- 1 tbsp butter - diced
- 1 tbsp Parmesan cheese - finely grated
- A pinch of salt and pepper

For serving:

- Fresh parsley – chopped
- A pinch of basil

DIRECTIONS

1. Preheat a water bath to 164ºF.
2. In a large bowl, crack the eggs and whisk quickly. When they are well mixed, add butter, Parmesan, salt, and pepper. Stir well.
3. Pour the mixture into a medium vacuum pouch and seal.
4. Put the bag in a water bath. Cook for 10 minutes.
5. After 10 minutes remove the bag from the bath and shake it well. That way, the eggs will start to get that "omelet look".
6. Put the bag back in the bath and cook for another 10 minutes.
7. When the eggs are finally cooked, transfer them to a plate.
8. Add a dash of basil and parsley and serve.

52. BACON 'N' CHEESE EGG BITES

 1 HOUR   7 MIN   6

NUTRITION:
CAL: 212 | FAT: 16 | PROTEIN: 13

INGREDIENTS

- 2 slices cooked bacon - split
- 6 eggs
- 2 oz. cream cheese
- 2 oz. Gruyere cheese - grated
- A pinch of salt and pepper

DIRECTIONS

1. Preheat a water bath to 172ºF.
2. Mix the eggs, salt, pepper, and both kinds of cheese into a blender. You want a consistent and smooth texture.
3. Put each piece of bacon into one jar. Then pour the egg mixture. Seal with the lids.
4. Place the jars in the water bath and cook sous vide for about an hour.
5. Remove the bits from jars with the help of a spoon or a knife.
6. Serve with your favorite salad.

53. SOFT BOILED EGGS

 46 MIN   11 MIN   2

NUTRITION:
CAL: 148 | FAT: 12 | PROTEIN: 10

INGREDIENTS
- 4 large eggs

DIRECTIONS
1. Preheat a water bath to 145°F.
2. Use a slotted spoon to kindly place the eggs in the bath. Cook for 45 minutes.
3. When the cooking time is finished, smoothly remove the eggs from the bath (once again use a slotted spoon).
4. Serve immediately.

54. TOAST WITH FLAWLESSLY POACHED EGGS

 1.5 HOUR   11 MIN   4

NUTRITION:
CAL: 369 | FAT: 17 | PROTEIN: 23

INGREDIENTS
- 8 large eggs

For toast:
- 8 slices toast
- 8 slices smoked salmon/ham
- 8 slices tomato
- A dash basil or lettuce leaves, salt, and pepper

DIRECTIONS
1. Preheat a water bath to 147°F.
2. Put the eggs directly into the bath and cook for 90 minutes.
3. In the meantime, prepare sandwiches – put a smoked salmon or ham on each toast.
4. Top every toast with one slice of tomato and a dash of basil or lettuce leaves.
5. When the eggs are done, remove them from the water bath.
6. Crack each egg on a toast and sprinkle with seasonings.
7. Serve.

55. POACHED EGGS WITH AVOCADO TOAST

 20 MIN   6 MIN   4

NUTRITION:
CAL: 181 | FAT: 9 | PROTEIN: 9

INGREDIENTS
- 4 eggs

For avocado toast:
- 4 slices toasted bread of your choice
- 1 Avocado - sliced
- Fresh chives
- A pinch of salt and pepper

DIRECTIONS
1. Preheat a water bath to 167°F.
2. Gently lower all the eggs into the bath, making sure they don't crack.
3. Cook for 15 minutes.
4. Remove the eggs.
5. Put the eggs in an ice bowl (half ice, half water) and hold them there for about 1 minute.
6. Place avocado slices on every toast and crack one egg over each slice. Sprinkle with chives, salt, and pepper.
7. Serve.

3. VEGETABLE AND SIDES

56. VEGAN STEEL CUT OATS

 3 HOUR   6 MIN   3

NUTRITION:
CAL: 85 | FAT: 2 | PROTEIN: 3

INGREDIENTS

- 2 cups water
- ½ cup steel cut oats
- ½ tsp salt
- Cinnamon and maple syrup for topping

DIRECTIONS

1. Prepare the sous vide water bath by using your immersion circulator and raise the temperature to 180 °F.
2. Take a heavy-duty resealable zipper bag and add all the listed ingredients except the cinnamon and maple syrup
3. Seal the bag using the immersion method and submerge underwater.
4. Cook for about 3 hours.
5. Once cooked, remove it and transfer the oats to your serving bowl.
6. Serve with a sprinkle of cinnamon and some maple syrup.

57. HONEY ROASTED CARROTS

 75 MIN   6 MIN   4

NUTRITION:
CAL: 154 | FAT: 13 | PROTEIN: 2

INGREDIENTS

- 1 lb baby carrots
- 4 tbsps butter
- 1 tbsp agave nectar
- 3 tbsps honey
- ¼ tsp salt
- ¼ tsp ground cardamom

DIRECTIONS

1. Prepare the sous vide water bath using your immersion circulator and increase the temperature to 185 °F
2. Add the carrots, honey, whole butter, salt, and cardamom to a resealable bag
3. Seal using the immersion method. Cook for 75 minutes and once done, remove it from the water bath.
4. Strain the glaze by passing through a fine mesh.
5. Set it aside.
6. Take the carrots out from the bag and pour any excess glaze over them. Serve with a little bit of seasonings.

58. FENNEL PICKLE WITH LEMON

 30 MIN   10 MIN   5

NUTRITION:
CAL: 56 | FAT: 1 | PROTEIN: 5

INGREDIENTS

- 2 medium bulb fennels, trimmed up and cut into ¼ inch thick slices
- 1 cup white wine vinegar
- 2 tbsps beet sugar
- Juice and zest from 1 lemon
- 1 tsp salt

DIRECTIONS

1. Prepare the sous vide water bath using your immersion circulator and raise the temperature to 180°F
2. Take a large bowl and add the vinegar, sugar, lemon juice, salt, lemon zest, and whisk them well.
3. Transfer the mixture to your resealable zip bag.
4. Add the fennel and seal using the immersion method.
5. Submerge underwater and cook for 30 minutes.
6. Transfer to an ice bath and allow the mixture to reach the room temperature.
7. Serve!

59. GARLIC CITRUS ARTICHOKES

 1.5 HOUR 31 MIN 4

NUTRITION:
CAL: 108 | FAT: 11 | PROTEIN: 2

INGREDIENTS

- 12 pieces baby artichokes
- 4 tbsps freshly squeezed lemon juice
- 4 tbsps butter
- 2 fresh garlic cloves, minced
- 1 tsp fresh lemon zest
- salt and black pepper, to taste
- Chopped up fresh parsley for garnishing

DIRECTIONS

1. Prepare the sous vide water bath using your immersion circulator and raise the temperature to 180°F
2. Take a large bowl and add cold water and 2 tbsps of lemon juice.
3. Peel and discard the outer tough layer of your artichoke and cut them into quarters.
4. Transfer to the cold-water bath and let it sit for a while.
5. Take a large skillet and put it over medium high heat.
6. Add in the butter to the skillet and allow the butter to melt.
7. Add the garlic alongside 2 tbsps of lemon juice and the zest.
8. Remove from heat and season with a bit of pepper and salt.
9. Allow it to cool for about 5 minutes.
10. Then, drain the artichokes from the cold water and place them in a large resealable bag. Add in the butter mixture as well.
11. Seal it up using the immersion method and submerge underwater for about 1 and a ½ hour.
12. Once cooked, transfer the artichokes to a bowl and serve with a garnish of parsley.

60. HONEY TRUFFLE SUNCHOKES

 1.5 HOUR 16 MIN 4

NUTRITION:
CAL: 105 | FAT: 10 | PROTEIN: 5

INGREDIENTS

- 8 oz peeled Sunchokes, sliced into ¼ inch thick pieces
- 3 tbsps unsalted butter
- 2 tbsps agave nectar
- 1 tsp truffle oil
- Salt and black pepper, to taste

DIRECTIONS

1. Prepare the sous vide water bath using your immersion circulator and raise the temperature to 180°F
2. Take a heavy-duty resealable zip bag and add the butter, nectar, sunchokes, and truffle oil and mix them well.
3. Sprinkle some salt and pepper, and then seal using the immersion method.
4. Submerge it underwater and cook for 1 ½ hour.
5. Once cooked, transfer the contents to a skillet.
6. Put the skillet over medium-high heat and cook for 5 minutes more until the liquid has evaporated.
7. Season with pepper and salt to adjust the flavor if needed and serve!

61. ITALIAN PICKLED VEGETABLES

 1 HOUR 10 MIN 6

NUTRITION:
CAL: 35 | FAT: 3 | PROTEIN: 4

INGREDIENTS

- 1 cup cauliflower, cut up into ½-inch pieces
- 1 stemmed and seeded bell pepper, cut up into ½-inch pieces
- 1 cup carrots, cut up into ½-inch pieces
- ½ thinly sliced white onion
- 2 cups white wine vinegar
- 1 cup water
- ½ cup beet sugar
- 3 tbsps salt
- 1 tbsp black peppercorns
- 2 seeded and stemmed Serrano peppers, cut up into ½-inch pieces

DIRECTIONS

1. Prepare the sous vide water bath using your immersion circulator and raise the temperature to 180°F
2. Take a large bowl and mix in vinegar, sugar, salt, water, and peppercorns.
3. Transfer the mixture to a large resealable zipper bag and add the cauliflower, onion, serrano peppers, vinegar mixture, bell pepper, and carrots.
4. Seal it up using the immersion method and submerge underwater, cook for about 1 hour.
5. Once cooked, take it out from the bag and serve.

62. ALFREDO VEGAN CAULIFLOWER

 1.5 HOUR 16 MIN 6

NUTRITION:
CAL: 108 | FAT: 34 | PROTEIN: 13

INGREDIENTS

- 4 cups chopped cauliflower
- 2 cups water
- 2/3 cup cashews
- 2 garlic cloves
- ½ tsp dried oregano
- ½ tsp dried basil
- ½ tsp dried rosemary
- 4 tbsps nutritional yeast
- Salt, and pepper to taste

DIRECTIONS

1. Prepare the sous vide water bath using your immersion circulator and increase the temperature to 170°F
2. Take a heavy-duty resealable zip bag and add the cashews, cauliflower, oregano, water, garlic, rosemary, and basil.
3. Seal using the immersion method. Submerge underwater and cook for 90 minutes.
4. Transfer the cooked contents to a blender and puree.
5. Use the Alfredo over your favorite pasta.

63. MARINATED MUSHROOMS

 1 HOUR 21 MIN 2

NUTRITION:
CAL: 40 | FAT: 3 | PROTEIN: 6

INGREDIENTS

- 10 large button mushrooms
- 3 tbsps truffle oil
- 3 tbsps olive oil
- 1 tbsp chopped fresh thyme
- 1 clove thinly sliced garlic

DIRECTIONS

1. Prepare the sous vide water bath using your immersion circulator and raise the temperature to 185°F
2. Take a large bowl and add the truffle oil, mushrooms, olive oil, garlic, and thyme
3. Season with some pepper and salt.
4. Transfer the mushroom mixture to a large Sous-vide resealable zip bag and add the mixture to the bag.

- Salt, and pepper to taste

5. Seal it up using the immersion method. Submerge underwater and cook for 1 hour.
6. Once cooked, drain the mushrooms and discard the cooking liquid.
7. Take a large skillet and put it over medium heat for 3 minutes.
8. Add the mushrooms and sear for about 1 minute to brown it.
9. Transfer the cooked mushroom to a serving plate and season with pepper and salt.
10. Top it up with thyme. Serve!

64. CANNELLINI BEANS WITH HERBS

3 HOUR | 16 MIN | 5

NUTRITION:
CAL: 234 | FAT: 22 | PROTEIN: 4

INGREDIENTS
- 1 cup cannellini beans (dried) soaked overnight in salty cold water
- 1 cup water
- ½ cup olive oil
- 1 peeled carrot, cut up into 1-inch dice
- 1 celery stalk, cut up into 1-inch dice
- 1 quartered shallot
- 4 crushed garlic cloves
- 2 fresh rosemary sprigs
- 2 bay leaves
- Salt, and pepper to taste

DIRECTIONS
1. Prepare the sous vide water bath using your Sous-vide immersion circulator and raise the temperature to 190ºF
2. Drain the soaked beans and rinse them.
3. Transfer to a heavy-duty resealable zip bag and add the olive oil, celery, water, carrot, shallot, garlic, rosemary, and bay leaves.
4. Season with pepper and salt.
5. Seal using the immersion method and cook for 3 hours.
6. Once cooked, remove the beans and check for seasoning.
7. Discard the rosemary and serve!

65. BUDDHA'S DELIGHT

1 HOUR | 21 MIN | 6

NUTRITION:
CAL: 186 | FAT: 6 | PROTEIN: 10

INGREDIENTS
- 1 cup vegetable broth
- 2 tbsps tomato paste
- 1 tbsp grated ginger
- 1 tbsp rice wine
- 1 tbsp rice wine vinegar
- 1 tbsp agave nectar
- 2 tsps Sriracha sauce
- 3 minced garlic cloves
- 2 boxes cubed tofu

DIRECTIONS
1. Prepare your sous vide water bath using your immersion circulator and raise the temperature to 185ºF
2. Take a medium bowl and add all the listed ingredients except the tofu.
3. Mix well.
4. Transfer the mixture to a heavy-duty resealable zipper bag and top with the tofu.
5. Seal it up using the immersion method. Cook for 1 hour.
6. Pour the contents into a serving bowl and serve!

66. SOUS VIDE NAVY BEANS

3 HOUR | 15 MIN | 8

NUTRITION:
CAL: 160 | FAT: 14 | PROTEIN: 2

INGREDIENTS

- 1 cup dried and soaked navy beans
- 1 cup water
- ½ cup olive oil
- 1 peeled carrot, cut up into 1-inch dices
- 1 stalk celery, cut up into 1-inch dices
- 1 quartered shallot
- 4 cloves crushed garlic
- 2 sprigs fresh rosemary
- 2 pieces bay leaves
- salt, to taste
- Freshly ground black pepper, to taste

DIRECTIONS

1. Prepare your sous vide water bath using your immersion circulator and raise the temperature to 190°F
2. Carefully drain and rinse your beans and add them alongside the rest of the ingredients to a heavy-duty zip bag.
3. Seal using the immersion method and submerge it underwater. Cook for about 3 hours.
4. Once cooked, taste the beans.
5. If they are firm, then cook for another 1 hour and pour them in a serving bowl.
6. Serve!

67. BUTTERED RADISHES

46 MIN | 6 MIN | 4

NUTRITION:
CAL: 84 | FAT: 8 | PROTEIN: 2

INGREDIENTS

- 1 lb radishes, cut up in half lengthwise
- 3 tbsps butter
- ½ tsp sea salt

DIRECTIONS

1. Prepare your sous vide water bath using your immersion circulator and raise the temperature to 190°F
2. Add your radish halves, butter, and salt in a resealable zipper bag and seal it up using the immersion method.
3. Submerge underwater and cook for 45 minutes.
4. Once cooked, strain the liquid and discard.
5. Serve the radishes in a bowl!

68. SOUS-VIDE RHUBARB

46 MIN | 6 MIN | 4

NUTRITION:
CAL: 15 | FAT: 2 | PROTEIN: 2

INGREDIENTS

- 2 cups rhubarb
- 1 tbsp Grand Marnier
- 1 tsp beet sugar
- ½ tsp salt
- ½ a tsp freshly ground black pepper

DIRECTIONS

1. Prepare the sous vide water bath to a temperature of 140°F using your immersion circulator.
2. Take a large heavy-duty resealable zip bag and add all the listed ingredients. Whisk everything well.
3. Seal the bag using the immersion method/water displacement method.
4. Place it under your preheated water and cook for about 40 minutes.
5. Once cooked, take the bag out from the water bath, take the contents out and place it on a serving plate.
6. Serve warm!

69. CHINESE BLACK BEAN SAUCE

1.5 HOURS | 21 MIN | 4

NUTRITION:
CAL: 35 | FAT: 1 | PROTEIN: 2

INGREDIENTS

- 4 cups halved green beans
- 3 minced garlic cloves
- 2 tsps rice wine vinegar
- 1½ tbsps prepared black bean sauce
- 1 tbsp olive oil

DIRECTIONS

1. Prepare the sous vide water bath using your immersion circulator and raise the temperature to 170ºF
2. Add all the listed ingredients into a large mixing bowl alongside the green beans. Coat everything evenly.
3. Take a heavy-duty zip bag and add the mixture.
4. Zip the bag using the immersion method and submerge it underwater.
5. Cook for about 1 hour and 30 minutes.
6. Once cooked, take it out and serve immediately!

70. CHIPOTLE & BLACK BEANS

6 HOURS | 10 MIN | 5

NUTRITION:
CAL: 67 | FAT: 2 | PROTEIN: 3

INGREDIENTS

- 1 cup dry black beans
- 2 2/3 cup water
- 1 tbsp olive oil
- 1/3 cup freshly squeezed orange juice
- 2 tbsps orange zest
- 1 tsp salt
- 1 tsp cumin
- ½ tsp chipotle chili powder

DIRECTIONS

1. Prepare the sous vide water bath using your immersion circulator and raise the temperature to 193ºF
2. Take a heavy-duty resealable plastic bag and add the listed ingredients into the bag.
3. Submerge it underwater and cook for 6 hours.
4. Once cooked, take the bag out from the water bath.
5. Pour the contents into a nice sauté pan and place it over medium heat.
6. Simmer until the amount has been reduced.
7. Once your desired texture is achieved, remove from the heat and serve!

71. PICKLED MIXED VEGGIES

40 MIN | 10 MIN | 4

NUTRITION:
CAL: 48 | FAT: 2 | PROTEIN: 4

INGREDIENTS

- 12 oz. beets, cut up into ½-inch slices
- ½ Serrano pepper, seeds removed
- 1 garlic clove, diced
- 2/3 cup white vinegar
- 2/3 cup filtered water
- 2 tbsps pickling spice

DIRECTIONS

1. Prepare the sous vide water bath using your immersion circulator and raise the temperature to 190ºF
2. Take 4-6 oz' mason jar and add the Serrano pepper, beets, and garlic cloves
3. Take a medium stock pot and add the pickling spice, filtered water, white vinegar, and bring the mixture to a boil
4. Remove the stock and strain the mix over the beets in the jar.
5. Fill them up.
6. Seal it loosely and submerge it underwater. Cook for 40 minutes. Allow the jars to cool and serve!

72. ROOT VEGETABLES MIX

3 HOURS | 15 MIN | 4

NUTRITION:
CAL: 68 | FAT: 4 | PROTEIN: 5

INGREDIENTS

- 1 peeled turnip, cut up into 1-inch pieces
- 1 peeled rutabaga, cut up into 1-inch pieces
- 8 pieces petite carrots peeled up and cut into 1-inch pieces
- 1 peeled parsnip, cut up into 1-inch pieces
- ½ red onion, cut up into 1-inch pieces and peeled
- 4 pieces garlic, crushed
- 4 sprigs fresh rosemary
- 2 tbsps olive oil
- salt, and black pepper to taste
- 2 tbsps unsalted butter

DIRECTIONS

1. Prepare the sous vide water bath using your immersion circulator and raise the temperature to 185ºF
2. Take two large heavy-duty resealable zipper bags and divide the vegetables and the rosemary between the bags.
3. Add 1 tbsp of oil to the bag and season with some salt and pepper.
4. Seal the bags using the immersion method. Submerge underwater and cook for 3 hours
5. Take a skillet and place it over high heat and add in the oil.
6. Once done, add the contents of your bag to the skillet. Cook the mixture for about 5-6 minutes until the liquid comes to a syrupy consistency.
7. Add the butter to your veggies and toss them well. Keep cooking for another 5 minutes until they are nicely browned.
8. Serve!

73. PICKLED CARROTS

3 HOURS | 15 MIN | 4

NUTRITION:
CAL: 107 | FAT: 1 | PROTEIN: 2

INGREDIENTS

- 10-12 pieces petite carrots, peeled with the stems trimmed
- 1 cup white wine vinegar
- ½ cup beet sugar
- 3 tbsps salt
- 1 tsp black peppercorns
- 1/3 cup ice cold water
- 4 sprigs fresh thyme
- 2 peeled garlic cloves

DIRECTIONS

1. Preheat the sous vide water bath to 190ºF
2. Take a medium-sized saucepan and add the vinegar, salt, sugar, and peppercorns and place it over medium heat.
3. Then, let the mixture reach the boiling point and keep stirring until the sugar has dissolved alongside the salt
4. Remove the heat and add the cold water.
5. Allow the mixture to cool down to room temperature.
6. Take a resealable bag and add the thyme, carrots, and garlic alongside the brine solution and seal it up using the immersion method.
7. Submerge underwater and cook for 90 minutes.
8. Once cooked, remove the bag from the water bath and place into an ice bath.
9. Carefully take the carrots out from the bag and serve.

74. SOUS VIDE GARLIC TOMATOES

45 MIN | 5 MIN | 4

NUTRITION:
CAL: 89 | FAT: 8 | PROTEIN: 1

INGREDIENTS

- 4 pieces cored and diced tomatoes
- 2 tbsps olive oil
- 3 minced garlic cloves
- 1 tsp dried oregano
- 1 tsp fine sea salt

DIRECTIONS

1. Prepare the sous vide water bath using your immersion circulator and raise the temperature to 145ºF
2. Add all the listed ingredients to the resealable bag and seal using the immersion method.
3. Submerge underwater and let it cook for 45 minutes.
4. Once cooked, transfer the tomatoes to a serving plate.
5. Serve with some vegan French bread slices.

75. SWEET CURRIED WINTER SQUASH

1.5 HOURS | 21 MIN | 4

NUTRITION:
CAL: 65 | FAT: 5 | PROTEIN: 1

INGREDIENTS

- 1 medium winter squash
- 2 tbsps unsalted butter
- 1 to 2 tbsps Thai curry paste
- ½ tsp salt
- Fresh cilantro for serving
- Lime wedges for serving

DIRECTIONS

1. Preheat the sous vide water bath to 185ºF
2. Slice up the squash into half lengthwise and scoop out the seeds alongside the inner membrane. Keep the seeds for later use.
3. Slice the squash into wedges of about 1 ½-inch thickness.
4. Take a large heavy-duty bag resealable zip bags and add the squash wedges, curry paste, butter and salt and seal it using the immersion method.
5. Submerge it underwater and let it cook for 1 ½ hour.
6. Once cooked, remove the bag from water and give it a slight squeeze until it is soft.
7. If it is not soft, then add to the water once again and cook for 40 minutes more.
8. Transfer the cooked dish to a serving plate and drizzle with a bit of curry butter sauce from the bag.
9. Top your squash with a bit of cilantro, lime wedges and serve!

76. TENDER DOENJANG-SPICED EGGPLANT

45 MIN | 6 MIN | 4

NUTRITION:
CAL: 146 | FAT: 15 | PROTEIN: 2

INGREDIENTS

- 4 large eggplant, cut into wedges
- 1/4 cup peanut oil
- 2 tbsps doenjang paste
- 2 tbsps light soy sauce
- 1 tbsp brown sugar
- 1 tbsp sesame seeds

DIRECTIONS

1. Preheat sous vide water bath to 185ºF.
2. Whisk the Doenjang paste, peanut oil, soy sauce, and sugar together in a mixing bowl.
3. Add the eggplant and toss to coat evenly, then transfer to a sous vide bag and vacuum tight. Cook for 45 minutes.
4. Drain the eggplant wedges from the cooking liquid.
5. Sear the eggplants on a hot grilling pan.
6. Top with sesame seeds and serve.

77. GARLICKY BRUSSELS SPROUTS

1 HOUR | 11 MIN | 2

NUTRITION:
CAL: 326 | FAT: 26 | PROTEIN: 13

INGREDIENTS

- 1 lb. Brussels sprouts, trimmed
- 1/4 cup olive oil
- 2 tbsps garlic, minced
- 1 tbsp sea salt

DIRECTIONS

1. Preheat a sous vide water bath to 185°F.
2. Add all ingredients to a sous vide bag and seal airtight.
3. Add to water bath and cook for 1 hour.
4. Serve immediately with your favorite dish.

78. SOUS VIDE ARTICHOKES

1 HOUR | 11 MIN | 2

NUTRITION:
CAL: 258 | FAT: 25 | PROTEIN: 6

INGREDIENTS

- 4 artichokes, trimmed down to their hearts
- 1/4 cup olive oil
- 1 tbsp sea salt

DIRECTIONS

1. Preheat a sous vide water bath to 185°F.
2. Toss artichokes with all ingredients until well-coated in a large mixing bowl.
3. Place in a vacuum sealable bag and vacuum airtight.
4. Add to water bath and cook for 1 hour.
5. Serve immediately with your favorite dish.

79. TENDER GARLIC ASPARAGUS

1 HOUR | 6 MIN | 4

NUTRITION:
CAL: 62 | FAT: 4.5 | PROTEIN: 4

INGREDIENTS

- 1 lb. asparagus, cleaned and dried with a paper towel
- 2 tsps olive oil
- 1 tbsp garlic powder
- 1 tsp sea salt

DIRECTIONS

1. Preheat a sous vide water bath to 135°F.
2. Toss asparagus with all ingredients until well-coated in a large mixing bowl.
3. Place asparagus, lined flat, in a vacuum sealable bag and vacuum airtight.
4. Cook for 1 hour.
5. Serve immediately with your favorite dish.

80. TANGY GARLIC CHILI TOFU

4 HOUR | 11 MIN | 2

NUTRITION:
CAL: 357 | FAT: 29 | PROTEIN: 2

INGREDIENTS

- 1 block super firm tofu
- 1/4 cup brown sugar
- 1/4 cup soy sauce
- 1/4 cup toasted sesame oil
- 2 tbsps chili garlic paste

DIRECTIONS

1. Preheat a sous vide water bath to 180ºF.
2. Press out liquid from tofu.
3. Cut tofu into thick chunks, about 2 inches each.
4. Preheat a frying pan on medium, spray with non-stick cooking spray, and cook until golden on each side.
5. Mix soy sauce, brown sugar, toasted sesame oil, and chili garlic paste together until well-blended in a mixing bowl.
6. Toss tofu in sauce to coat well.
7. Transfer tofu and sauce to a sous vide bag and seal.
8. Submerge in sous vide bath and cook for 4 hours.
9. Remove and serve immediately.

81. YUMMY STEAK FRIES

1.5 HOUR | 11 MIN | 4

NUTRITION:
CAL: 221 | FAT: 6 | PROTEIN: 4

INGREDIENTS

- 5 russet Potatoes
- 1/2 stick unsalted butter

For the seasoning mix:

- 1 tsp garlic powder
- 1 tsp chili powder
- 1/2 tsp smoked paprika
- 1/2 tsp sea salt
- 1/2 tsp black pepper

DIRECTIONS

1. Preheat a sous vide water bath to 190ºF.
2. Cut potatoes in half and lengthwise into wedges.
3. Melt butter in the microwave.
4. Mix together seasonings in a separate bowl.
5. Place potatoes in a resealable plastic bag, toss in butter until covered evenly.
6. Toss in seasoning mix and toss to coat again.
7. Seal and lower bag into the water bath
8. Cook for 90 minutes. Then remove and place on a baking sheet broil for 2-3 minutes on each side. Serve hot!

82. RICH AND CREAMY POLENTA

1 HOUR | 5 MIN | 6

NUTRITION:
CAL: 126 | FAT: 5 | PROTEIN: 3.5

INGREDIENTS

- 1/2 cup dry yellow polenta
- 2 cups chicken or vegetable stock
- 1/4 cup butter, unsalted
- Sea salt
- 1/4 cup pecorino Romano cheese, for serving

DIRECTIONS

1. Preheat a sous vide water bath to 182ºF.
2. Add polenta, stock, butter and a pinch of sea salt to a resealable plastic bag and seal.
3. Submerge the bag in the water bath and cook for 1 hour.
4. Remove from the water bath and add to a mixing bowl.
5. Fold in cheese until well-incorporated and serve warm.

83. TENDER LEEKS WITH HERBED BUTTER

1 HOUR | 11 MIN | 4

NUTRITION:
CAL: 102 | FAT: 11 | PROTEIN: 2

INGREDIENTS

- 4 baby leeks (or 2 large)
- 4 tbsps butter, salted
- 1 tsp Herbs de Provence

DIRECTIONS

1. Preheat a sous vide water bath to 180°F.
2. Wash leeks and cut off ends. If using large leeks, split down the middle, then cut again in half, making four pieces per leek. Baby leeks can be left intact.
3. Melt butter in microwave, add herbs, and mix.
4. Put leeks and butter into large zipper-lock bag, swirl the butter mixture around to evenly coat the leeks. Remove excess air and seal shut.
5. Place in sous vide bath and cook for one hour.
6. Serve as a tender side dish for any main course.

84. TANGY TENDER MUSHROOMS

30 MIN | 11 MIN | 2

NUTRITION:
CAL: 90 | FAT: 4 | PROTEIN: 4

INGREDIENTS

- 1 lb. button mushrooms cleaned, rinsed, and cut into bite-size pieces
- 2 tbsps soy sauce
- 2 tbsps olive oil
- 1 tbsp balsamic vinegar
- 1/2 tsp black pepper
- 1/2 tsp sea salt, plus more to taste

DIRECTIONS

1. Preheat your sous vide water bath to 176°F.
2. Combine mushrooms with the rest of ingredients, in a large mixing bowl, and toss to coat evenly.
3. Place the mixture in a sealable plastic bag; seal using the water displacement method or use a vacuum sealer.
4. Add mushrooms to the water bath and cook for 30 minutes.
5. Remove the bag from the water bath and serve immediately with your favorite meal.

85. EASY FLAVOR-PACKED PICKLES

2.5 HOURS | 11 MIN | 4

NUTRITION:
CAL: 105 | FAT: 4 | PROTEIN: 4

INGREDIENTS

- 20 small cucumbers, stems removed
- 4 medium mason jars
- 20 black peppercorns
- 4 garlic cloves, smashed
- 4 tsps fresh dill

For the Pickling Brine:

- 2-1/2 cups white wine vinegar
- 2-1/2 cups water
- 1/2 cup sugar, granulated
- 2 tbsps pickling salt

DIRECTIONS

1. Preheat a sous vide water bath to 140°F.
2. Whisk brine ingredients together in a large mixing bowl until well-combined.
3. Place 5 cucumbers, 5 peppercorns, 1 garlic clove, and 1 tsp dill in each Mason jar.
4. Fill each jar with brine and seal lid tight.
5. Submerge mason jars in water bath and cook for 2 hours 30 minutes.
6. Remove from the water bath and allow to cool to room temperature. Refrigerate overnight or up to 3 days to brine. Serve with your favorite meals.

86. HOT CHILI CHUTNEY

6 HOURS | 20 MIN | 3

NUTRITION:
CAL: 161 | FAT: 1 | PROTEIN: 1.7

INGREDIENTS

- 5 medium jalapeños
- 2 medium red bell peppers
- 1 medium red onion, chopped
- 1/2 tbsp rosemary
- 1 bay leaf
- 1/2 tsp ground cinnamon
- 1/4 tsp sea salt
- 1/4 tsp black pepper
- 1/2 cup brown sugar
- 1 tbsp balsamic vinegar

DIRECTIONS

1. Preheat a sous vide water bath to 182°F.
2. Roast the peppers under a broiler until skins are completely charred.
3. Transfer the peppers to a bowl, cover with plastic wrap, and let sit about 15 to 20 minutes or until cool enough to handle.
4. Peel away the charred outer skins, cut the peppers in half, core, seed, and finely chop the flesh.
5. Add peppers and remaining ingredients to a cooking pouch and vacuum seal.
6. Submerge the pouch in water bath and cook for 5 hours.
7. Remove from the water bath and quick chill by submerging in ice water for 30 minutes.
8. Serve right away, or refrigerate in the pouch, unopened, for up to a week.

87. HOLIDAY CRANBERRY SAUCE

2 HOURS | 3 MIN | 4

NUTRITION:
CAL: 161 | FAT: 1 | PROTEIN: 1.7

INGREDIENTS

- 1 package frozen cranberries (or fresh)
- 1-2 tbsps raw honey
- 1 cinnamon stick
- 2 fresh cloves
- 1 orange, sliced thin
- 1/2 tbsp cinnamon
- 1/2 tsp nutmeg

DIRECTIONS

1. Preheat a sous vide water bath to 185°F
2. Place cranberries in a sealed bag along with remaining ingredients and cook for about 2 hours.
3. Remove and transfer to an ice bath for 5 - 10 minutes.
4. Serve with your favorite meals; alternatively, you can refrigerate for up to 14 days.

88. GREEN BEANS ALMANDINE

1.5 HOUR | 15 MIN | 4

NUTRITION:
CAL: 89 | FAT: 7 | PROTEIN: 3.5

INGREDIENTS

- 3 cups fresh green beans
- 2 tbsps olive oil
- 1 tbsp lemon zest
- 1 tsp salt
- 2 tbsps lemon juice
- 1/2 cup toasted almonds

DIRECTIONS

1. Preheat your sous vide water bath to 180°F. Clean and trim the green beans and mix with lemon zest and olive oil. Roughly chop the almonds.
2. Place the whole mixture in the sous vide bag, seal, and place in your preheated container. Set the timer for 1-1/2 hours.
3. Put the cooked green beans on a plate, top with lemon juice, and season with salt.
4. Mix in the almonds and serve.

89. FRAGRANT TOMATO SAUCE

1.5 HOUR | 11 MIN | 4

NUTRITION:
CAL: 221 | FAT: 6 | PROTEIN: 4

INGREDIENTS

- 2 lbs. ripe tomatoes
- 2 tbsps olive oil
- 1/2 cup onion, chopped
- 2 garlic cloves, minced
- 3 sprigs fresh oregano, stemmed
- 6 large basil leaves, chopped
- 1 whole green pepper, seeded and cut into four large pieces

DIRECTIONS

1. Heat olive oil to medium in a sauté pan.
2. Add onion, garlic, and oregano, and cook until fragrant, about 5 to 7 minutes, and set aside to cool.
3. Preheat a sous vide water bath to 120ºF.
4. Add olive oil mix, tomatoes, and remaining ingredients to a resealable plastic bag, and seal airtight.
5. Cook for 50 minutes.
6. Remove bag from the water, open and let cool for a few minutes.
7. Remove peppers and discard.
8. Remove and peel the tomatoes.
9. Add peeled tomatoes and the remaining contents of the bag to a food processor or blender and process until desired texture is achieved.
10. Serve with your favorite dishes.

90. CREAMY BÉARNAISE SAUCE

30 MIN | 15 MIN | 4

NUTRITION:
CAL: 89 | FAT: 4 | PROTEIN: 5

INGREDIENTS

For the reduction:

- 1 bunch fresh tarragon, chopped
- 2 medium shallots, minced
- 1/2 cup white wine vinegar
- 1/2 cup dry white wine
- 6 whole black peppercorns

For the sauce:

- 3 egg yolks
- 2 cups, premium French butter
- 3-4 tbsps reduction
- Sea salt and pepper, to taste

DIRECTIONS

1. Preheat a sous vide water bath to 140ºF
2. In a small saucepan, combine tarragon, shallots, vinegar, pepper and wine over medium-high heat.
3. Bring to simmer and cook until reduced by half.
4. Remove from heat, strain liquid, and set it aside to cool.
5. Place reduction, butter and egg yolks in a resealable plastic bag - DO NOT seal.
6. Place the bag in the water bath to cook for 30 minutes.
7. Pour the sauce into a food processor or blender, and process until thickened.
8. Season with sea salt and pepper and serve immediately.

91. APPLE BUTTERNUT SQUASH SOUP

2 HOURS | 11 MIN | 4

NUTRITION:
CAL: 86 | FAT: 4.6 | PROTEIN: 3

INGREDIENTS

- 1 medium butternut squash
- 1 large tart apple
- 1/2 yellow onion
- 1 tsp sea salt
- 3/4 cup light cream

DIRECTIONS

1. Preheat your sous vide bath to 185°F. Core and slice the apple, peel and slice the butternut squash, slice the onion.
2. Place the butternut squash, apple, and onion in a sous vide bag. Seal and place the bag in your preheated container and set your timer for 2 hours.
3. Once cooked, place the ingredients in a blender and blend until smooth. Add the remaining ingredients and puree again.

92. GLAZED CARROTS

1 HOUR | 11 MIN | 4

NUTRITION:
CAL: 67 | FAT: 2.1 | PROTEIN: 0.8

INGREDIENTS

- 1 lb. baby carrots
- 2 tsps butter
- 2 tsps honey
- Salt and pepper

DIRECTIONS

1. Preheat your sous vide water bath to 185°F.
2. Place all the ingredients in the sous vide bag including salt and pepper to taste.
3. Seal and place the bag in your preheated container and set your timer for 1 hour.
4. When the carrots are cooked, put them on a plate to cool for a few minutes, and drizzle with cooking juices. Serve.

93. PARMESAN GARLIC ASPARAGUS

16 MIN | 6 MIN | 4

NUTRITION:
CAL: 125 | FAT: 12 | PROTEIN: 2.9

INGREDIENTS

- 1 bunch green asparagus, trimmed
- 4 tbsp. unsalted butter, cut into cubes
- Sea salt
- 1 tbsp. pressed garlic
- 1/4 cup shaved Parmesan cheese

DIRECTIONS

1. Preheat your sous vide water bath to 185°F.
2. Use paper towels to pat the salmon dry
3. Place the asparagus in a single layer row in the bag or bags you're going to use to sous vide. Put a tbsp. of butter in each of the corners, the pressed garlic in the middle, salt to taste, and seal the bag. Move the bag around to get garlic to disperse evenly.
4. Place the bag in your preheated water and set the timer for 14 minutes.
5. Top the cooked asparagus with some of the liquid from the bag and the parmesan cheese.
6. Serve immediately.

94. SWEET POTATOES WITH COCONUT CHILI

1 HOUR | 11 MIN | 4

NUTRITION:
CAL: 164 | FAT: 4.1 | PROTEIN: 2

INGREDIENTS

- 4 sweet potatoes
- 2 tbsps coconut oil, melted
- ½ tsp chili powder
- ½ tsp cumin powder
- ¼ tsp salt
- 2 tbsps chopped cilantro, for garnish

DIRECTIONS

1. Preheat your sous vide bath to 190ºF.
2. Peel and cut sweet potatoes into 1-inch-thick roundels.
3. Mix melted coconut oil and spices in a bowl. Add sweet potato and mix well, making sure to cover the roundels in the oil and spice.
4. Place in a large zipper-lock bag (or multiple smaller zipper-lock bags), remove excess air and seal.
5. Place in sous vide bath and cook for 60 minutes.
6. Serve garnished with some chopped cilantro.

95. GARLIC AND ROSEMARY RISOTTO

46 MIN | 11 MIN | 4

NUTRITION:
CAL: 268 | FAT: 5.2 | PROTEIN: 7.9

INGREDIENTS

- 1 cup Arborio rice
- 1 tsp olive oil
- 2 tbsps jarred, roasted minced garlic
- 3 cups chicken or vegetable broth
- 1 sprig fresh rosemary
- 1/3 cup grated Romano cheese

DIRECTIONS

1. Preheat your sous vide water bath to 185ºF. Discard the stems from the rosemary and mince the leaves.
2. Place all ingredients except for cheese in a resealable bag.
3. Place the bag in your preheated container and set your timer for 45 minutes.
4. When the rice is cooked, place it in a bowl and fluff with a fork.
5. Mix in the cheese and serve immediately.

96. LEMON AND PARMESAN BROCCOLI

52 MIN | 11 MIN | 5

NUTRITION:
CAL: 63 | FAT: 4.8 | PROTEIN: 1.7

INGREDIENTS

- 1 head broccoli
- 2 tbsps butter
- Salt and pepper
- Parmesan cheese, for sprinkling
- 1 lemon

DIRECTIONS

1. Preheat your sous vide water bath to 185ºF. Cut the head of broccoli into large pieces.
2. Put the broccoli and butter in a sous vide bag. Salt and pepper to taste.
3. Place the bag in your preheated container and set your timer for 45 minutes.
4. Transfer broccoli to a plate and add the lemon juice and top with cheese to serve.

97. BLACKENED BRUSSELS SPROUTS WITH GARLIC AND BACON

1 H 25 | 16 MIN | 6

NUTRITION:
CAL: 45 | FAT: 2 | PROTEIN: 4

INGREDIENTS

- 2 lbs. Brussels sprouts
- 3 cloves garlic, chopped
- 3 strips bacon
- Bacon fat, from cooking the bacon
- Salt and pepper

DIRECTIONS

1. Preheat your sous vide water bath to 183ºF.
2. Wash the Brussels sprouts and use paper towels to pat them dry.
3. Heat a skillet on medium heat for a few min. When it's hot added in the bacon. Cook the bacon until crispy, flipping halfway through. Remove the bacon and add in the garlic
4. Cook the garlic in the pan with the bacon fat until fragrant, about 1 minute. Then place the bacon fat and garlic in a bowl.
5. Put the Brussels sprouts in the bag or bags you're going to use to sous vide along with the bacon fat, a little fresh ground pepper, and garlic. Shake the bag around so everything, is well mixed and seal the bag.
6. Place the bag in your preheated water and set the timer for 50 minutes.
7. At the 35-minute mark preheat your oven to 400ºF and line a large rimmed baking sheet with parchment paper.
8. Place the cooked mixture on the baking sheet, making sure the Brussels sprouts are in a single layer. Put the baking sheet in the oven and cook the Brussels sprouts for 5 to 7 min. The sprouts should blacken a little bit when they're ready.
9. Serve immediately.

98. ASIAN INSPIRED BOK CHOY

20 MIN | 11 MIN | 4

NUTRITION:
CAL: 98 | FAT: 1| PROTEIN: 9

INGREDIENTS

- 1 lb. baby bok choy, cut in half lengthwise
- 1 tbsp. ginger, minced
- 2 cloves garlic, minced
- 1 tbsp. toasted sesame oil
- 1 tbsp. canola oil
- 1 tbsp. soy sauce
- 1 tbsp. fish sauce
- 1 tsp. red pepper flake
- 1 tbsp. toasted sesame seed
- 1 tbsp. cilantro leaves

DIRECTIONS

1. Preheat your sous vide water bath to 176ºF.
2. Put the garlic and ginger in a large heat proof container.
3. Put the sesame oil and canola oil in a small pot and heat it on medium heat. You want the oil to get so hot that it just starts to smoke.
4. Take the pot off the heat and pour it into the container with the garlic and ginger.
5. Mix in the bok choy, red pepper flakes, fish sauce, and soy sauce.
6. Place the entire mixture in the bag you're going to use to sous vide and seal the bag.
7. Place the bag in your preheated water and set the timer for 20 minutes.
8. Place the cooked bok choy on a plate or in a bowl, and top with the cilantro and sesame seeds.
9. Serve immediately.

99. ROSEMARY AND GARLIC POTATOES

1 HOUR | 6 MIN | 4

NUTRITION:
CAL: 365 | FAT: 10.5 | PROTEIN: 5

INGREDIENTS

- 1 lb. baby bok choy, cut in half lengthwise
- 1 tbsp. ginger, minced
- 2 cloves garlic, minced
- 1 tbsp. toasted sesame oil
- 1 tbsp. canola oil
- 1 tbsp. soy sauce
- 1 tbsp. fish sauce
- 1 tsp. red pepper flake
- 1 tbsp. toasted sesame seed
- 1 tbsp. cilantro leaves

DIRECTIONS

1. Preheat your sous vide water bath to 176°F.
2. Put the garlic and ginger in a large heat proof container.
3. Put the sesame oil and canola oil in a small pot and heat it on medium heat. You want the oil to get so hot that it just starts to smoke.
4. Take the pot off the heat and pour it into the container with the garlic and ginger.
5. Mix in the bok choy, red pepper flakes, fish sauce, and soy sauce.
6. Place the entire mixture in the bag you're going to use to sous vide and seal the bag.
7. Place the bag in your preheated water and set the timer for 20 minutes.
8. Place the cooked bok choy on a plate or in a bowl, and top with the cilantro and sesame seeds.
9. Serve immediately.

100. CANDIED SWEET POTATOES

1.5 HOUR | 6 MIN | 6

NUTRITION:
CAL: 151 | FAT: 8 | PROTEIN: 2

INGREDIENTS

- 4 cups sweet potatoes, peeled and cubed into ½ inch pieces
- 4 tbsp. unsalted butter, cut into small pieces
- 4 tbsp. brown sugar
- 1 tsp. ginger root, finely minced
- 1 pinch cinnamon
- 1 pinch cayenne pepper
- 1 pinch ground clove
- salt and pepper to taste
- 1 cup mini marshmallows
- 1 to 2 tbsp. brown sugar, optional addition for topping

DIRECTIONS

1. Preheat your sous vide water bath to 183°F.
2. Put the sweet potatoes in the bag you're going to use to sous vide along with the butter, ginger, cinnamon, cayenne, clove, and salt and pepper. Massage the bag to evenly disperse the butter and seal bag.
3. Place the bag in your preheated water and set the timer for 1 hour 30 minutes.
4. Place the cooked sweet potatoes in a bowl and top with the brown sugar and marshmallows.
5. Serve immediately.

101. PICKLED ASPARAGUS

30 MIN | 20 MIN | 4

NUTRITION:
CAL: 40 | FAT: 2 | PROTEIN: 2

INGREDIENTS

- 12 oz. asparagus, woody ends trimmed
- 2/3 cup white wine vinegar
- 2/3 cup water
- 3 tbsp. sugar
- 1 tbsp. sea salt
- ½ tsp. whole peppercorns
- ½ tsp. yellow or brown mustard seeds
- ¼ tsp. coriander seeds
- 2 cloves garlic, peeled and sliced in half lengthwise
- 1 bay leaf
- fresh chili pepper, sliced in half

DIRECTIONS

1. Preheat your sous vide water bath to 190ºF.
2. Place everything but the asparagus in small pot and heat on high heat until it boils. Carefully stir the mixture until the sugar dissolves.
3. Place the asparagus in a single layer row in the bag you're going to use to sous vide along with the heated mixture and seal the bag.
4. Place the bag in your preheated water and set the timer for 10 min.
5. While asparagus is cooking, prepare an ice bath, (half ice half water.)
6. Place the cooked asparagus, still in the bag in the ice bath and let it chill for 15 minutes before serving.

102. SPICY PICKLED VEGETABLE MEDLEY

50 MIN | 11 MIN | 6

NUTRITION:
CAL: 35 | FAT: 2| PROTEIN: 2

INGREDIENTS

- 1 cup apple cider vinegar
- ½ cup sriracha
- ¼ cup granulated sugar
- 4 tsp. salt
- 4 tsp. red pepper flake
- 1 cup baby beets, cut into quarters lengthwise
- 1 cup carrot, sliced ¼ inch
- 1 cup persian cucumbers, sliced ¼ inch thick
- 1 cup shallot, sliced ¼ inch thick

DIRECTIONS

1. Preheat your sous vide water bath to 176ºF.
2. Mix together everything but the vegetables in a measuring cup.
3. Place the beets in a bag, the carrots in a bag, and the cucumbers and shallots in bag. Pour and equal amount of the liquid in each bag.
4. Place the beets bag in your preheated water. Set timer for 30 min.
5. Add the carrots bag and cook the carrots bag for 15 minutes.
6. Add the cucumber and shallots bag and cook for 5 minutes
7. While the vegetables are cooking, prepare and ice bath, which is half ice half water.
8. Place the cooked vegetables, still in the bag in the ice bath and let it chill for 15 minutes before serving.

103. TURMERIC PICKLED CAULIFLOWER

3 HOURS | 11 MIN | 6

NUTRITION:
CAL: 95 | FAT: 2 | PROTEIN: 2

INGREDIENTS

- 4 cups cauliflower florets
- 1 cup white wine vinegar
- 1 cup water
- 1/4 cup sugar
- 1 tbsp. salt
- 1 thumb-sized piece turmeric sliced
- a few sprigs dill
- 1 tbsp. black peppercorns

DIRECTIONS

1. Preheat your sous vide water bath to 140ºF.
2. Place everything but the dill and cauliflower in a small pot and bring to a simmer on medium heat. Stir the mixture carefully until the sugar dissolves.
3. Place the cauliflower and dill in the bag you're going to use to sous vide along with the heated mixture and seal the bag.
4. Place the bag in your preheated water and set the timer for 3 hours.
5. Towards the end of the cooking process, prepare and ice bath, which is half ice half water.
6. Place the cooked cauliflower, still in the bag in the ice bath and let it chill for 15 minutes before serving.

104. SIMPLE HONEY GLAZED CARROTS

50 MIN | 6 MIN | 3

NUTRITION:
CAL: 345 | FAT: 34| PROTEIN: 6

INGREDIENTS

- 6-8 medium to large sized carrots, washed and peeled
- 3 tbs. unsalted butter
- 2 tbs. honey
- 1 cinnamon stick
- sea salt to taste

DIRECTIONS

1. Preheat your sous vide water bath to 185ºF.
2. Place the all the ingredients in the bag you're going to use to sous vide and seal the bag.
3. Place the bag in your preheated water and set the timer for 45 minutes.
4. Towards the end of the cooking process, heat a skillet on high heat until it's hot.
5. Place the cooked carrots in the skillet and sear for a total of 1 to 2 minutes, making sure to sear both sides. Top the carrots with a little more honey to serve.

105. GARLIC CHEESE RISOTTO

43 MIN | 6 MIN | 4

NUTRITION:
CAL: 345 | FAT: 34| PROTEIN: 6

INGREDIENTS

- 1 cup Arborio rice
- 1 tsp. olive oil
- 2 tbsp. roasted minced garlic (jarred)
- 3 cups chicken or vegetable broth
- 1 sprig fresh rosemary, leaves only, minced
- Salt and pepper to taste
- 1/3 cup grated Romano cheese

DIRECTIONS

1. Preheat your sous vide water bath to 183ºF.
2. Place the first 6 ingredients in a sous vide bag.
3. Place the bag in your preheated water and set the timer for 45 minutes.
4. Place the cooked risotto in 4 bowls and fluff it with a fork.
5. Mix in the cheese and serve.

106. SOUS VIDE TOMATOES

47 MIN | 7 MIN | 3

NUTRITION:
CAL: 48 | FAT: 2 | PROTEIN: 0.9

INGREDIENTS

- 4 medium on-the-vine tomatoes
- salt and freshly ground black pepper
- 2 tbsp. olive oil
- 2 tbsp. balsamic vinegar, plus more for serving
- 1 sprig fresh rosemary, plus more for serving

DIRECTIONS

1. Preheat your sous vide water bath to 140ºF.
2. Bring water to a boil in a big pot on high heat. Prepare an ice bath
3. Slice a small X in the top of each tomato and put them in the water. Allow the tomatoes to cook for around 1 minutes, until the skin starts to peel off. Then quickly put the tomatoes in the prepared ice bath.
4. When the tomatoes cool down, take off the skins. Season the tomatoes with salt and pepper to taste.
5. Place the tomatoes in the bag you're going to use to sous vide along with the olive oil, balsamic vinegar, and rosemary. Then seal the bag.
6. Place the bag in your preheated water and set the timer for 45 minutes.
7. Place the cooked tomatoes on a plate, sprinkle with a little more balsamic vinegar and top with more rosemary to serve.

107. ARTICHOKE & ROASTED RED PEPPER RISOTTO

1 HOUR | 11 MIN | 4

NUTRITION:
CAL: 158 | FAT: 7 | PROTEIN: 7

INGREDIENTS

- 1 cup Arborio rice
- 3 cups vegetable or chicken broth
- 1, 14 oz. can artichoke hearts, drained and chopped
- 1,12 oz. jar roasted red peppers, drained and chopped
- 1 tbsp olive oil
- 4 cloves garlic, peeled and pressed or finely chopped
- 1 tsp. Italian seasoning
- Ground black pepper, to taste

DIRECTIONS

1. Preheat your sous vide water bath to 183ºF.
2. Place the first 8 ingredients in the sous vide bag.
3. Place it in your preheated water and set the timer for 1 hour.
4. Place the cooked risotto in 4 bowls and fluff it with a fork.
5. Mix in the cheese and serve.

108. TURKEY & MUSHROOM RISOTTO

1 HOUR | 6 MIN | 4

NUTRITION:
CAL: 199 | FAT: 6 | PROTEIN: 21

INGREDIENTS

- 1 cup Arborio rice
- 1 tsp. olive oil
- 1 small yellow onion, peeled and diced
- 8 to 10 Crimini mushrooms, wiped clean and sliced
- 8 oz. cooked turkey or chicken, diced (leftovers work well!)
- 2 tbsp. roasted minced garlic (jarred)
- 3 cups turkey or chicken broth
- 1 sprig fresh rosemary, leaves only, minced
- Salt and pepper to taste
- 1/3 cup grated Romano cheese

DIRECTIONS

1. Preheat your sous vide water bath to 183ºF.
2. Heat up the olive oil in a frying pan on medium heat. Cook the onion and mushrooms until they become tender, about 5 min.
3. Place the first 9 ingredients in the bag you're going to use to sous vide.
4. Place the bag in your preheated water and set the timer for 1 hour.
5. Place the cooked risotto in 4 bowls and fluff it with a fork.
6. Mix in the cheese and serve.

109. VEGETABLE RISOTTO

1 HOUR | 6 MIN | 4

NUTRITION:
CAL: 105 | FAT: 5.7 | PROTEIN: 1.9

INGREDIENTS

Risotto:

- 1 cup Arborio rice
- 3 cups vegetable or mushroom broth
- ½ tsp. butter
- 2, 4 oz. cans mushroom stems and pieces, chopped
- 1 sprig fresh rosemary, leaves minced
- salt and pepper to taste

Spring Vegetables:

- 1 lb. spring vegetables like asparagus, broccoli, peppers, summer squash, cut into bite sized pieces, peeled if necessary
- Salt and pepper to taste
- 1 to 2 tbsp. butter
- fresh or dried herbs of choice

DIRECTIONS

1. Preheat your sous vide water bath to 183ºF.
2. Place the risotto ingredients in the sous vide bag and the spring vegetable ingredients in a separate one and seal them.
3. Place the bags in your preheated water and set the timer for 45 min.
4. Place the cooked risotto in 4 bowls and fluff it with a fork.
5. Mix in the cheese and vegetables, and serve.

110. FENNEL RISOTTO

46 MIN | 15 MIN | 4

NUTRITION:
CAL: 106 | FAT: 2 | PROTEIN: 2

INGREDIENTS

- 1 cup Arborio rice
- 3 cups vegetable broth
- 1 glass white wine
- 1 tbsp. olive oil
- salt and pepper
- 4 fennel bulbs – trimmed cut in half
- a little butter
- Freshly grated Parmesan cheese, for serving

DIRECTIONS

1. Preheat your sous vide water bath to 183°F.
2. Place the first 5 ingredients in the sous vide bag and the fennel and a little butter in a separate bag, and seal them.
3. Place the bags in your preheated water and set the timer for 45 min.
4. Place the cooked risotto in 4 bowls and fluff it with a fork.
5. Mix in the cheese and fennel, and serve.

111. ROASTED RED PEPPER EGG WHITE BITES

1 HOUR | 11 MIN | 6

NUTRITION:
CAL: 54 | FAT: 3 | PROTEIN: 7.9

INGREDIENTS

- 6 egg whites
- 1/4 cup cream cheese
- 1/2 cup cottage cheese
- 1/4 tsp. salt
- 1/4 tsp. pepper
- 2 tbsp. finely chopped roasted red pepper
- 2 green onions, green parts only, finely chopped
- Butter or oil

DIRECTIONS

1. Preheat your sous vide water bath to 172°F.
2. Place the first 5 ingredients in a blender or food processor and blend until smooth.
3. Use butter or oil to grease 6, 4 oz. mason jars.
4. Pour in an equal amount of the egg mixture and place an equal amount of roasted red pepper in the mason jars.
5. Use a butter knife to stir the mixture.
6. Use your fingertips to tighten the lids.
7. Place the jars in your preheated water and set the timer for 1 hour.
8. Allow the cooked egg bites to cool for a few minutes.
9. Serve the cooked egg bites in the jars or use a knife to remove them and put them on plates.

112. BALSAMIC MUSHROOMS AND MIXED HERBS

1 HOUR | 10 MIN | 6

NUTRITION:
CAL: 45 | FAT: 3 | PROTEIN: 4

INGREDIENTS

- 1 lb cremini mushrooms, stems removed
- 1 tbsp olive oil
- 1 tbsp apple balsamic vinegar
- 1 tsp black pepper, freshly ground
- 1 tsp fresh thyme, minced
- 1 garlic clove, minced
- 1 tsp salt

DIRECTIONS

1. Preheat your water bath to 140 °F
2. Add all the listed ingredients into a heavy-duty resalable zip bag
3. Seal bag using the immersion method, submerge it
4. Cook for 1 hour
5. Serve and enjoy!

113. CARAMELIZED ONION AND BROCCOLI PALEO EGG BITES

1.5 HOUR | 21 MIN | 6

NUTRITION:
CAL: 95 | FAT: 5 | PROTEIN: 7.8

INGREDIENTS

- 6 eggs
- 1/4 tsp. salt
- 1 cup broccoli florets cut pieces
- 1/2 cup yellow onion, minced
- 1 tbsp. olive oil
- 1/4 tsp. garlic powder
- 2 tbsp. water
- 2 tbsp. finely chopped roasted red pepper

DIRECTIONS

1. Preheat your sous vide water bath to 172ºF.
2. Place the first 2 ingredients in a blender and blend on medium-high speed. Blend until the mixture turns to a creamy color and the is homogenized.
3. Pour the olive oil into a small frying pan and heat it on medium-high heat until the oil moves around the pan freely. Put in the onions, a pinch of salt, garlic powder, and broccoli in the pan and mix until the vegetables are coated with oil. Reduced the temperature to medium heat and cook for 3 to 4 minutes.
4. Pour the water into the pan and stir the mixture. Cook for another minute, until all the water evaporates.
5. Take the pan off the heat and allow the mixture to cool.
6. Pour in an equal amount of the egg mixture. Place an equal amount of roasted red pepper and the onion mixture in the mason jars.
7. Use a butter knife to stir the mixture.
8. Use your fingertips to tighten the lids.

114. PARMESAN AND SCALLION OMELET

20 MIN | 10 MIN | 1

NUTRITION:
CAL: 245 | FAT: 21.2 | PROTEIN: 12

INGREDIENTS

- 2 large eggs
- 1 tbsp. minced scallion greens
- 1 tbsp. finely grated Parmesan cheese
- 1 tbsp. unsalted butter, diced
- Salt and pepper
- Chopped fresh parsley, for serving

DIRECTIONS

1. Preheat your sous vide to 165ºF.
2. Whisk the eggs in a medium bowl. Then whisk in the parmesan, butter, scallions, and salt and pepper to taste.
3. Place the mixture in the bag that you're going to use to sous vide and seal it.
4. Place the bags in your preheated water and set the timer for 10 min.
5. After the 10 minutes gentle fold the eggs into the shape of an omelet and cook for 10 more minutes.
6. Place the cooked omelet on a plate and top with the parsley to serve.

115. FANTASTIC EARLY MORNING ARTICHOKE

30 MIN | 15 MIN | 2

NUTRITION:
CAL: 130 | FAT: 11 | PROTEIN: 2

INGREDIENTS

- 1 whole artichoke
- 2 tbsps butter
- 1 clove garlic, sautéed
- 1 tsp of sea salt

DIRECTIONS

1. Preheat your water bath to 180 ºF
2. Peel outer leaves and stems of the artichoke
3. Then cut up the artichokes in half from bloom end to the stem end and season it with salt and garlic
4. Add all the listed ingredients into a heavy-duty resalable zip bag
5. Seal bag using the immersion method, submerge it
6. Cook for 30 minutes. Serve and enjoy

4. POULTRY

116. EASY CHICKEN CORDON BLEU

1.5 HOURS | 6 MIN | 4

NUTRITION:
CAL: 93 | FAT: 5| PROTEIN: 12

INGREDIENTS

- 2 boneless, skinless chicken breasts
- 1 tsp sea salt
- 1 tsp black pepper
- 4 Swiss cheese slices
- 2 slices uncured ham
- Binding string

DIRECTIONS

1. Prepare a sous vide water bath to 140ºF.
2. Butterfly chicken breasts and place them between two sheets of plastic wrap.
3. Tenderize flat using a meat tenderizer.
4. Remove plastic wrap and season the chicken with salt and pepper.
5. Lay Swiss cheese in a single layer down the middle of each chicken breast.
6. Place a layer of uncured ham on top of the cheese.
7. Roll each chicken breast up like a jelly roll, beginning at the narrowest edge. Use binding string on each end to hold together.
8. Place the chicken rolls in a vacuum bag, seal, and cook for 1 hour 30 minutes.
9. Allow chicken to rest for 5 minutes, and slice to serve warm.

117. MOIST DELICIOUS THANKSGIVING TURKEY

2.5 HOURS | 10 MIN | 10

NUTRITION:
CAL: 702 | FAT: 25| PROTEIN: 108

INGREDIENTS

- 8 lbs. turkey
- 2 tsp salt
- 1 stick unsalted butter
- 8 garlic cloves, minced
- 4 sprigs sage
- 4 sprigs thyme
- 4 sprigs rosemary

DIRECTIONS

1. Defrost turkey according to the instructions on the packaging.
2. Preheat a sous vide water bath to 149ºF.
3. Remove the packaged gizzards inside the turkey cavity.
4. Remove the thighs and drumsticks with a boning knife, then remove the wings of the turkey.
5. Cut out the rib cage, with kitchen shears, and save for stock or gravy.
6. Cut the breast in half, down the middle with boning knife, and keep the bone in.
7. Place the thighs and wings in one gallon vacuum bag and do not overlap.
8. Place drumsticks in another bag, turkey breast in a third and fourth bag.
9. Add 2 smashed cloves garlic, 1 sprig of each herb, and two tbsps of butter to each bag.
10. Seal with a vacuum sealer or use the water displacement method.
11. Take care that the turkey pieces inside the bags are completely submerged during sous vide.
12. Cook for 2 hours 30 minutes; legs will be most tender when cooked at 4 to 6 hours.
13. Here, you can crisp in a cast iron skillet for 3 minutes on each side and serve immediately with your favorite trimmings.

118. HARISSA CHICKEN

2 HOURS | 15 MIN | 2

NUTRITION:
CAL: 273 | FAT: 20 | PROTEIN: 23.5

INGREDIENTS

- 2 boneless, skinless chicken breasts
- 1 tbsp harissa, powdered; or 1/2 tbsp harissa paste
- 1/2 tsp cayenne pepper
- 2 garlic cloves, minced
- Sea salt, to taste
- 1 preserved lemon, chopped
- 4 tbsps olive oil, divided

DIRECTIONS

1. Add all ingredients to a resealable bag and marinate for 30 minutes. Use only half the olive oil.
2. Preheat the sous vide water bath to 141°F.
3. Seal the bag and add chicken to sous vide water bath and cook for 2 hours.
4. Heat remaining olive oil in a frying pan on medium-high.
5. Remove chicken from water bath and sear on both sides for 2 minutes.
6. Serve with juices over couscous and enjoy!

119. ITALIAN-STYLE CHICKEN MARSALA

2.5 HOURS | 15 MIN | 4

NUTRITION:
CAL: 290 | FAT: 5.6 | PROTEIN: 26.6

INGREDIENTS

- 4 chicken breasts
- 2 sprigs fresh thyme
- 1 tsp sea salt
- 1 tsp black pepper

For the chicken Marsala topping:

- 1 cup unbleached flour
- 1 tbsp olive oil
- 3 cups sliced baby portabella mushrooms
- 3/4 cup Marsala wine
- 3/4 cup chicken stock
- 3 tbsps butter
- 4 tbsps chopped Italian parsley

DIRECTIONS

1. Preheat a sous vide water bath to 141°F
2. Lightly salt and pepper the chicken breasts and place in a vacuum bag with thyme and seal.
3. Add to water bath and cook for 2 hours.
4. Heat olive oil in a sauté pan over high heat.
5. Preheat oven to warm.
6. Remove the sous vide chicken breasts from the sous vide bath, pat dry with a paper towel, and dredge them in the flour.
7. Sear the chicken breasts for 1 minute per side.
8. Remove and place on a baking sheet in the warm oven.
9. Turn heat to medium high for the sauté pan and melt 1 tbsp of butter.
10. Add mushrooms and cook until they brown and release their liquid; about 4 to 6 minutes.
11. Turn heat down to medium and add the Marsala wine to the pan; simmer for 1 minute, scraping the bottom of the pan to dislodge the browned bits.
12. Add the chicken stock and simmer for 10 minutes to reduce sauce.
13. Fold the remaining 2 tbsps of butter into the sauce and plate the seared chicken breasts.
14. Spoon the Marsala sauce evenly over the chicken breasts.
15. Garnish with Italian parsley and serve.

120. RICH AND TASTY DUCK À L'ORANGE

2.5 HOURS | 15 MIN | 2

NUTRITION:
CAL: 338 | FAT: 24.3 | PROTEIN: 23

INGREDIENTS

- 2 small duck breasts
- 1 orange, sliced
- 4 garlic cloves, smashed
- 1 shallot, smashed
- 4 thyme sprigs
- 1/2 tbsp black peppercorns
- 1 tbsp sherry vinegar
- 1/4 cup red wine, like Merlot
- 2 tbsps butter
- Sea salt, to taste

DIRECTIONS

1. Preheat a sous vide water bath to 135ºF.
2. Add the duck breasts with slices of orange, garlic, shallots, thyme and peppercorns to a vacuum bag.
3. Seal and cook for 2 hours 30 minutes.
4. Preheat a frying pan to medium high heat.
5. Remove duck from bag and set bag aside.
6. Fry the duck breast, skin side down, for 30 seconds.
7. Remove duck breast from pan and keep warm.
8. Add vinegar and red wine to frying pan to deglaze leftover fat.
9. Add the contents of the vacuum bag and cook for about 6 minutes over medium heat.
10. Fold in the butter and season with salt and pepper.
11. Slice the duck breast into 2-inch medallions, top with sauce, and serve.

121. SPICY HONEY SRIRACHA WINGS

46 MIN | 6 MIN | 2

NUTRITION:
CAL: 355 | FAT: 22.3 | PROTEIN: 28

INGREDIENTS

- 1 lb. chicken wings
- 1/2 tsp sea salt
- 1/2 tsp paprika
- 1/2 tsp garlic
- 1/2 tsp ginger

For the Glaze:

- 1 tbsp sesame oil
- 2 tbsps soy sauce
- 2 tbsps honey

DIRECTIONS

1. Preheat a sous vide water bath to 140ºF
2. Mix spices in a mixing bowl and toss wings to coat.
3. Add wings to a vacuum bag.
4. Cook the wings for 40 minutes.
5. Combine glaze ingredients in a large mixing bowl.
6. Transfer chicken wings in an ice bath.
7. For crispy wings, fry in a cast iron skillet on high heat for 1 to 2 minutes, or until golden.
8. Toss the wings in the glaze and serve hot.

122. AROMATIC ROSEMARY CHICKEN

2 HOURS | 50 MIN | 4

NUTRITION:
CAL: 135 | FAT: 4.3 | PROTEIN: 23

INGREDIENTS

- 4 chicken breasts

For the brine:

- 2 cups chicken stock
- 4 tbsps salt
- 2 tbsps brown sugar

For the rosemary sauce:

- 1 stick of butter
- 2 tsps rosemary, chopped
- 1 tsp garlic powder
- ½ tsp paprika
- ½ tsp sea salt
- ½ tsp black pepper
- 1 tbsp olive oil

DIRECTIONS

1. Add chicken to a shallow dish with brine, cover, and refrigerate for 50 minutes.
2. Preheat the sous vide water bath to 141°F
3. Combine rosemary sauce ingredients in a mixing bowl.
4. Add chicken breasts to a vacuum bag and seal.
5. Add to sous vide bath and cook for 2 hours.
6. Add rosemary sauce to a pan on medium-high heat and brown for 5 minutes.
7. Remove chicken from bags, coat with butter, and brown in a frying pan on medium-high, on both sides, for 2 minutes.
8. Serve drizzled with sauce and enjoy!

123. TEMPTING TERIYAKI CHICKEN

1.5 HOURS | 30 MIN | 1

NUTRITION:
CAL: 150 | FAT: 3.1 | PROTEIN: 27.1

INGREDIENTS

- 1 skinless, boneless chicken breast
- 1/2 tsp ginger juice
- 2 tbsps sugar, plus 1 tsp
- 1/2 tsp salt
- 2 tbsps soy sauce
- 2 tbsps sake or mirin

DIRECTIONS

1. Dry the chicken with a paper towel and then coat with the ginger juice.
2. Mix 1 tsp sugar and salt in a small bowl, and sprinkle on both sides of the chicken.
3. Add the chicken to a vacuum bag and seal; set aside to marinate for 30 minutes or overnight.
4. Preheat a sous vide water bath to 140°F
5. Add chicken and cook sous vide for 1 hour 30 minutes.
6. Combine the remaining sugar, soy sauce and sake in a small saucepan, bring to a boil, and cook until the sauce is thick, forming large shiny bubbles.
7. Remove sauce and place on warm until chicken is done.
8. Plate chicken, top with teriyaki sauce, and serve!

124. CHICKEN BREAST WITH CREAMY MUSHROOM SAUCE

1.5 HOURS | 35 MIN | 2

NUTRITION:
CAL: 653 | FAT: 62 | PROTEIN: 24

INGREDIENTS

- 2 boneless, skinless chicken breasts
- 1/8 tsp sea salt
- For the mushroom cream sauce:
- 3 shallots, finely chopped
- 2 large cloves garlic, minced
- 1 tsp olive oil
- 2 tbsps butter
- 1 cup button mushrooms, sliced
- 2 tbsps port wine
- 1/2 cup chicken stock
- 1 cup heavy cream
- 1/4 tsp fresh ground black pepper

DIRECTIONS

1. Preheat a sous vide water bath to 140ºF
2. Salt chicken breasts evenly, place in vacuum bag, and seal.
3. Cook for 1 hour 30 minutes.
4. Add the olive oil to a frying pan on medium heat.
5. Add shallots and cook for 3 minutes.
6. Add the butter and garlic and stir for 1 minute.
7. Turn stove up to medium-high and add the mushrooms; cook until they release liquid and it evaporates.
8. Add the port wine and cook until it's nearly evaporated.
9. Add the stock and cook for 2 minutes, then fold in the cream until well-incorporated.
10. Cook over medium heat until the sauce thickens and finish with pepper.
11. Remove chicken from sous vide bath and plate.
12. Top with mushroom sauce and enjoy!

125. DUCK BREAST WITH AMARENA CHERRY SAUCE

1 HOUR | 16 MIN | 4

NUTRITION:
CAL: 573 | FAT: 32.9 | PROTEIN: 45.5

INGREDIENTS

- 4 duck breasts
- 1 small jar Amarena cherries in syrup
- 1 cup red wine
- 4 sprigs thyme
- 5 tbsps butter

DIRECTIONS

1. Preheat a sous vide water bath to 145ºF. Wash and dry the duck, and then cut the skin off of it. Salt and pepper the duck to taste. Place the duck in the sous vide bag with 1 tbsp of butter and 1 sprig of thyme on each breast.
2. Seal the bag, then place in the preheated container and set timer for 1 hour.
3. Place cherries and wine in a pan and bring to a boil over high heat.
4. Reduce the temperature to medium heat and simmer until the sauce becomes thick. Take the pan off the heat.
5. When the duck is cooked, pat it dry and heat a skillet on medium heat with a tbsp of butter.
6. Once the skillet is hot, add in the duck and sear it for about a minute per side. Serve topped with the cherry sauce.

126. DUCK LEG CONFIT

8 HOURS | 6 HOURS | 2

NUTRITION:
CAL: 200 | FAT: 11.5 | PROTEIN: 18.8

INGREDIENTS

- 2 duck legs
- 2 tsps salt
- Bay leaf
- Sprig of thyme
- 2 thin orange slices
- 1 clove garlic
- Salt and pepper
- 2 tbsps duck fat or olive oil

DIRECTIONS

1. Place all the ingredients in a medium size bowl and mix until the salt dissolves. Place the duck in the bowl and refrigerate for 6 hours covered.
2. Preheat a sous vide water bath to 176°F
3. Take the duck out of the mixture and pat it dry using a paper towel. Salt and pepper the duck to taste and place it in the sous vide bag with the oil or fat.
4. Seal the bag and place it in your preheated container and set your timer for 8 hours.
5. When the duck is almost done cooking, preheat your broil to high.
6. When the duck is done cooking, broil it until skin side becomes crispy.

127. LEMON HERB TURKEY BREAST

8 HOURS | 6 HOURS | 2

NUTRITION:
CAL: 542 | FAT: 20.9 | PROTEIN: 67

INGREDIENTS

- 1 lb. chicken wings
- 1/2 tsp sea salt
- 1/2 tsp paprika
- 1/2 tsp garlic
- 1/2 tsp ginger
- 1/2 tsp black pepper

For the glaze:

- 1 tbsp sesame oil
- 2 tbsps soy sauce
- 2 tbsps honey

DIRECTIONS

1. Preheat a sous vide water bath to 143°F
2. Combine all the ingredients except for the turkey and flour in a bowl. Place the turkey in the sous vide bag along with the marinade mixture. Seal the bag and place in the water bath. Cook for 4 hours.
3. When the turkey is cooked, put the flour in a small saucepan along with 1 tbsp of oil. Heat the mixture over medium heat, stirring constantly for about 1 minute. Pour in the juices from the bag and use a whisk to remove any lumps from the gravy.
4. Slice the turkey thin and serve with the gravy.

128. FILIPINO ADOBO CHICKEN

4 HOURS | 15 MIN | 2

NUTRITION:
CAL: 445 | FAT: 25 | PROTEIN: 46.8

INGREDIENTS

- 1-1/2 lbs. chicken thighs and drumstick
- 6 pieces dried bay leaves
- 1 cup soy sauce
- 1 head garlic crushed
- 1 tbsp whole peppercorn
- 1/4 cup vinegar
- 1/2 cup chicken broth

DIRECTIONS

1. Preheat a sous vide water bath to 155°F
2. Place the chicken and all the other ingredients in the sous vide bag.
3. Place the bag in your preheated container and set your timer for 4 hours.
4. Serve chicken with the sauce from the bag.

129. SPICY CURRIED CHICKEN THIGHS

2 HOURS | 15 MIN | 4

NUTRITION:
CAL: 390 | FAT: 29 | PROTEIN: 28

INGREDIENTS

- 8 pieces boneless, skinless chicken thighs
- 8 garlic cloves
- 6 tbsps olive oil
- 2 tbsps cumin
- 2 tbsps coriander
- 2 tsps salt
- 2 tsps allspice
- 2 tsps turmeric
- 1 tsp curry
- 1 tsp ground ginger
- 1 tsp ground pepper
- 1/4 tsp cayenne

DIRECTIONS

1. Preheat a sous vide water bath to 165ºF
2. Place all the ingredients except for the chicken thighs in a blender or food processor. Blend until the ingredients form a thick paste. Coat the chicken with the paste. Place in a sous vide bag and seal. Put the chicken in the sous vide for 2 hours. Towards the end of the cooking process, preheat your broiler.
3. When the chicken is cooked, take it out of the bag and place it under the broiler. Broil each side until it browns, no more than 2 minutes per side.

130. CHICKEN TIKKA MASALA

2 HOURS | 15 MIN | 4

NUTRITION:
CAL: 603 | FAT: 52.3 | PROTEIN: 25

INGREDIENTS

- 4 boneless, skinless chicken breasts
- 2 tbsps butter
- Pinch of salt and pepper
- 2 cups crushed or strained tomatoes
- 2 cups heavy cream
- 1-inch piece peeled ginger cut into chunks
- 4 garlic cloves
- 1-1/2 tbsps honey
- 1 tbsp paprika
- 1 tbsp cumin
- 3 tsps turmeric
- 2 tsps coriander
- 1-1/2 tsps salt

DIRECTIONS

1. Preheat a sous vide water bath to 146ºF. Cut the ginger into chunks.
2. Salt and pepper the chicken to taste and place it in the sous vide bag with the butter and seal. Blend all the remaining ingredients in a blender until smooth. Place the sauce in another sous vide bag.
3. Place both bags in your preheated container and set your timer for 2 hours.
4. When the chicken is cooked, remove from bag and slice it. Then, top the chicken with the sauce and serve.

131. TURKEY BREAST WITH PECANS

2 HOURS | 15 MIN | 4

NUTRITION:
CAL: 390 | FAT: 30 | PROTEIN: 28

INGREDIENTS

- 8 pieces boneless, skinless chicken thighs
- 8 garlic cloves
- 6 tbsps olive oil
- 2 tbsps cumin
- 2 tbsps coriander
- 2 tsps salt
- 2 tsps allspice
- 2 tsps turmeric
- 1 tsp curry
- 1 tsp ground ginger
- 1 tsp ground pepper
- 1/4 tsp cayenne

DIRECTIONS

1. Preheat a sous vide water bath to 165ºF
2. Place all the ingredients except for the chicken thighs in a blender or food processor. Blend until the ingredients form a thick paste. Coat the chicken with the paste. Place in a sous vide bag and seal. Put the chicken in the sous vide for 2 hours. Towards the end of the cooking process, preheat your broiler.
3. When the chicken is cooked, take it out of the bag and place it under the broiler. Broil each side until it browns, no more than 2 minutes per side.

131. TURKEY BREAST WITH PECANS

14 HOURS | 15 MIN | 4

NUTRITION:
CAL: 94 | FAT: 6 | PROTEIN: 10

INGREDIENTS

- 1 turkey leg
- 1 tbsp olive oil
- 1 tbsp garlic salt
- 1 tsp black pepper
- 3 sprigs thyme
- 1 tbsp rosemary

DIRECTIONS

1. Prepare a sous vide water bath and set to 146º F. Season the turkey with garlic, salt and pepper. Place it in a vacuum-sealable bag.
2. Release air by the water displacement method, seal and submerge the bag in the bath. Cook for 14 hours. Once done, remove the legs and pat it dry.

131. TURKEY BREAST WITH PECANS

40 MIN | 15 MIN | 2

NUTRITION:
CAL: 489 | FAT: 21 | PROTEIN: 67

INGREDIENTS

- 1 lb turkey breasts, skinless and boneless
- 1 tbsp butter
- 3 tbsp fresh orange juice
- ½ cup chicken stock
- 1 tsp Cayenne pepper
- Salt and black pepper to taste

DIRECTIONS

1. Rinse the turkey breasts under cold running water and pat dry. Set aside.
2. In a medium bowl, combine orange juice, chicken stock, Cayenne pepper, salt, and pepper. Mix well and place the meat into this marinade. Refrigerate for 20 minutes.
3. Now, place the meat along with marinade into a large vacuum-sealable bag and cook for 40 minutes at 122ºF.
4. In a medium nonstick saucepan, melt the butter over a medium-high temperature. Remove the meat from the bag and add it to the saucepan. Fry for 2 minutes and remove from the heat.

134. THYME & ROSEMARY TURKEY LEGS

8 HOURS | 25 MIN | 2

NUTRITION:
CAL: 402 | FAT: 25 | PROTEIN: 40

INGREDIENTS

- 2 turkey legs
- 5 tsp butter, melted
- 10 garlic cloves, minced
- 2 tbsp dried rosemary
- 1 tbsp cumin
- 1 tbsp thyme

DIRECTIONS

1. Prepare a sous vide water bath to 134ºF.
2. Combine the garlic, rosemary, cumin, thyme and butter. Rub the turkey with the mixture.
3. Place the turkey in a vacuum-sealable bag. Release air by the water displacement method, seal and submerge the bag in the water bath. Cook for 8 hours
4. Once the timer has stopped, remove the turkey. Reserve the cooking juices. Heat the grill over high heat and put the turkey. Sprinkle the cooking juices. Turn around and sprinkle more juices. Set aside and allow to cool. Serve.

135. TURKEY BREAST WITH CLOVES

1 HOUR | 30 MIN | 6

NUTRITION:
CAL: 610 | FAT: 46 | PROTEIN: 45

INGREDIENTS

- 2 lbs turkey breast, sliced
- 2 garlic cloves, minced
- 1 cup olive oil
- 2 tbsp Dijon mustard
- 2 tbsp lemon juice
- 1 tsp fresh rosemary, finely chopped
- 1 tsp cloves, minced
- Salt and black pepper to taste

DIRECTIONS

1. In a large bowl, combine olive oil, with mustard, lemon juice, garlic, rosemary, cloves, salt, and pepper. Mix until well incorporated and add turkey slices. Soak and refrigerate for 30 minutes before cooking.
2. Remove from the refrigerator and transfer to 2 vacuum-sealable bags. Seal the bags and cook in a sous vide water bath for one hour at 149º F. Remove from the water bath and serve.

136. DILL & ROSEMARY TURKEY BREAST

1.5 HOUR | 25 MIN | 2

NUTRITION:
CAL: 438 | FAT: 16 | PROTEIN: 68

INGREDIENTS

- 1-lb boneless turkey breasts
- Salt and black pepper to taste
- 3 fresh dill sprigs
- 1 fresh rosemary sprig, chopped
- 1 bay leaf

DIRECTIONS

1. Prepare a sous vide water bath to 146ºF.
2. Heat a skillet over medium heat, Put the turkey and sear for 5 minutes. Reserve the Fat. Season the turkey with salt and pepper. Place the turkey, dill, rosemary, bay leaf and reserved Fat in a vacuum-sealable bag. Release air by the water displacement method, seal and submerge the bag in the water bath. Cook for 1 hour and 30 minutes.
3. Heat a skillet over high heat. Once the timer has stopped, remove the turkey and transfer into the skillet. Sear for 5 minutes.

136. DILL & ROSEMARY TURKEY BREAST

1.5 HOUR | 25 MIN | 2

NUTRITION:
CAL: 438 | FAT: 16| PROTEIN: 68

INGREDIENTS

- 1-lb boneless turkey breasts
- Salt and black pepper to taste
- 3 fresh dill sprigs
- 1 fresh rosemary sprig, chopped
- 1 bay leaf

DIRECTIONS

1. Prepare a sous vide water bath to 146ºF.
2. Heat a skillet over medium heat, Put the turkey and sear for 5 minutes. Reserve the Fat. Season the turkey with salt and pepper. Place the turkey, dill, rosemary, bay leaf and reserved Fat in a vacuum-sealable bag. Release air by the water displacement method, seal and submerge the bag in the water bath. Cook for 1 hour and 30 minutes.
3. Heat a skillet over high heat. Once the timer has stopped, remove the turkey and transfer into the skillet. Sear for 5 minutes.

137. ROASTED SWEET DUCK

1.5 HOUR | 25 MIN | 2

NUTRITION:
CAL: 219 | FAT: 8| PROTEIN: 34

INGREDIENTS

- 8 oz boneless duck breast
- ¼ tsp cinnamon
- ¼ tsp smoked paprika
- ¼ tsp cayenne pepper
- 1 tbsp thyme
- 1 tsp honey
- Salt and black pepper to taste

DIRECTIONS

1. Prepare a sous vide water bath to 134ºF. Pat dry the breast duck with a baking sheet and remove the skin, be careful not to cut the flesh. Season with salt.
2. Heat a frying pan over high heat. Sear the duck for 3-4 minutes. Remove and set aside.
3. In a bowl, combine the paprika, thyme, cayenne pepper and cinnamon, mix well. Marinade the duck breast with the mixture. Place it in a vacuum-sealable bag. Add 1 tbsp of honey. Release air by the water displacement method, seal and submerge the bag in the water bath. Cook for 3 hours and 30 minutes.
4. Once the timer has stopped, remove the bag and dry. Heat a skillet over high heat and sear the duck for 2 minutes. Flip it and cook for 30 seconds more. Allow cooling and serve.

138. THYME DUCK BREAST

1 HOUR | 1 HOUR | 3

NUTRITION:
CAL: 115 | FAT: 6| PROTEIN: 24

INGREDIENTS

- 3 duck breast, skin on
- 3 tsp thyme leaves
- 2 tsp olive oil
- Salt and black pepper to taste

DIRECTIONS

1. Make crosswise strips on the ducks and without cutting into the meat. Season the skin with salt and the meat side with thyme, pepper, and salt. Place the duck breasts in 3 separate vacuum-sealable bags. Release air and seal the bag. Refrigerate for 1 hour.
2. Make a water bath, place Sous Vide in it, and set to 135ºF. Remove the bag from the refrigerator and submerge the bag in the water bath. Set the timer for 1 hour.
3. Once the timer has stopped, remove and unseal the bag. Set a skillet over medium heat, add olive oil. Once it has heated, add duck and sear until skin renders and meat is golden brown. Remove and let sit for 3 minutes and then slice. Serve.

139. ORANGE GOOSE CONFIT

12 HOURS | 10 MIN | 4

NUTRITION:
CAL: 673 | FAT: 64| PROTEIN: 23

INGREDIENTS

- 3 bay leaves
- 4 goose legs
- 10 tsp salt
- 6 garlic cloves, smashed
- 1 fresh rosemary sprig, stemmed
- 1 cup goose Fat
- 1 tsp peppercorns
- Zest of 1 orange

DIRECTIONS

1. Brush the goose legs with the garlic, salt, peppercorns and rosemary. Cover and allow to chill in the fridge for 12 to 24 hours. Prepare a sous vide water bath to 172ºF. Remove the goose from the fridge and pat dry with kitchen towel.
2. Place the goose, goose Fat, bay leaves, peppercorn and orange zest in a vacuum-sealable bag. Release air by the water displacement method, seal and submerge the bag in the water bath. Cook for 12 hours.
3. Once the timer has stopped, remove the goose from the bag and clean the Fat excess. Heat a skillet over high heat and sear the goose for 5-7 minutes until crispy.

140. CHICKEN WINGS

7 HOURS | 20 MIN | 4

NUTRITION:
CAL: 258 | FAT: 28| PROTEIN: 2

INGREDIENTS

- 12 chicken wings
- ¼ cup vegetable oil
- 4 sprigs thyme
- 2 tsps crushed red pepper flakes
- Salt, to taste

DIRECTIONS

1. Preheat a sous vide water bath to 167ºF.
2. In a sous vide bag, combine the chicken wing with remaining ingredients.
3. Shake gently to coat the chicken and vacuum seal the bag.
4. Submerge in water and cook 7 hours.
5. Finishing steps:
6. Remove the bag with chicken from cooker.
7. Heat some oil in a large skillet.
8. Place the wings into a skillet and cook until the skin is crispy.
9. Serve.

141. SAGE INFUSED TURKEY

12 HOURS | 10 MIN | 4-6

NUTRITION:
CAL: 142 | FAT: 7| PROTEIN: 17

INGREDIENTS

- 2 turkey legs and thighs, with bone and skin
- 1 lemon, sliced
- 10 sage leaves
- 4 cloves garlic, halved
- Salt, to taste
- 1 tsp black peppercorns

DIRECTIONS

1. Preheat a sous vide water bath to 148ºF.
2. Season the turkey with salt and place in a Sous Vide bag.
3. Add the lemon slices, sage, garlic, and peppercorns.
4. Vacuum seal the bag and cook the turkey 12 hours.
5. Finishing steps:
6. Remove the turkey from the bag and pat dry.
7. Heat non-stick skillet over medium-high heat.
8. Sear the turkey until golden-brown.
9. Serve warm.

142. TURKEY BURGERS

1 HOUR | 20 MIN | 6

NUTRITION:
CAL: 310 | FAT: 13 | PROTEIN: 44

INGREDIENTS

- 2lb. ground lean turkey
- 1 shallot, chopped
- ½ cup parsley, chopped
- ½ cup sun-dried tomatoes, packed in oil, chopped
- 2 cloves garlic, minced
- 1 tsp dry mustard powder
- 1 tsp paprika powder
- Salt and pepper, to taste

DIRECTIONS

1. Combine all ingredients in a bowl.
2. Shape the mixture into 6 patties. Arrange the patties on a baking sheet lined with parchment paper. Freeze 4 hours.
3. Preheat a sous vide water bath to 145°F.
4. Place each patty in a Sous Vide bag and vacuum seal.
5. Place in a water bath 60 minutes.
6. Finishing steps:
7. Remove the bag from the cooker.
8. Open the bag and remove the patties.
9. Heat a grill pan over medium-high heat. Sear the patties for 1 minute per side.
10. Serve with fresh salad and fresh buns.

143. DUCK CONFIT

12 HOURS | 25 MIN | 2

NUTRITION:
CAL: 650 | FAT: 63 | PROTEIN: 17

INGREDIENTS

- 2 duck legs, skin on, bone in
- 3 sprigs marjoram
- 1 tbsp green peppercorns
- 1 tbsp fine salt
- ½ cup duck Fat
- 2 fresh bay leaves

DIRECTIONS

1. Rub the duck with marjoram, peppercorns, and salt.
2. Place in a clean vessel and refrigerate 24 hours.
3. Preheat a sous vide water bath to 170°F.
4. Remove the duck from a vessel, rinse, and pat dry. Place the duck into Sous Vide bag, along with duck Fat, and bay leaves.
5. Vacuum seal and cook 12 hours in a water bath.
6. Finishing steps:
7. When the timer goes off, remove the duck.
8. Heat the nonstick skillet and cook the duck, skin side down, 5 minutes. Serve.

144. CHICKEN BREAST MEAL

1 HOUR | 5 MIN | 1

NUTRITION:
CAL: 110 | FAT: 3 | PROTEIN: 21

INGREDIENTS

- 1-piece boneless chicken breast
- Salt and pepper as needed
- Garlic powder as needed

DIRECTIONS

1. Prepare a sous vide water bath to 150°F
2. Carefully drain the chicken breast and pat dry using a kitchen towel
3. Season the breast with garlic powder, pepper and salt
4. Place in a resealable bag and seal using the immersion method
5. Submerge and cook for 1 hour
6. Serve!

145. MOROCCAN CHICKEN SALAD

1 HOUR | 10 MIN | 2

NUTRITION:
CAL: 271 | FAT: 11 | PROTEIN: 33

INGREDIENTS

- 6 chicken tenderloins
- 4 cups pumpkin, cubed and roasted
- 4 cups rocket tomatoes
- 4 tbsps sliced almonds
- Juice of 1 lemon
- 2 tbsps olive oil
- 4 tbsps red onion, chopped
- 2 pinches paprika
- 2 pinches turmeric
- 2 pinches cumin
- 2 pinches salt

DIRECTIONS

1. Prepare your sous vide water bath to 140°F
2. Add all the spices and chicken in a zip-bag. Coat the chicken well
3. Seal using the immersion method and cook for 60 minutes
4. Sear for 1 minute on each side afterwards
5. Put the remaining ingredients in another bowl and toss well
6. Top them up with the chicken and serve!

146. KOREAN CHICKEN WINGS

2 HOURS | 20 MIN | 2

NUTRITION:
CAL: 243 | FAT: 15 | PROTEIN: 21

INGREDIENTS

- 8 chicken wings
- 2 tbsps low-sodium soy sauce
- 2 tbsps rice vinegar
- 2 tbsps light brown sugar
- ½ tsp ginger powder
- ½ tsp sesame oil
- 1 tbsp chili sauce
- A pinch of white pepper
- Salt and freshly ground black pepper as needed
- 1 scallion, finely chopped
- 1 tbsp unsalted peanuts, toasted and chopped

DIRECTIONS

1. Prepare a sous vide water bath to 147°F
2. Season the wings with pepper and salt.
3. Put the wings in the Sous Vide zip bag and seal using the immersion method and cook for 2 hours
4. While the wings are cooking, mix together vinegar, sugar, soy sauce, chili sauce, ginger powder, sesame oil, and white pepper in a medium saucepan.
5. Bring to a rapid simmer over medium heat and continue to simmer until reduced by half. Move to a large bowl and set aside.
6. Once the cooking is done, take out the bag from water. Remove the wings and pat dry them. Discard the cooking liquid and heat broiler to high
7. Move the wings to bowl with sauce and toss to coat. Place wings and remaining sauce onto a foil-lined rimmed baking sheet.
8. Broil wings for about 10 minutes or until slightly charred and sauce is sticky
9. Top with scallion and peanuts and serve.

147. PANKO CRUSTED CHICKEN

1 HOUR | 20 MIN | 4

NUTRITION:
CAL: 202 | FAT: 5 | PROTEIN: 27

INGREDIENTS

- 4 boneless chicken breasts
- 1 cup panko bread crumbs
- 1 lb. sliced mushrooms
- Small bunch of thyme
- 2 eggs
- Salt and pepper as needed
- Canola oil as needed

DIRECTIONS

1. Prepare a sous vide water bath to 150ºF
2. Season the chicken with salt, and thyme
3. Place the breast in a resealable bag and seal using the immersion method and cook for 60 minutes
4. Then, place a pan over medium heat, add the mushrooms and cook them until the water has evaporated
5. Add 3-4 sprigs of thyme and stir
6. Once cooked, remove the chicken from the bag and pat dry
7. Add the oil and heat it up over medium-high heat. Add the eggs into a container and dip the chicken in egg wash until well coated.
8. Add the panko bread crumbs in a shallow container and add some salt and pepper. Put the chicken to bread crumbs and coat until well covered.
9. Fry the chicken for 1-2 minutes per side and serve with the mushrooms

148. CLEMENTINE CHICKEN BREAST

2.5 HOURS | 20 MIN | 2

NUTRITION:
CAL: 114 | FAT: 4 | PROTEIN: 25

INGREDIENTS

- 2 chicken breasts, bone in, skin on
- 1½ tbsps freshly squeezed orange juice
- 1½ tbsps freshly squeezed lemon juice
- 1½ tbsps brown sugar
- 1 tbsp Pernod
- 1 tbsp olive oil
- 1 tbsp whole grain mustard
- 1 tsp fennel seeds
- 1 tsp salt
- ¾ tsp freshly ground black pepper
- 1 medium-sized fennel bulb, trimmed, thinly sliced up (reserve the fronds for later use)
- 2 clementines, unpeeled, cut into ¼ inch thick slices
- Chopped parsley for garnishing

DIRECTIONS

1. Prepare a sous vide water bath to 146ºF
2. Put the lemon juice, orange juice, Pernod, olive oil, fennel seeds, brown sugar, mustard, salt and pepper in a large bowl, give it a good mix
3. Put the chicken breast, sliced clementine and sliced fennel in a large, resealable zip bag and add the orange mixture
4. Seal using the immersion method and cook for 2½ hours
5. Set the broiler to high heat. Prepare a broiler safe baking dish and line it with aluminum foil
6. Once cooked, take the bag out from the water bath and transfer the contents to the baking sheet
7. Broil for 3-6 minutes to char slightly
8. Transfer the juice from the bag into a small saucepan and simmer for about 5-10 minutes
9. Put the chicken and vegetables on a platter and drizzle the sauce all over.
10. Sprinkle with parsley and fennel fronds and serve!

149. CHICKEN & MELTED LEEKS

45 MIN | 15 MIN | 4

NUTRITION:
CAL: 477 | FAT: 54 | PROTEIN: 79

INGREDIENTS

- 4 x 6 oz. skinless chicken breast
- Salt and pepper us needed
- 3 tbsps butter
- 1 large leek, cleaned and sliced crossways
- ½ cup panko
- 2 tbsps chopped parsley
- 1 oz. cheddar cheese
- 1 tbsp olive oil

DIRECTIONS

1. Prepare a sous vide water bath to 145ºF
2. Take the chicken breast and season it generously on both sides with salt and pepper and put in a zip bag
3. Seal using the immersion method and cook for 45 minutes
4. Take a skillet and add 2 tbsp of butter over medium heat, allow the butter to heat up and add the leeks
5. Stir to coat them
6. Season with salt and pepper
7. Then, lower down the heat to low and cook for additional 10 minutes
8. Put a clean skillet over a medium heat. Put in a tbsp of butter
9. Add the panko and toast, and stir well until the panko is hot
10. Spoon the panko mixture from the skillet into a separate bowl and add the cheddar cheese and chopped up parsley, mix well
11. Once the chicken breasts are thoroughly cooked, remove them from the bag and pat dry
12. Heat the olive oil over a high heat and sear the breasts for 1 minute
13. Serve each breast on the melted leek, and top with the toasted panko/cheese mix

150. MOROCCAN CHICKEN MEAL

1 HOUR | 15 MIN | 2

NUTRITION:
CAL: 554 | FAT: 19 | PROTEIN: 52

INGREDIENTS

- 6 chicken tenderloin
- 4 cups pumpkin, cut into cubes and roasted
- 4 cups rocket lettuce
- 4 tbsps sliced almonds
- Juice of 1 lemon
- 2 tbsps olive oil
- 4 tbsps red onion, chopped
- 2 pinches paprika
- 2 pinches turmeric
- 2 pinches cumin
- 2 pinches salt

DIRECTIONS

1. Prepare a sous vide water bath to 140ºF
2. Put the chicken and the seasoning in a heavy-duty, resealable bag
3. Seal it using the immersion/water displacement method
4. Submerge the bag and let it cook for about 60 minutes
5. Once done, take the chicken out from the bag and sear the tenderloins in a very hot pan, allowing 1 minute per side
6. Put all the remaining ingredients in a serving bowl and toss them well
7. Cover the chicken with your salad and serve!

151. CHICKEN PUDDING WITH ARTICHOKE HEARTS

1 HOUR 20 MIN 3

NUTRITION:
CAL: 180| FAT: 15 | PROTEIN: 8

INGREDIENTS

- 1-lb chicken breast, boneless and skinless
- 2 medium-sized artichokes
- 2 tbsp butter
- 2 tbsp olive oil
- 1 lemon, juiced
- A handful of fresh parsley leaves, finely chopped
- Salt and black pepper to taste
- ½ tsp chili pepper

DIRECTIONS

1. Thoroughly rinse the meat and pat dry with a kitchen paper.
2. Using a sharp paring knife cut the meat into smaller pieces and remove the bones.
3. Rub with olive oil and set aside.
4. Heat the sauté pan over medium heat.
5. Turn the heat down slightly to medium and add the meat.
6. Cook for about three minutes to get it a little golden on both sides.
7. Remove from the heat and transfer to a large vacuum-sealable bag.
8. Seal the bag and cook for one hour at 149ºF.
9. Meanwhile, prepare the artichoke.
10. Cut the lemon onto halves and squeeze the juice in a small bowl.
11. Divide the juice in half and set aside.
12. Using a sharp paring knife, trim off the outer leaves until you reach the yellow and soft ones.
13. Trim off the green outer skin around the artichoke base and steam.
14. Make sure to remove the 'hairs' around the artichoke heart.
15. They are inedible so simply throw them away.
16. Cut artichoke into half-inch pieces.
17. Rub with half of the lemon juice and place in a heavy-bottomed pot.
18. Add enough water to cover and cook until completely fork-tender.
19. Remove from the heat and drain.
20. Chill for a while – to a room temperature.
21. Cut each piece into thin strips.
22. Now combine artichoke with chicken meat in a large bowl.
23. Stir in salt, pepper, and the remaining lemon juice.
24. Melt the butter over medium heat and drizzle over pudding.
25. Sprinkle with some chili pepper and serve.

152. ALMOND BUTTERNUT SQUASH & CHICKEN SALAD

1 HOUR | 20 MIN | 2

NUTRITION:
CAL: 475 | FAT: 8| PROTEIN: 52

INGREDIENTS

- 6 chicken tenderloins
- 4 cups butternut squash, cubed and roasted
- 4 cups rocket tomatoes
- 4 tbsp sliced almonds
- Juice of 1 lemon
- 2 tbsp olive oil
- 4 tbsp red onion, chopped
- 1 tbsp paprika
- 1 tbsp turmeric
- 1 tbsp cumin
- Salt to taste

DIRECTIONS

1. Prepare a sous vide water bath to 138ºF.
2. Place the chicken and all the spices in a vacuum-sealable bag.
3. Shake well.
4. Release air by the water displacement method, seal and submerge the bag in the water bath.
5. Cook for 60 minutes.
6. Once the timer has stopped, remove the bag and transfer to a heated skillet.
7. Sear for 1 minute each side. In a bowl, combine the remaining ingredients.
8. Serve with the chicken on top.

153. CHICKEN & WALNUT SALAD

1 HOUR | 20 MIN | 2

NUTRITION:
CAL: 475 | FAT: 8| PROTEIN: 52

INGREDIENTS

- 2 skinless chicken breasts, boneless
- Salt and black pepper to taste
- 1 tbsp corn oil
- 1 apple, cored and diced
- 1 tsp lime juice
- ½ cup white grapes, cut in half
- 1 stick rib celery, diced
- 1/3 cup mayonnaise
- 2 tsp Chardonnay wine
- 1 tsp Dijon mustard
- 1 head Romaine lettuce
- ½ cup walnuts, toasted and chopped

DIRECTIONS

1. Prepare a sous vide water bath to 146ºF.
2. Place the chicken in a vacuum-sealable bag and season with salt and pepper.
3. Release air by the water displacement method, seal and submerge the bag in the water bath.
4. Cook for 2 hours.
5. Once the timer has stopped, remove the bag and discard the cooking juices. In a large bowl, toss the apple slices and the lime juice.
6. Add the celery and white grapes. Mix well.
7. In another bowl, stir the mayonnaise, Dijon mustard and Chardonnay wine.
8. Pour the mixture over the fruit and mix well. Chop the chicken and put in a medium bowl, season with salt and combine well.
9. Pour the chicken in the salad bowl. Collocate the romaine lettuce in salad bowls and set the salad on top.
10. Garnish with walnuts.

154. SWEET & SOUR CHICKEN WINGS

2 HOURS | 20 MIN | 2

NUTRITION:
CAL: 475 | FAT: 33 | PROTEIN: 36

INGREDIENTS

- 12 chicken wings
- Salt and black pepper to taste
- 1 cup chicken batter
- ½ cup water
- ½ cup tamari sauce
- ½ minced onion
- 5 garlic cloves, minced
- 2 tsp ginger powder
- 2 tbsp brown sugar
- ¼ cup mirin
- Sesame seeds for garnish
- Cornstarch slurry (mixed 1 tbsp cornstarch and 2 tbsp water)
- Olive oil for frying

DIRECTIONS

1. Prepare a sous vide water bath to 147°F.
2. Place the chicken wing in a vacuum-sealable bag and season with salt and pepper.
3. Release air by the water displacement method, seal and submerge the bag in the water bath. Cook for 2 hours.
4. Once the timer has stopped, remove the bag and dry it. Heat a frying pan with oil.
5. In a bowl, combine 1/2 cup of chicken batter and 1/2 cup of water.
6. Pour the remaining chicken batter in another bowl.
7. Soak the wings in the wet batter then in the dry batter.
8. Fry for 1-2 minutes until crispy and golden brown.
9. For the sauce, heat a saucepan and pour all the ingredients.
10. Cook until bubble.
11. Stir the wings in the sauce.
12. Top with sesame seeds and serve.

155. TURKEY AND QUINOA

1 HOUR | 10 MIN | 4

NUTRITION:
CAL: 602 | FAT: 17 | PROTEIN: 75

INGREDIENTS

- 2 lbs turkey breasts, skinless, boneless and cubed
- 2 tbsps avocado oil
- 1 cup quinoa, cooked
- 1 cup chicken stock
- 2 spring onions, chopped
- ½ tsp garam masala
- ½ tsp sweet paprika
- ½ tsp chili powder
- ½ tsp turmeric powder
- A pinch of salt and black pepper

DIRECTIONS

1. In a sous vide bag, mix the turkey with the oil, quinoa and the other ingredients, seal the bag and cook in the water bath at 170 °F for 1 hour.
2. Divide everything between plates and serve.

156. TURKEY WITH MUSHROOMS

1 HOUR | 10 MIN | 4

NUTRITION:
CAL: 242 | FAT: 10 | PROTEIN: 33

INGREDIENTS

- 1-lb turkey breast, skinless, boneless and sliced
- 1 cup mushrooms, halved
- 1 tbsp balsamic vinegar
- 2 tbsps lemon juice
- 1 tbsp olive oil
- 1 tsp chili powder
- ¼ cup cilantro, chopped

DIRECTIONS

1. In a large sous vide bag, mix the turkey with the mushrooms and the other ingredients, seal the bag, cook in the water bath at 175 ºF for 1 hour, divide everything between plates and serve.

157. TURKEY WITH LIME SAUCE

1 HOUR | 10 MIN | 4

NUTRITION:
CAL: 253 | FAT: 11 | PROTEIN: 31

INGREDIENTS

- 1-lb turkey breast, skinless, boneless and roughly cubed
- 1 tbsp avocado oil
- Juice of 1 lime
- 1 tbsp chives, chopped
- 1 tbsp lime zest, grated
- 2 spring onions, chopped
- A pinch of salt and black pepper

DIRECTIONS

1. In a sous vide bag, mix the turkey with the lime juice and the other ingredients, seal the bag and cook in the water bath at 180 ºF for 1 hour.
2. Divide everything between plates and serve.

158. TURKEY WITH LENTILS

1 HOUR | 10 MIN | 4

NUTRITION:
CAL: 559 | FAT: 21 | PROTEIN: 72

INGREDIENTS

- 2 lbs turkey breast, boneless, skinless and roughly cubed
- 2 tbsps olive oil
- 1 cup canned lentils, drained and rinsed
- ½ cup chicken stock
- ½ tsp sweet paprika
- ½ tsp chili powder
- ½ tsp cumin, ground
- A pinch of salt and black pepper
- 1 tbsp parsley, chopped

DIRECTIONS

1. In a large sous vide bag, mix the turkey with the lentils, oil and the other ingredients, seal the bag and cook in the water bath at 175 ºF for 50 minutes.
2. Divide the mix between plates and serve.

159. CHICKEN AND LEEKS

1 HOUR | 10 MIN | 4

NUTRITION:
CAL: 256 | FAT: 19 | PROTEIN: 67

INGREDIENTS

- 2 lbs chicken breast, skinless, boneless and cubed
- 2 tbsps avocado oil
- 1 cup leeks, sliced
- 2 spring onions, chopped
- Juice of ½ lemon
- ½ tsp hot paprika
- ½ cup chicken stock
- ½ tsp cumin, ground
- A pinch of salt and black pepper
- 1 tbsp chives, chopped

DIRECTIONS

1. Divide the chicken, leeks and the other ingredients into 2 sous vide bags, seal them, submerge in the water bath, cook at 180 °F for 1 hour, divide everything between plates and serve.

160. TURMERIC DUCK

1 HOUR | 10 MIN | 4

NUTRITION:
CAL: 498 | FAT: 29 | PROTEIN: 55

INGREDIENTS

- 2 spring onions, chopped
- 2 lbs duck breast, skinless, boneless and sliced
- 1 tsp turmeric powder
- 2 garlic cloves, minced
- 1 tbsp lime juice
- 1 tbsp lime zest, grated
- 2 tbsps olive oil
- A pinch of salt and black pepper
- 1 tbsp oregano, chopped

DIRECTIONS

1. In a large sous vide bag, mix the duck with the spring onions, turmeric and the other ingredients, seal the bag and cook in the water bath at 180 °F for 1 hour and 10 minutes.
2. Divide the mix between plates and serve.

5.PORK

161. PORK HOAGIES

12 HOURS | 15 MIN | 4

NUTRITION:
CAL: 184 | FAT: 13 | PROTEIN: 25

INGREDIENTS

- 1 lb. boneless pork shoulder chops
- 1 tbsp dry rub + additional tsp for later use
- ¼ cup BBQ sauce
- 4 hoagie rolls
- 1 cup prepped fried pickles for topping

DIRECTIONS

1. Preheat a sous vide water bath to 187°F
2. Slice up the pork into bite-sized portions and season with 1 tbsp of dry rub.
3. Transfer the chops to a large resealable zipper bag and seal using the immersion method.
4. Cook for 12 hours.
5. Once cooked, remove the pork from the bag and shred it.
6. Season using the dry rub
7. Serve by topping the hoagie rolls with soft fried pickles and a drizzle of BBQ sauce.

162. BACON POTATO MIX

1.5 HOURS | 30 MIN | 6

NUTRITION:
CAL: 197 | FAT: 9 | PROTEIN: 8

INGREDIENTS

- 1 ½ lb. Yukon potatoes, sliced up into ¾ inch pieces
- ½ cup chicken stock
- Salt and pepper, as needed
- 4 oz. thick bacon cut up into ¼ inch thick strips
- ½ cup onion, chopped
- 1/3 cup apple cider vinegar
- 4 thinly sliced scallions

DIRECTIONS

1. Preheat a sous vide water bath to 185°F
2. Take a heavy-duty resealable bag and add the potatoes alongside stock.
3. Season with some salt and seal it using the immersion method. Submerge and cook for about 1 and a ½ hour.
4. Place a large-sized skillet over medium-high heat.
5. Add the bacon and cook for 5-7 minutes.
6. Transfer it to a kitchen towel and dry it. Reserve the Fat.
7. Return the heat to the skillet and add the onions. Cook for 1 minute.
8. Take a skillet and place it over medium heat, remove the bag from the water bath and pour the stock and potatoes from the bag into the skillet.
9. Add the cooked bacon and vinegar.
10. Bring the mixture to a simmer.
11. Add the scallions and season with a bit of pepper and salt.

163. MOLASSES PORK LOIN

4 HOURS | 15 MIN | 6

NUTRITION:
CAL: 245 | FAT: 7 | PROTEIN: 31

INGREDIENTS

- 2 lbs. pork loin roast
- 1-piece bay leaf
- 3 oz. molasses
- ½ oz. soy sauce

DIRECTIONS

1. Preheat a sous vide water bath to 142°F
2. Transfer the pork loin and bay leaf into a resealable zip bag.
3. Take a small bowl and mix the molasses, soy, lemon peel, honey, bay leaf, scallions, garlic powder, mustard, and ginger.

- ½ oz. honey
- Juice of 2 lemons
- 2 strips lemon peel
- 4 chopped scallions
- ½ tsp garlic powder
- ¼ tsp Dijon mustard
- ¼ tsp ground ginger
- 1 oz. crushed corn chips
- Green onion for Servings, sliced

4. Ladle 1/3 of the mixture over the pork loin.
5. Seal using the immersion method. Cook for 4 hours.
6. Once cooked, take the pork out from the water bath and add the remaining glaze to a saucepan.
7. Boil all over high heat and cook until reduced to glaze.
8. Pour glaze over pork loin and toss crushed corn chips over all.
9. Serve with the sliced green onion

164. JAPANESE PORK CUTLET

1 HOUR | 15 MIN | 3

NUTRITION:
CAL: 245 | FAT: 7 | PROTEIN: 31

INGREDIENTS

- 3 pork loin chops
- Salt and pepper as needed
- 1 cup flour
- 2 whole eggs
- Panko crumbs as needed to coat the chops

DIRECTIONS

1. Preheat a sous vide water bath to 140ºF
2. Make tiny slits on the loin body and trim any excess Fat. Season with salt and pepper.
3. Transfer to a resealable zip bag and seal using the immersion method. Submerge and cook for 1 hour.
4. Once cooked, remove the loin chops from the bag and pat them dry.
5. Dredge the loin in flour, egg and finally panko crumbs.
6. Heat up the oil to 450ºF and fry chops for 1 minute. Put on a cooling rack and slice.
7. Serve on top of the steamed rice with vegetables

165. APPLE BUTTER PORK TENDERLOIN

2 HOURS | 10 MIN | 3

NUTRITION:
CAL: 100 | FAT: 2 | PROTEIN: 8

INGREDIENTS

- 1 pork tenderloin
- 1 jar apple butter
- Fresh rosemary sprigs
- Salt and pepper, as needed

DIRECTIONS

1. Preheat a sous vide water bath to 145ºF
2. Season the pork with salt and pepper.
3. Spread apple butter on pork.
4. Transfer to a resealable zip bag and add the rosemary sprigs.
5. Seal using the immersion method and cook for 2 hours.
6. Once done, remove the pork from the bag and pat dry.
7. Season with salt and pepper and apply apple butter generously.
8. Sear on hot grill.
9. Slice and serve!

166. PORK CHOP WITH CORN

1 HOUR | 15 MIN | 4

NUTRITION:
CAL: 165 | FAT: 7 | PROTEIN: 28

INGREDIENTS

- 4 pieces pork chop
- 1 small red bell pepper, diced
- 1 small yellow onion, diced
- 3 ears corn kernels
- ¼ cup cilantro, chopped
- Salt and pepper, as needed
- 1 tbsp vegetable oil

DIRECTIONS

1. Preheat a sous vide water bath to 140ºF
2. Season the pork chop with salt.
3. Transfer to a resealable zip bag and seal using the immersion method. Cook for 1 hour.
4. Take a pan and put it over medium heat, add the oil and allow the oil to heat up
5. Add the onion, corn, and bell pepper.
6. Sauté for a while until barely browned.
7. Finish the corn mix with cilantro and set it aside.
8. Wipe the pan clean and place the pan over medium heat.
9. Add the oil and sear the pork chop for 1 minute per side.
10. Slice and serve with the salad.

167. MANGO SALSA & PORK

2 HOURS | 25 MIN | 4

NUTRITION:
CAL: 428 | FAT: 15 | PROTEIN: 48

INGREDIENTS

- 2 lbs. pork tenderloin
- ¼ cup light brown sugar
- 1 tbsp ground allspice
- ½ tsp cayenne pepper
- ¼ tsp ground cinnamon
- ¼ tsp ground cloves
- salt and black pepper, as needed
- 2 tbsps canola oil
- 2 pitted and peeled mangoes, finely diced
- ¼ cup fresh cilantro, chopped
- 1 red bell pepper, stemmed, seeded, and finely diced
- 3 tbsps red onion, finely diced
- 2 tbsps freshly squeezed lime juice
- 1 small jalapeno seeded and finely diced

DIRECTIONS

1. Preheat a sous vide water bath to 135ºF
2. Take a medium bowl and mix the sugar, allspice, cinnamon, cayenne, cloves, 2 tsps of salt, and 1 tsp of pepper.
3. Rub the mixture over the tenderloins.
4. Take a large-sized skillet and put it over medium heat, add the oil and once the oil simmers, transfer the pork and sear for 5 minutes, browning all sides.
5. Transfer to a plate and rest for 10 minutes.
6. Transfer the pork chop to a resealable zipper bag and seal using the immersion method. Cook for 2 hours.
7. Once cooked, take the bag out and allow it to rest for a while, take the chop out and slice it.
8. Prepare the salsa by mixing the mango, cilantro, bell pepper, onion, lime juice, and jalapeno in a mixing bowl.
9. Serve the sliced pork with salsa with a seasoning salt and pepper.

168. LEMONGRASS PORK CHOPS

2 HOURS | 20 MIN | 2

NUTRITION:
CAL: 238 | FAT: 16 | PROTEIN: 24

INGREDIENTS

- 2 (10-oz) bone-in pork rib chops
- 2 tbsps coconut oil
- 1 stalk sliced lemon grass
- 1 tbsp minced shallot
- 1 tbsp soy sauce
- 1 tbsp mirin
- 1 tbsp rice wine vinegar
- 1 tbsp light brown sugar
- 1 tsp minced fresh ginger
- 1 tsp fish sauce
- 1 tsp salt
- 1 tsp minced garlic

DIRECTIONS

1. Preheat a sous vide water bath to 140ºF
2. Take a food processor and add 1 tbsp of coconut oil, lemon grass, soy sauce, shallot, vinegar, mirin, brown sugar, garlic, fish sauce, ginger, and salt.
3. Process for 1 minute.
4. Place the pork chops into a resealable zip bag alongside soy-lemon grass mixture and seal using the immersion method. Cook for 2 hours.
5. Once cooked, remove the bag and take the pork chops out, pat them dry.
6. Heat a grill to high heat and sear the chops until well browned.
7. Allow it to rest for 2-3 minutes.
8. Serve!

169. PORK & ZUCCHINI RIBBONS

3 HOURS | 20 MIN | 2

NUTRITION:
CAL: 311 | FAT: 19 | PROTEIN: 18

INGREDIENTS

- 2 (6-oz) bone-in pork loin chops
- Salt and black pepper as needed
- 3 tbsps olive oil
- 1 tbsp freshly squeezed lemon juice
- 2 tsps red wine vinegar
- 2 tsps honey
- 2 tbsps rice bran oil
- 2 medium zucchinis, sliced into ribbons
- 2 tbsps pine nuts, toasted up

DIRECTIONS

1. Preheat a sous vide water bath to 140ºF
2. Take the pork chops and season it with salt and pepper, transfer to a heavy-duty zip bag and add 1 tbsp of oil.
3. Seal using the immersion method and cook for 3 hours.
4. Prepare the dressing by whisking lemon juice, honey, vinegar, 2 tbsps of olive oil and season with salt and pepper.
5. Once cooked, remove the bag from the water bath and discard the liquid.
6. Heat up rice bran oil in a large skillet over high heat and add the pork chops, sear until browned (1 minute per side
7. Once done, transfer it to a cutting board and allow to rest for 5 minutes.
8. Take a medium bowl and add the zucchini ribbons with dressing
9. Thinly slice the pork chops and discard the bone.
10. Place the pork on top of the zucchini.
11. Top with pine nuts and serve!

170. HERBED PORK LOIN

2 HOURS | 20 MIN | 4

NUTRITION:
CAL: 205 | FAT: 11 | PROTEIN: 23

INGREDIENTS

- 1 lb. pork tenderloin, trimmed
- Salt and fresh ground pepper as needed
- 1 tbsp chopped fresh basil + additional for servings
- 1 tbsp chopped fresh parsley + additional for servings
- 1 tbsp chopped fresh rosemary + additional for servings
- 2 tbsps unsalted butter

DIRECTIONS

1. Preheat a sous vide water bath to 134°F.
2. Season the tenderloin with pepper and salt
3. Rub herbs (a mixture of basil, parsley and rosemary all over the tenderloin and transfer to a resalable zip bag
4. Add 1 tbsp of butter
5. Seal using the immersion method. Submerge underwater and cook for 2 hours
6. Once cooked, remove the bag and remove the pork from the bag
7. Place a large-sized skillet over medium-high heat
8. Add the remaining butter and herb mixture and allow the butter to heat up
9. Add the pork and sear it well for 1-2 minutes each side, making sure to keep scooping the butter over the pork
10. Remove the heat and transfer the pork to a cutting board
11. Allow it to rest for 5 minutes and slice into medallions. Serve.

171. RED PEPPER SALAD & PORK CHOP

1 HOUR | 15 MIN | 4

NUTRITION:
CAL: 204 | FAT: 12 | PROTEIN: 24

INGREDIENTS

- 4 pork chops
- 1 small red bell pepper, diced
- 1 small yellow onion, diced
- 2 cups frozen corn kernels
- ¼ cup cilantro, chopped
- Salt and pepper as needed
- Vegetable oil as needed

DIRECTIONS

1. Prepare a sous vide water bath to 140°F
2. Season the pork carefully with salt
3. Transfer the pork to a resealable zip bag and seal using the immersion method. Submerge underwater and cook for 1 hour
4. Take a pan and put it over medium heat and add the oil, allow it to heat up
5. Add the onion, red pepper, corn and sauté for a while until they are slightly browned
6. Season with salt and pepper
7. Finish the corn mix with a garnish of chopped cilantro, keep it aside
8. Remove the pan from heat and wipe the oil
9. Place it back to medium-high heat
10. Put the oil and allow it to heat up
11. Transfer the cooked pork chops to the pan and sear each side for 1 minute. Serve the pork chops with the salad!

172. FRAGRANT NONYA PORK BELLY

7 HOURS | 10 MIN | 4

NUTRITION:
CAL: 154 | FAT: 8 | PROTEIN: 23

INGREDIENTS

- 1 lb. pork belly
- ¼ cup chopped shallots
- 3 sliced garlic cloves
- ½ tbsp coriander seeds
- 2-star anise
- 4 large dried shiitake mushrooms
- 2 tbsps coconut aminos
- 2 tsps brown sugar
- ½ tsp salt
- ¼ tsp ground white pepper

DIRECTIONS

1. Prepare a sous vide water bath to 176ºF
2. Chop up the pork belly into 1-inch cubes and transfer to a bowl.
3. Add the remaining ingredients and whisk them well.
4. Transfer to a resealable zip bag and seal using the immersion method.
5. Cook for 7 hours and remove the bag.
6. Transfer the solids to servings dish and discard the star anise.
7. Tip the cooking liquid to a small pan and reduce it over medium heat.
8. Pour the sauce over pork belly and serve!

173. ITALIAN SAUSAGE & AUTUMN GRAPE

1 HOUR | 10 MIN | 4

NUTRITION:
CAL: 186 | FAT: 13 | PROTEIN: 14

INGREDIENTS

- 2 ½ cups seedless purple grapes with stem removed
- 1 tbsp chopped fresh rosemary
- 2 tbsps butter
- 4 whole sweet Italian sausages
- 2 tbsps balsamic vinegar
- Salt and ground black pepper, as needed

DIRECTIONS

1. Prepare a sous vide water bath to 160ºF
2. Take a plastic bag and add the grapes, rosemary, butter, and sausage in one layer.
3. Seal using the immersion method. Cook for 1 hour.
4. Remove the sausage to servings platter and pour the grapes and liquid in a saucepan.
5. Add the balsamic vinegar and simmer for 3 minutes over medium-high heat and season the mixture with salt and pepper.
6. Grill the sausage on medium-high heat for 3-4 minutes and serve with the grapes

174. MUSHROOM MIXED PORK CHOPS

55 MIN | 5 MIN | 2

NUTRITION:
CAL: 337 | FAT: 22 | PROTEIN: 24

INGREDIENTS

- 2 thick-cut bone-in pork chops
- Salt and fresh ground pepper, as needed
- 2 tbsps unsalted butter, cold
- 4 oz. mixed wild mushrooms
- ¼ cup sherry
- ½ cup beef stock
- 1 tbsp steak marinade
- Chopped garlic for garnish

DIRECTIONS

1. Prepare a sous vide water bath to 140ºF
2. Take the pork chop and season it thoroughly with salt and pepper and transfer to a resealable zip bag, seal using the immersion method and cook for 55 minutes.
3. Remove the pork chop and pat dry, discard cooking liquid.
4. Take a large skillet and put it over medium-high heat, add 1 tbsp of butter and allow the butter to melt.
5. Add the pork chops and sear 1 minute per side and transfer to a platter.
6. Heat up the skillet once more and add the mushrooms, cook for 2-3 minutes.
7. Add the sherry and bring the mixture to a nice simmer, add the stock, and steak marinade and simmer until you have a thick sauce.

8. Remove the heat and swirl the remaining butter, season with salt and pepper and pour over the pork chops.
9. Garnish with chopped garlic and serve!

175. PORK CHEEK TACOS

12 HOURS | 15 MIN | 8

NUTRITION:
CAL: 150 | FAT: 6 | PROTEIN: 26

INGREDIENTS

- 2 lbs. skinless pork cheeks
- 1 tbsp ancho chili powder
- 1 tbsp salt
- 1 tbsp light brown sugar
- 2 tsps ground cumin
- 2 tsps garlic powder
- 1 tsp cayenne pepper
- 1 tsp freshly ground black pepper
- Corn tortillas
- Pickled red onion and fresh cilantro for servings

DIRECTIONS

1. Prepare a sous vide water bath to 180°F
2. Add the pork cheeks, chili powder, salt, brown sugar, garlic powder, cumin, cayenne, and black pepper to a resealable zipper bag and seal using the immersion method.
3. Cook for 12 hours.
4. Once cooked, remove the bag and take the pork out, reserve the cooking liquid.
5. Take the pork and shred the pork into 1-inch pieces and transfer to a large bowl.
6. Stir in the cooking liquid and serve on tortillas with a topping of pickled red onion and fresh cilantro.

176. HONEY MUSTARD PORK

3 HOURS | 20 MIN | 2

NUTRITION:
CAL: 737 | FAT: 36 | PROTEIN: 93

INGREDIENTS

- 2 pieces bone-in pork loin chops
- 3 tbsps olive oil
- 1 tbsp + 2 tsps whole grain mustard
- 1 tbsp + 1 tsp honey
- Salt and ground black pepper, as needed
- 1 tbsp freshly squeezed lemon juice
- 2 tsps red wine vinegar
- 2 tbsps rice bran oil
- 2 cups mixed baby lettuce
- 2 tbsps thinly sliced sundried tomatoes
- 2 tsps pine nuts, toasted

DIRECTIONS

1. Prepare a sous vide water bath to 140°F
2. Take a small bowl and mix in 1 tbsp olive oil, 1 tbsp mustard, 1 tbsp honey, and season with salt and pepper
3. Transfer to a resealable zip bag alongside the pork chop and toss well to coat it.
4. Seal using the immersion method and cook for 3 hours.
5. To prepare the dressing, add the lemon juice, vinegar, 2 tbsps of olive oil, 2 tsps of mustard and the remaining honey in a bowl. Season with salt and pepper.
6. Remove the bag and remove the pork chop, discard the liquid.
7. Take a large skillet over high heat and add bran oil, heat it up and wait until it starts to smoke. Add the pork chops and sear for 30 seconds per side.
8. Rest for 5 minutes.
9. Take a medium bowl and add the lettuce, sun-dried tomatoes and pine nuts, toss well with 3 quarter of the dressing.
10. Take the pork chops and transfer them to your servings plate and top with the salad and dressing.
11. Serve!

177. CIDER AND ROSEMARY PORK WITH CARAMEL SAUCE

45 MIN | 15 MIN | 2

NUTRITION:
CAL: 308 | FAT: 12 | PROTEIN: 46

INGREDIENTS

- 1 lb bone-in, double-cut pork chop
- 1 sprig of chopped rosemary
- salt as needed
- Ground black pepper as needed
- 1 chopped garlic clove
- 1 cup of hard cider
- 1 tbsp vegetable oil
- 1 tbsp dark brown sugar
- Sautéed cabbage, if desired
- Sautéed apples, if desired

DIRECTIONS

1. Prepare a sous vide water bath to 140 °F.
2. Season the pork chop with salt and pepper.
3. Rub the chop with rosemary and garlic.
4. Take a heavy-duty resealable bag and add a ½ cup of the hard cider and the pork chop.
5. Seal it using the immersion method.
6. Submerge it under water and cook for 45 minutes.
7. Once ready, remove the bag and pat the chops dry using a kitchen towel.
8. Take a cast-iron skillet and add the vegetable oil; swirl it gently.
9. Add the chops to the skillet and sear until golden brown (approximately 45 seconds per side)
10. Allow it to rest for about 5 minutes.
11. Pour the sauce into the skillet from the bag, and add the Remaining ½ cup of cider.
12. Add the brown sugar and keep stirring until the sugar has melted.
13. Simmer for 1 minute and pour the sauce over the pork chop.
14. Serve with cabbage and apple.

178. COCONUT PORK RIBS

8 HOURS | 20 MIN | 4

NUTRITION:
CAL: 287 | FAT: 25 | PROTEIN: 18

INGREDIENTS

- 1/3 cup unsweetened coconut milk
- 2 tbsps peanut butter
- 2 tbsps soy sauce
- 2 tbsps light brown sugar
- 2 tbsps dry white wine
- 2-inch fresh lemongrass
- 1 tbsp Sriracha
- 1-inch peeled fresh ginger
- 2 cloves garlic
- 2 tsps sesame oil
- 12 oz country-style pork ribs

DIRECTIONS

1. Prepare a sous vide water bath to 134°F.
2. Add coconut milk, peanut butter, brown sugar, soy sauce, wine, lemongrass, Sriracha, ginger, garlic, and sesame oil to a blender; blend until smooth.
3. Add ribs to a Ziploc bag, along with the sauce, and seal using the immersion method.
4. Cook for 8 hours.
5. Remove the bag and remove the ribs from the bag; transfer to a plate.
6. Pour the bag contents into a large skillet and place it over medium-high heat; bring to a boil and lower heat to medium-low. Simmer for 10-15 minutes.
7. Add ribs to the sauce and turn well to coat it.
8. Simmer for 5 minutes.

179. PORK CHEEK RAGOUT

10 HOURS | 20 MIN | 8

NUTRITION:
CAL: 445 | FAT: 24 | PROTEIN: 20

INGREDIENTS

- 2 lbs. skinless pork cheeks
- 2 finely diced carrots
- ½ white onion, finely diced
- 1 cup canned tomato sauce
- 1 cup canned diced tomatoes
- 3 sprigs oregano
- 3 garlic cloves, crushed
- 1 tsp granulated sugar
- 2 pieces bay leaves
- salt and black pepper, as needed
- Cooked pasta and fresh parsley for servings

DIRECTIONS

1. Prepare a sous vide water bath to 180°F
2. Add the pork cheeks, carrots, onion, tomato sauce, diced tomatoes, garlic, oregano, sugar, bay leaves, 1 tsp of pepper, 1 tbsp of salt to a heavy-duty re-sealable zip bag.
3. Seal using the immersion method. Cook for 10 hours.
4. Once done, remove the bag and then the pork, make sure to reserve the cooking liquid.
5. Shred using 2 forks into 1-inch pieces, transfer to large bowl and set it to the side.
6. Remove and discard the oregano from the cooking liquid, pour the contents to a food processor and pulse until the ingredients are uniformly chopped.
7. Take the sauce and season it well with pepper and salt, pour it over the pork toss to combine.
8. Toss the pasta with the mixture and serve with parsley!

180. PORK SLICES WITH NOODLE SALAD

20 HOURS | 20 MIN | 2

NUTRITION:
CAL: 330 | FAT: 28 | PROTEIN: 19

INGREDIENTS

- ½ lb boneless pork leg
- 1 tbsp olive oil
- 1 tbsp freshly squeezed lime juice
- 1 tbsp fish sauce
- 1 tbsp soy sauce
- 1 tbsp rice vinegar
- 1 tbsp palm sugar
- 2 vermicelli noodle nests
- ½ thinly sliced scallion
- 2 tbsps roasted peanuts chopped up
- 2 tbsps chopped fresh cilantro
- 2 tbsps chopped fresh mint

DIRECTIONS

1. Prepare a sous vide water bath to 176°F
2. Add the pork leg to a resealable zip bag alongside the olive oil.
3. Seal using the immersion method and cook for 12 hours.
4. Prepare your dressing by mixing the lime juice, soy sauce, fish sauce, rice vinegar, and palm sugar in a small-sized bowl, give the whole mixture a nice stir.
5. Once cooked, take the pork out from the water bath and allow it to cool.
6. Shred using forks into bite-sized pieces.
7. Bring a large pot of water and bring it to a boil over high heat, add the vermicelli noodle and cook for 2-3 minutes.
8. Transfer to a bowl and add the scallions, mint, cilantro, peanuts, dressing, and pork to the noodle and toss well.
9. Serve!

181. PORK CHILI VERDE

24 HOURS | 20 MIN | 8

NUTRITION:
CAL: 227 | FAT: 6 | PROTEIN: 23

INGREDIENTS

- 2 lbs. boneless pork shoulder cut up into 1-inch pieces
- 1 tbsp salt
- 1 tbsp ground cumin
- 1 tsp fresh ground black pepper
- 1 tbsp olive oil
- 1 lb. tomatillos
- 3 poblano pepper, finely seeded and diced
- ½ white onion finely diced
- 1 jalapeno seeded and diced
- 3 garlic cloves, crushed
- 1 bunch roughly chopped cilantro
- 1 cup chicken broth
- ½ cup fresh squeezed lime juice
- 1 tbsp Mexican oregano

DIRECTIONS

1. Prepare a sous vide water bath to 150ºF
2. Season the pork with salt, cumin, and pepper.
3. Take a large skillet and place it over medium high heat, add the oil and allow it to heat up.
4. Add the pork and sear for 5-7 minutes.
5. Increase the heat back to medium-high and add the tomatillos, poblano pepper, onion, jalapeno, and garlic. Cook for 5 minutes until slightly charred.
6. Transfer the whole prepared mixture to a food processor and add the cilantro, lime juice, chicken broth, oregano, and process for 1 minute.
7. Transfer the sauce to a resealable zip bag alongside the pork and seal using the immersion method. Submerge it underwater and cook for 24 hours.
8. Once cooked, remove the bag and transfer the contents to a servings bowl. Sprinkle some salt and pepper and serve over rice.

182. GARLIC & GINGER PORK KEBOBS

4 HOURS | 20 MIN | 4

NUTRITION:
CAL: 154 | FAT: 8 | PROTEIN: 23

INGREDIENTS

- 1 lb. boneless pork shoulder cut up into 1-inch pieces
- 1 tbsp salt
- 1 tbsp minced salt
- 1 tbsp minced fresh ginger
- 1 tbsp garlic, minced
- 1 tsp cumin
- 1 tsp coriander
- 1 tsp garlic powder
- 1 tsp brown sugar
- 1 tsp fresh ground black pepper

DIRECTIONS

1. Prepare a sous vide water bath to 150ºF
2. Rub the pork with salt, garlic, ginger, cumin, coriander, garlic powder, pepper, and brown sugar, and transfer to a resealable bag.
3. Seal using the immersion method and cook for 4 hours.
4. Heat up the grill to medium-high heat and remove the pork from the bag once cooking is done, pierce it into skewers.
5. Grill for 3 minutes until browned all around
6. Serve!

183. CREAM-POACHED PORK LOIN

4 HOURS | 20 MIN | 4

NUTRITION:
CAL: 585 | FAT: 33 | PROTEIN: 48

INGREDIENTS

- 1 – 3 lbs. boneless pork loin roast
- salt and pepper as needed
- 2 thinly sliced onion
- ¼ cup cognac
- 1 cup whole milk
- 1 cup heavy cream

DIRECTIONS

1. Prepare a sous vide water bath to 145°F
2. Season the pork with pepper and salt, take a large iron skillet and place it over medium-heat for 5 minutes.
3. Add the pork and sear for 15 minutes until all sides are browned.
4. Transfer to a platter, add the onion to the rendered Fat (in the skillet and cook for 5 minutes.
5. Add the cognac and bring to a simmer. Allow it to cool for 10 minutes.
6. Add the pork, onion, milk, and cream to a resealable zipper bag and seal using the immersion method. Submerge underwater and cook for 4 hours.
7. Once cooked, remove the bag from the water and take the pork out, transfer the pork to cutting board and cover it to keep it warm.
8. Pour the bag contents to a skillet and bring the mixture to a simmer over medium heat, keep cooking for 10 minutes and season with salt and pepper.
9. Slice the pork and serve with the cream sauce.

184. HOISIN GLAZED PORK TENDERLOIN

3 HOURS | 15 MIN | 1

NUTRITION:
CAL: 154 | FAT: 6 | PROTEIN: 24

INGREDIENTS

- 1-piece pork tenderloin, trimmed
- 1 tsp salt
- ½ tsp freshly ground black pepper
- 3 tbsps hoisin sauce

DIRECTIONS

1. Prepare a sous vide water bath to 145°F
2. Take the tenderloins and season it with pepper and salt and transfer to a resealable zip bag.
3. Seal using the immersion method and cook for 3 hours.
4. Remove the bag and then the pork, brush with hoisin sauce.
5. Heat up your grill to high grill and add the tenderloin, sear for 5 minutes until all sides are caramelized.
6. Allow it to rest and slice the tenderloin into medallions, serve!

185. SWEET PORK BELLY

8 HOURS | 10 MIN | 4

NUTRITION:
CAL: 308 | FAT: 12 | PROTEIN: 46

INGREDIENTS

- 2 lbs pork belly
- 1 tsp Chinese five-spice powder
- 2 tsps salt
- 1 tsp ground white pepper
- 3 tbsps white vinegar

DIRECTIONS

1. Prepare a sous vide water bath to 158°F
2. Using a sharp paring knife, slide cuts through the pork belly skin 1 inch apart horizontally. Be careful to only cut through the skin and not too deep into the underlying Fatty layer.
3. Insert 2 skewers, crisscrossed, into the pork belly.
4. In a small bowl, mix together Chinese five-spice powder, salt, and white pepper. Rub

the underside of the pork belly generously with half of the salt mixture.

5. Place pork belly in a large cooking pouch. Seal pouch tightly after removing the excess air. Place pouch in sous vide bath and set the cooking time for 6-8 hours.
6. Preheat the oven broiler to high. Arrange a rack on a baking sheet.
7. Remove pouch from the sous vide bath and open carefully. Remove pork belly from pouch and pat dry pork belly with paper towels.
8. Generously sprinkle underside of pork belly with remaining salt mixture. Flip the belly over and coat with a very thin layer of vinegar.
9. Place pork belly on the rack that is on the baking sheet. Broil for 10-15 minutes, rotating baking sheet occasionally.
10. Transfer pork belly to a cutting sheet and cut into bite-sized pieces with a large knife. Serve immediately.

186. TENDER PORK CHOPS

2 HOURS   5 MIN   2

NUTRITION:
CAL: 248 | FAT: 16 | PROTEIN: 24

INGREDIENTS

- 2 pork chops
- 1 tbsp canola oil
- 1 tbsp butter
- 4 garlic cloves
- 1 tsp rosemary
- 1 tsp thyme
- Salt and pepper, as needed

DIRECTIONS

1. Preheat a sous vide water bath to 140ºF.
2. Season the pork with pepper and salt. Place pork chops into the zip-lock bag.
3. Remove all the air from the bag before sealing. Place bag into the hot water bath and cook for 2 hours.
4. Remove pork from bag and pat dry with paper towel.
5. Heat oil and butter in a pan over high heat with rosemary, thyme, and garlic.
6. Place pork chops in a pan sear until lightly brown, about 1 minute on each side.
7. Serve and enjoy.

187. BONE- IN PORK CHOP

2 HOURS   5 MIN   2

NUTRITION:
CAL: 237 | FAT: 15 | PROTEIN: 24

INGREDIENTS

- 2 pork chops, bone in
- 1 tsp. olive oil
- 1/8 tsp. tarragon
- 1/8 tsp. thyme
- Black pepper
- Salt

DIRECTIONS

1. Fill and preheat a sous vide water bath to 145 ºF.
2. Season pork chops with pepper and salt.
3. Rub tarragon, olive oil, and thyme over pork chops.
4. Place pork chops into the zip-lock bag and remove all the air from the bag before sealing.
5. Place bag into the hot water bath and cook for 2 hours.
6. Remove pork chops from bag and sear until lightly brown.
7. Serve and enjoy.

188. PORK CHOPS WITH MUSHROOMS

2 HOURS | 10 MIN | 4

NUTRITION:
CAL: 292 | FAT: 22 | PROTEIN: 24

INGREDIENTS

- 4 pork chops, boneless
- 4 tbsp butter
- 2 garlic cloves, minced
- 1 tbsp flour
- 1 cup chicken broth
- 8 oz. crimini mushrooms, sliced
- 1 large shallot, sliced
- Pepper
- Salt

DIRECTIONS

1. Preheat a sous vide water bath to 140°F.
2. Place the chops into a zip-lock bag. Place bag into a water bath and cook for 2 hours.
3. Remove chops from bag and pat dry with paper towel.
4. Season the chop with salt and pepper.
5. Heat 2 tbsp. butter in a pan. Sear the chops on both the sides.
6. Add remaining 2 tbsp. butter in a pan. Add sliced mushrooms to the pan and cook for 4-5 minutes stirring occasionally.
7. Add shallots cook for 2 minutes until tender, add garlic and stir for 1 minute constantly then add flour.
8. Stir well until mixture is evenly coated over mushrooms, add chicken broth stir for 1 minute.
9. Season with salt and pepper.
10. Serve and enjoy.

189. HERB RUB PORK CHOPS

2 HOURS | 10 MIN | 4

NUTRITION:
CAL: 318 | FAT: 25 | PROTEIN: 24

INGREDIENTS

- 4 pork chops, bone in
- 1/4 cup olive oil
- 1 tsp black pepper
- 1 tbsp balsamic vinegar
- 1 lemon zest
- 2 garlic cloves, minced
- 6 thyme sprigs, remove stems
- 1/4 cup chives
- 1/4 cup rosemary
- 10 basil leaves
- 1/4 cup parsley
- 1/2 tsp salt

DIRECTIONS

1. Preheat a sous vide water bath to 140°F.
2. Add herbs to the food processor and process until chopped.
3. Add garlic, olive oil, pepper, salt, vinegar, and lemon zest and blend until smooth paste.
4. Rub herb mixture over pork chops. Place pork chops into the zip-lock bag and remove all the air from the bag before sealing.
5. Place bag into the hot water bath and cook for 2 hours.
6. Remove pork chops from the water bath and broil for 3-4 minutes.
7. Serve and enjoy.

190. PORK LOIN

4 HOURS | 5 MIN | 4

NUTRITION:
CAL: 597 | FAT: 48 | PROTEIN: 36

INGREDIENTS

- 2 lbs. pork loin roast
- 2 tbsp sweet and sour sauce
- 1 tsp black pepper
- 1 tsp garlic powder
- 1/2 tsp chipotle powder
- 1 tsp salt

DIRECTIONS

1. Fill and preheat a sous vide water bath to 153° F.
2. In a small bowl, mix together chipotle powder, garlic powder, black pepper, and salt.
3. Rub spice mixture over the pork loin roast.
4. Place pork into the zip-lock bag and remove all the air from the bag before sealing.
5. Place bag into the hot water bath and cook for 4 hours.
6. Remove pork from bag and coat outside with sweet and sour sauce.
7. Broil pork for 5 minutes until lightly brown.
8. Serve and enjoy.

191. LEMON PORK CHOPS

6 HOURS | 5 MIN | 4

NUTRITION:
CAL: 597 | FAT: 48 | PROTEIN: 36

INGREDIENTS

- 4 pork chops, bone in
- 1 lemon, sliced
- 4 fresh thyme sprigs, chopped
- 1 tbsp. olive oil
- Salt and pepper, as needed

DIRECTIONS

1. Fill and preheat a sous vide water bath to 138° F.
2. Season pork chops with pepper and salt.
3. Place pork chops into the zip-lock bag with thyme and lemon slices. Drizzle with olive oil.
4. Remove all air from the bag before sealing.
5. Place bag into the hot water bath and cook for 6 hours.
6. Remove pork chops from bag and pat dry with paper towel.
7. Using kitchen torch sear the pork chops until caramelizing.
8. Serve and enjoy.

192. FIVE SPICE PORK

48 HOURS | 5 MIN | 4

NUTRITION:
CAL: 161 | FAT: 6 | PROTEIN: 23

INGREDIENTS

- 1 lb. pork belly
- 1 bacon slice
- 1 tsp Chinese 5 spice powder
- Salt and pepper, as needed

DIRECTIONS

1. Fill and preheat a sous vide water bath to 140° F.
2. Add pork belly into the zip-lock bag with bacon slice and seasoning.
3. Remove all the air from the bag before sealing.
4. Place bag into the hot water bath and cook for 48 hours.
5. Remove pork from bag and broil until crisp.
6. Serve and enjoy.

193. BBQ PORK RIBS

18 HOURS | 5 MIN | 2

NUTRITION:
CAL: 653 | FAT: 19 | PROTEIN: 14

INGREDIENTS

- 1 rack back ribs, cut into rib portions
- 2 tbsp Worcestershire sauce
- 1/3 cup brown sugar
- 1 1/2 cups BBQ sauce

DIRECTIONS

1. Fill and preheat a sous vide water bath to 160º F.
2. Whisk brown sugar in 1 cup BBQ sauce and Worcestershire sauce.
3. Place ribs into the large mixing bowl then pour marinade over ribs and toss well.
4. Place ribs into the zip-lock bag and remove all the air from the bag before sealing.
5. Place bag into the hot water bath and cook for 18 hours.
6. Remove ribs from bag and place on baking tray.
7. Brush ribs with remaining BBQ sauce and broil for 5 minutes.
8. Serve and enjoy.

194. BBQ BABY BACK RIBS

24 HOURS | 5 MIN | 2

NUTRITION:
CAL: 335 | FAT: 15 | PROTEIN: 14

INGREDIENTS

- 1 rack baby back pork ribs
- 6 tbsp Chipotle BBQ sauce
- Salt and pepper, as needed

DIRECTIONS

1. Fill and preheat a sous vide water bath to 143º F.
2. Cut rib rack in half and season with pepper and salt.
3. Brush BBQ sauce over the pork ribs.
4. Place ribs into the zip-lock bag and remove all the air from the bag before sealing.
5. Place bag into the hot water bath and cook for 24 hours.
6. Remove ribs from bag and grill for 1 minute.
7. Serve and enjoy.

195. PORK CARNITAS

20 HOURS | 10 MIN | 12

NUTRITION:
CAL: 529 | FAT: 41| PROTEIN: 38

INGREDIENTS

- 6 lb. pork shoulder
- 2 tbsp anise
- 2 bay leaves
- 2 cinnamon sticks
- 3 tbsp garlic, minced
- 4 bacon slices
- 1/3 cup brown sugar
- 2 orange juices
- 1 onion, chopped
- 1 tbsp sea salt

DIRECTIONS

1. Fill and preheat a sous vide water bath to 175º F.
2. In a small bowl, mix together anise, sugar, salt, garlic, and orange juice.
3. Place pork into the zip-lock bag then pours orange juice mixture over pork.
4. Add cinnamon, bay leaves, bacon, and onions into the bag.
5. Seal bag and place into the hot water bath and cook for 20 hours.
6. Heat large pan over medium-high heat.
7. Remove pork from bag and place on pan and shred using a fork.
8. Cook shredded pork until crispy.
9. Serve and enjoy.

196. PULLED PORK

18 HOURS | 10 MIN | 4

NUTRITION:
CAL: 570 | FAT: 40| PROTEIN: 38

INGREDIENTS

- 2 lb. pork shoulder, boneless
- 1/2 cup taco seasoning
- 1 onion, diced
- 1/4 cup cilantro, chopped

DIRECTIONS

1. Fill and preheat a sous vide water bath to 165° F.
2. Season pork with half taco seasoning.
3. Place pork into the zip-lock bag and remove all the air from the bag before sealing.
4. Place bag into the hot water bath and cook for 18 hours.
5. Remove pork from bag and pat dry with paper towel.
6. Season pork with remaining taco seasoning.
7. Place pork in preheated 350 F/ 176 C oven and cook for 30 minutes.
8. Remove pork from oven and using fork shred the pork.
9. Garnish with cilantro and serve.

197. SIMPLE SLICED PORK BELLY

3 HOURS | 10 MIN | 2

NUTRITION:
CAL: 570 | FAT: 40| PROTEIN: 38

INGREDIENTS

- 4 oz. pork belly, sliced
- 3 bay leaves
- 1 tbsp garlic salt
- 1 tbsp whole black peppercorns
- 1 1/2 tbsp. olive oil

DIRECTIONS

1. Fill and preheat a sous vide water bath to 145° F.
2. Add sliced pork belly, bay leaves, garlic salt, peppercorns, and 1 tbsp. olive oil into the large zip-lock bag.
3. Remove all the air from the bag before sealing.
4. Place bag into the hot water bath and cook for 3 hours.
5. Heat remaining oil in a pan over medium heat.
6. Remove pork from bag and sear in hot oil for 2 minutes on each side.
7. Serve and enjoy.

198. PERFECT PORK CHOP

50 MIN | 5 MIN | 4

NUTRITION:
CAL: 643 | FAT: 45| PROTEIN: 43

INGREDIENTS

- 20 oz. pork rib chop, bone in
- 2 tbsp butter
- Salt and pepper, as needed

DIRECTIONS

1. Preheat a sous vide water bath to 140°F.
2. Season pork chops with pepper and salt.
3. Place pork chops into the zip-lock bag and remove all the air from the bag before sealing.
4. Place bag into the hot water bath and cook for 45 minutes.
5. Heat butter into the pan over medium heat.
6. Remove pork chop from the bag and pat dry with paper towel.
7. Sear pork chops in hot butter until lightly brown from both the sides.
8. Serve and enjoy.

199. SWEET AND SPICY PORK RIBS

20 HOURS | 5 MIN | 6

NUTRITION:
CAL: 536 | FAT: 36 | PROTEIN: 24

INGREDIENTS

- 2 full racks baby back pork ribs, cut in half
- 1/2 cup jerk seasoning mix

DIRECTIONS

1. Preheat a sous vide water bath to 145°F.
2. Season pork rib rack with half jerk seasoning and place in large zip-lock bag.
3. Remove all the air from the bag before sealing.
4. Place bag into the hot water bath and cook for 20 hours.
5. Remove meat from bag and rub with remaining seasoning and place on a baking tray.
6. Broil for 5 minutes. Slice and serve.

200. BRINED PORK BELLY

12 HOURS | 10 MIN | 4

NUTRITION:
CAL: 257 | FAT: 6 | PROTEIN: 23

INGREDIENTS

- 1-lb skinless pork belly
- 4 cups water
- ½ cup light brown sugar
- ½ cup salt
- 2 tbsps whole black peppercorns
- 6 fresh thyme sprigs
- 1 tbsp vegetable oil

DIRECTIONS

1. Add water, brown sugar, salt, peppercorns, and thyme to a large pan and bring to a boil. Remove from heat and refrigerate for at least 5 hours. After 5 hours, place pork belly in brine, cover, and refrigerate again for 24 hours.
2. Preheat a sous vide water bath to 158°F.
3. Remove pork belly from brine and place in a large cooking pouch. Seal pouch tightly after removing the excess air. Place pouch in sous vide bath and set the cooking time for 12 hours. Cover the sous vide bath with plastic wrap to minimize water evaporation. Add water intermittently to keep the water level up.
4. Remove pouch from the sous vide bath and immediately plunge into a large bowl of ice water. Set aside to cool completely. Transfer the pouch to the refrigerator for at least 4 hours.
5. After 4 hours, remove pork belly from pouch and cut into ¾-inch thick slices.
6. In a large, non-stick skillet, heat oil over medium heat and sear pork pieces for 10 minutes. Serve immediately.

201. SZECHUAN PORK BELLY BITES

10 HOURS | 15 MIN | 4

NUTRITION:
CAL: 313 | FAT: 7 | PROTEIN: 29

INGREDIENTS

- 1¼ lb pork belly strips, rind removed and cut into 1-inch pieces
- 1 tbsp clear honey
- Pinch of freshly ground white pepper
- Peel of 1 Mandarin orange
- 1-star anise pod
- Pinch of sea salt
- 2 tbsps Szechuan peppercorns, ground with a

DIRECTIONS

1. 1Preheat a sous vide water bath to 158°F.
2. Place pork belly strips, honey, and a pinch of white pepper in a large cooking pouch. Squish the pouch to coat the pork well.
3. Add orange peel and star anise pod. Seal pouch tightly after removing the excess air. Place pouch in sous vide bath and set the cooking time for 9-10 hours.
4. Preheat conventional oven to 400°F.
5. Mix salt and ground Szechuan peppercorns together in a small bowl. Remove pouch and open carefully.
6. Remove pork pieces from pouch and pat dry pork pieceswith paper towels. Coat the Fatty side of each pork piece with the salt mixture.

- pestle and mortar
- 1 bottle BBQ sauce (of your choice)

7. Arrange pork pieces on a baking sheet and coat pieces with BBQ sauce. Bake for 5 minutes.
8. Insert a cocktail stick into each piece and serve immediately.

202. PORK TENDERLOIN

2 HOURS | 10 MIN | 4

NUTRITION:
CAL: 205 | FAT: 11 | PROTEIN: 23

INGREDIENTS

- 1-lb pork tenderloins
- 1½ tbsps dry rub of your choice
- 1½ tbsps salt
- Freshly ground black pepper, to taste
- 2 tbsps butter

DIRECTIONS

1. Preheat a sous vide water bath to 140ºF.
2. Season pork tenderloin with dry rub, salt, and black pepper generously.
3. Divide pork tenderloins and butter into 2 cooking pouches. Seal pouches tightly after removing the excess air. Place pouches in sous vide bath and set the cooking time for 2 hours.
4. Remove pouches from the sous vide bath and open carefully. Remove pork tenderloins from pouches and pat dry pork tenderloins with paper towels.
5. Heat a cast iron skillet and sear pork tenderloin until browned. Serve immediately.

203. COUNTRY PORK RIBS WITH DIJON

24 HOURS | 15 MIN | 6

NUTRITION:
CAL: 888| FAT: 62 | PROTEIN: 67

INGREDIENTS

- 3 lbs country style pork ribs
- 1 tbsp ground rosemary
- 1 tbsp garlic powder
- 1 tbsp onion powder
- 2 tbsps salt
- 1 tbsp ground black pepper
- 1 tbsp cornstarch
- 2 tbsps water
- 3 tbsps Dijon mustard
- 1 tbsp vegetable oil

DIRECTIONS

1. Preheat a sous vide water bath to 165ºF.
2. Mix rosemary, spices, salt, and black pepper together in a small bowl.
3. Rub pork ribs generously with spice mixture.
4. Place ribs in a cooking pouch. Seal pouch tightly after removing the excess air. Place pouch in sous vide bath and set the cookingtime for 24 hours. Cover the sous vide bath with plastic wrap tominimize water evaporation. Add water intermittently to keep the water level up.
5. In a small bowl, dissolve cornstarch into water. Set aside.
6. Remove pouch from the sous vide bath and open carefully.
7. Remove ribs from pouch, reserving cooking liquid in pan, pat dry ribs with paper towels.
8. Place the pan of cooking liquid on medium-high heat. Add cornstarch mixture and Dijon mustard to pan and beat until well combined. Cook until desired thickness is reached.
9. Heat oil in a skillet over high heat and sear ribs until browned on both sides. Serve ribs topped with sauce.

204. SIMPLE PORK CHOPS

4 HOURS | 15 MIN | 4

NUTRITION:
CAL: 208 | FAT: 11 | PROTEIN: 28

INGREDIENTS

- 4 (1½-inch thick) bone-in pork rib chops
- salt and freshly ground black pepper, to taste
- 2 tbsps vegetable oil
- 2 tbsps butter, divided
- 2 garlic cloves
- 4 thyme or rosemary sprigs
- 2 shallots, thinly sliced

DIRECTIONS

1. Preheat a sous vide water bath to 140ºF.
2. Season pork chops generously with salt and black pepper.
3. Place pork chops in a cooking pouch. Seal pouch tightly after removing the excess air. Place pouch in sous vide bath and set the cooking time for 3-4 hours.
4. Remove pouch from the sous vide bath and open carefully. Remove chops from pouch and pat dry with paper towels.
5. In a heavy, large cast iron skillet, heat oil and 1 tbsp of butter over high heat and sear chops for 45 seconds. Flip pork chops and add remaining butter, garlic, herb sprigs, and shallots to the skillet. Cook for 45 seconds, occasionally pouring the butter over the chops.
6. Serve pork chops topped with sauce left in skillet.

205. GARLIC & HERB RUBBED PORK CHOPS

2 HOURS | 20 MIN | 4

NUTRITION:
CAL: 316 | FAT: 24 | PROTEIN: 26

INGREDIENTS

- 4 (1½-inch thick) large bone-in pork chops ¼ cup fresh chives
- ¼ cup fresh rosemary, stems removed
- ¼ cup fresh parsley
- 6 fresh thyme sprigs, stems removed
- 10 large basil leaves
- 2 garlic cloves, minced
- Zest of 1 lemon
- ¼ cup olive oil
- 1 tbsp white balsamic vinegar
- ½ tsp salt
- 1 tsp freshly cracked black pepper

DIRECTIONS

1. Preheat a sous vide water bath to 140ºF.
2. In a food processor, add herbs and pulse until finely chopped. Add garlic, lemon zest, olive oil, vinegar, salt, and black pepper and pulse until a smooth paste is formed. Rub chops evenly with herb mixture.
3. Place chops in a cooking pouch. Seal pouch tightly after removing the excess air. Place pouch in sous vide bath and set the cooking time for 2 hours.
4. Preheat the oven broiler to high. Grease a baking sheet.
5. Remove pouch from the sous vide bath and open carefully. Remove chops from pouch.
6. Transfer chops onto prepared baking sheet and broil for 3-4 minutes per side. Serve immediately.

206. THAI PORK CHOPS WITH GREEN CURRY

2 HOURS | 15 MIN | 4

NUTRITION:
CAL: 308 | FAT: 23 | PROTEIN: 25

INGREDIENTS

- 4 boneless pork loin chops
- 2 Thai green chili peppers, minced
- 2 tbsps fresh ginger, minced
- 3 garlic cloves, minced
- 4 tbsps oil

DIRECTIONS

1. In a large bowl, add Thai chilies, ginger, garlic, ginger, 4 tbsps oil, and salt. Add pork chops and toss to coat well. Let sit for 1-2 hours.
2. Preheat a sous vide water bath to 135ºF.
3. In a cooking pouch, place chops with some of marinade. Seal pouch tightly after removing the excess air. Place pouch in sous vide bath and set the cooking time for 2 hours.

- 1 tsp salt
- 1 can coconut milk
- 3 tbsps green curry paste
- 2 tomatoes, chopped
- 4 tbsps fresh Thai basil, minced
- Vegetable oil, as required

4. For green curry sauce: while pork chops are in sous vide bath, add coconut milk and green curry paste to a small pan and cook until just starting to boil. Reduce heat to low and simmer for 10 minutes.
5. In a bowl, mix together tomatoes and basil. Set aside.
6. Remove pouch from the sous vide bath and open carefully. Remove chops from pouch and pat dry chops with paper towels.
7. In a cast iron skillet, heat a little vegetable oil over high heat and sear pork chops for 30-60 seconds per side.
8. Divide chops onto serving plates and top with tomato mixture. Drizzle with green curry sauce and serve.

207. PORK CHOPS WITH APPLE CIDER SAUCE

12 HOURS | 20 MIN | 4

NUTRITION:
CAL: 324 | FAT: 24 | PROTEIN: 25

INGREDIENTS

- 4 extra-thick pork chops
- Salt and freshly ground black pepper, to taste
- 5 tbsps butter, divided
- 8 thyme sprigs
- 2 apples, cored and sliced
- 2 garlic cloves, finely chopped
- 2/3 cup hard apple cider
- 1 tbsp whole grain mustard
- 1 tsp cider vinegar
- 1 tsp sugar

DIRECTIONS

1. Preheat a sous vide water bath to 140°F.
2. Season pork chops lightly with salt and black pepper.
3. Divide chops, 4 tbsps of butter, and thyme sprigs into 4 cooking pouches with each pouch containing 1 pork chop, 1 tbsp of butter, and 2 thyme sprigs. Seal pouches tightly after removing the excess air. Place pouches in sous vide bath and set the cooking time for 12 hours.
4. For sauce: add apples and remaining tbsp of butter to a pan and cook over medium-high heat until apples just begin to soften.
5. Remove pouches from the sous vide bath and open carefully. Remove the chops from the pouches, reserving the cooking liquid.
6. Heat a grill pan over high heat and sear chops until browned on both sides.
7. Add garlic, apple cider, mustard, cider vinegar, sugar, and ½ cup of reserved cooking liquid to pan of apples and simmer for a few minutes or until desired sauce thickness is reached.
8. Divide chops onto serving plates and top evenly with the apple sauce. Serve immediately

208. CHAR SUI (CHINESE PORK)

12 HOURS | 20 MIN | 4

NUTRITION:
CAL: 523 | FAT: 74 | PROTEIN: 60

INGREDIENTS

For Pork Shoulder:

- large pork shoulder
- 2 tbsps caster sugar
- 2 cubes Chinese red fermented bean curd
- 2 tsps Chinese rose wine
- 1 tbsp mild honey
- 1 tbsp oyster sauce
- 1 tbsp hoisin sauce
- 1 tsp soy sauce

DIRECTIONS

1. Preheat a sous vide water bath to 155°F.
2. For pork shoulder: in a large bowl, add all ingredients for pork shoulder except the meat and mix until well combined. Add pork shoulder and coat generously with marinade.
3. Place the pork shoulder in a cooking pouch with the marinade. Seal pouch tightly after removing the excess air. Place pouch in sous vide bath and set the cooking time for 15 hours. Cover the sous vide bath with plastic wrap to minimize water evaporation. Add water intermittently to keep the water level up.
4. Preheat the oven broiler to high.
5. Remove pouch from the sous vide bath and open carefully. Remove pork shoulder from pouch, reserving 1-2 tbsps of the cooking liquid.

- 1 tsp Chinese five spice powder
- ¼ tsp ground white pepper

For Glaze:
- 1 tbsp honey

6. For glaze: in a small bowl, mix together reserved cooking liquid and honey. Coat pork shoulder with glaze mixture.
7. Transfer pork shoulder onto a roasting pan. Broil until charred on both sides.
8. Remove from oven. Cut into slices of the desired size and serve.

209. SMOKEY PULLED PORK SHOULDER

25 HOURS | 20 MIN | 4

NUTRITION:
CAL: 929 | FAT: 44 | PROTEIN: 101

INGREDIENTS

For Spice Rub:
- ¼ cup dark brown sugar
- ¼ cup paprika
- 3 tbsps salt
- 2 tbsps granulated garlic powder
- 1 tbsp whole yellow mustard seed
- 1 tbsp whole coriander seed
- 1 tbsp dried oregano
- 1 tsp freshly ground black pepper
- 1 tsp red pepper flakes
- ½ tsp Prague Powder

For Pork:
- 1 (5-7 lb) boneless pork shoulder
- ½ tsp liquid smoke
- salt, to taste

DIRECTIONS

1. Preheat a sous vide water bath to 165°F.
2. For Spice Rub: in a spice grinder, add all ingredients for spice rub in batches and grind until a fine powder is formed.
3. Rub pork evenly with half of spice mixture.
4. Place pork shoulder and liquid smoke in a large cooking pouch. Seal pouch tightly after removing the excess air. Place pouch in sous vide bath and set the cooking time for 18-24 hours. Cover the sous vide bath with plastic wrap to minimize water evaporation. Add water intermittently to keep the water level up.
5. Preheat oven to 300°F. In the oven, arrange a rack in the lower-middle position. Arrange another rack on a rimmed baking sheet.
6. Remove pouch from the sous vide bath and open carefully. Remove pork shoulder from pouch.
7. Rub remaining spice mixture evenly onto the surface of the pork. Place pork on the wire rack that is on the rimmed baking sheet. Roast for 1½ hours.
8. Remove pork from oven and transfer to a cutting board. With 2 forks, shred meat into bite-size pieces.
9. Season pulled pork with salt and serve immediately.

210. PULLED PORK SHOULDER

36 HOURS | 25 MIN | 4

NUTRITION:
CAL: 765 | FAT: 32 | PROTEIN: 82

INGREDIENTS

For Pork:
- 4-lb bone-in pork shoulder, trimmed of large Fat pieces
- Salt and freshly ground black pepper, to taste
- 3 whole garlic cloves, peeled
- 1 bay leaf
- 1 tsp dried thyme, crushed
- ¼ tsp celery salt

DIRECTIONS

1. Preheat a sous vide water bath to 149°F.
2. Season pork shoulder evenly with salt and pepper.
3. Place pork shoulder, whole garlic cloves, bay leaf, thyme, and celery salt in a large cooking pouch. Roll the pork around in the bag to coat with seasonings.
4. Seal pouch tightly after removing the excess air. Place pouch in sous vide bath and set the cooking time for 36 hours. Cover the sous vide bath with plastic wrap to minimize water evaporation. Add water intermittently to keep the water level up.
5. For barbecue sauce: add all barbecue sauce ingredients to a pan over medium-high heat and bring to a boil. Reduce heat to low and simmer for 30 minutes, stirring occasionally. Remove from heat and set aside to cool at room temperature. Transfer sauce into a bowl and refrigerate until serving.

- For Barbecue Sauce:
- 1 cup ketchup
- ¼ cup red onion, finely chopped
- 1 garlic clove, minced
- ¼ cup fresh orange juice
- 1 tbsp fresh lemon juice
- 2 tbsps molasses
- 2 tbsps apple cider vinegar
- 1 tbsp tomato paste
- 1 tsp yellow mustard
- 1 tsp liquid smoke
- 1 tsp Worcestershire sauce
- ¼ tsp celery salt

For Pickled Onion:

- ½ red onion, thinly sliced
- 1 tbsp apple cider vinegar
- 1½ tsps raw (turbinado) sugar
- ¼ tsp salt
- 1½ tbsps boiling water

For Serving:

- 4 dinner rolls, halved

6. Remove pouch from the sous vide bath and open carefully. Remove pork shoulder from pouch, reserving cooking liquid in a large bowl.
7. With 2 forks, shred pork into small pieces. Discard all large Fat pieces and bones. Transfer pork into a bowl with reserved cooking liquid and refrigerate overnight.
8. For pickled onion: in a small bowl, mix together sliced onion, vinegar, sugar, and salt. Add boiling water and stir to combine. Set aside at room temperature to cool. Refrigerate before serving.
9. For sandwiches: Add sauce to a medium pan over medium-high heat and cook for 2-3 minutes or until warmed. Add 1 lb of shredded pork and stir to combine. Reduce heat to low and simmer for 4-5 minutes or until heated completely.
10. Place pork mixture over each roll evenly. Top with pickled onion and serve.

211. MISO PORK MEATBALLS

2 HOURS | 20 MIN | 4

NUTRITION:
CAL: 155 | FAT: 9| PROTEIN: 24

INGREDIENTS

- 1-lb ground pork
- 1/3 cup mushrooms, minced finely
- 1/3 cup fresh cilantro, chopped
- 1/3 cup scallions, minced finely
- 1 lemongrass stalk (white, tender, inner part), minced finely
- 2 garlic cloves, finely chopped
- 1 tbsp fish sauce
- 1 tbsp miso
- 1½ tsps cornstarch
- 1 tsp salt
- Few grinds of black pepper
- 3-4 tbsps sesame seeds

DIRECTIONS

1. In a large bowl, add all ingredients except sesame seeds and mix until well combined. Refrigerate mixture for at least 1 hour.
2. With slightly damp hands, make golf-ball sized meatballs from pork mixture. Arrange meatballs onto a baking sheet lined with parchment and freeze for at least 1½-2 hours.
3. Preheat a sous vide water bath to 150°F.
4. Place meatballs in a large cooking pouch with space around each meatball. Seal pouch tightly after removing the excess air. Place pouch in sous vide bath and set the cooking time for 2-3 hours.
5. Remove pouch from the sous vide bath and open carefully. Remove meatballs from pouch and pat dry with paper towels. Evenly coat meatballs with sesame seeds.
6. Heat a non-stick skillet over medium-high heat and fry meatballs until browned on both sides.
7. Serve immediately.

212. PORK SAUSAGE

4 HOURS | 10 MIN | 4

NUTRITION:
CAL: 979 | FAT: 72 | PROTEIN: 60

INGREDIENTS

- 3 lbs raw, natural casing sausages
- 6-oz beer
- 2-6 tsps salt
- 1 tbsp butter

DIRECTIONS

1. Preheat a sous vide water bath to 171°F.
2. Place sausages in a single layer in cooking pouches. Add a few tbsps of beer and 2 tsps of salt to each pouch. Seal pouches tightly after removing the excess air. Place pouches in sous vide bath and set the cooking time for 4 hours.
3. Remove pouches from the sous vide bath and open carefully. Remove sausages from pouch and pat dry with paper towels.
4. In a skillet, melt butter over medium heat and cook sausages for 3 minutes, flipping occasionally.
5. Serve immediately.

213. ITALIAN SAUSAGE WITH PEPPERS & ONION

3 HOURS | 20 MIN | 4

NUTRITION:
CAL: 468 | FAT: 34| PROTEIN: 24

INGREDIENTS

For Sausage:
- 8 Italian sausage links
- For Vegetables:
- 1 orange bell pepper
- 1 red bell pepper
- 1 poblano pepper
- 2 onions, cut into ½-¾-inch thick slices
- Salt and freshly ground black pepper, to taste
- Canola oil, as required

DIRECTIONS

1. Preheat a sous vide water bath to 140°F.
2. Place sausages in cooking pouches in a single layer. Seal pouches tightly after removing the excess air. Place pouches in sous vide bath and set the cooking time for 2-3 hours.
3. Preheat the grill to high heat.
4. While the sausages are in the sous vide bath, cut into the sides of each pepper, leaving them whole. Sprinkle each of the peppers and onion with salt and pepper and drizzle with oil.
5. Grill peppers and onions until they begin to brown.
6. Remove from grill and set aside to cool slightly. After cooling, cut peppers into ½-inch strips.
7. Remove pouches from the sous vide bath and open carefully. Remove sausages from pouch and pat dry with paper towels.
8. Sear sausages over high heat on the grill for 1-2 minutes per side.
9. Divide peppers and onions onto serving plates and top with sausages.

214. ROSEMARY PORK CHOPS

2 HOURS | 15 MIN | 4

NUTRITION:
CAL: 168 | FAT: 9 | PROTEIN: 24

INGREDIENTS

- 1-lb bone-in, double-cut pork chop
- salt and freshly ground black pepper, to taste
- 1 garlic clove, finely chopped
- 1 fresh rosemary sprig, finely chopped
- 1 cup hard cider, divided
- 1 tbsp vegetable oil
- 1 tbsp dark brown sugar
- Sautéed apples, for serving
- Sautéed cabbage, for serving

DIRECTIONS

1. Preheat a sous vide water bath to 140°F.
2. Season pork chop generously with salt and pepper then rub with garlic and rosemary.
3. Place pork chop and ½ cup of hard cider in a cooking pouch. Seal pouch tightly after removing the excess air. Place pouch in sous vide bath and set the cooking time for 45-120 minutes.
4. Remove pouch from the sous vide bath and open carefully. Remove pork chop from pouch, reserving the cooking liquid. Pat dry the pork chop with paper towels.
5. In a cast iron skillet, heat oil over medium-high heat and sear pork chop for 30-45 seconds per side. Transfer pork chop to a serving platter.
6. In the same skillet used for the pork chop, add reserved cooking liquid, remaining hard cider, and sugar and bring to a rapid simmer for 1 minute, stirring continuously.
7. Place sauce over pork chop and serve alongside sautéed apples and cabbage.

215. PORK CHOPS WITH MIXED MUSHROOMS

55 MIN | 10 MIN | 4

NUTRITION:
CAL: 158 | FAT: 9 | PROTEIN: 12

INGREDIENTS

- 8-oz thick-cut, bone-in pork chops
- Salt and freshly ground black pepper, to taste
- 2 tbsps cold unsalted butter, divided
- 4 oz mixed wild mushrooms
- ¼ cup sherry
- 1 tbsp steak marinade
- ½ cup beef broth
- Chopped garlic chives, for garnishing

DIRECTIONS

1. Preheat a sous vide water bath to 140°F.
2. Season pork chops generously with salt and pepper.
3. Place pork chops in a cooking pouch. Seal pouch tightly after removing the excess air. Place pouch in sous vide bath and set the cooking time for 45 minutes.
4. Remove pouch from the sous vide bath and open carefully. Remove pork chops from pouch and pat dry with paper towels.
5. In a large skillet, melt 1 tbsp of butter over medium-high heat and sear pork chops for 1 minute on each side. Transfer chops to a plate and cover with foil to keep warm.
6. In the same skillet used for the pork chops, add the mushrooms and cook for 2-3 minutes, stirring occasionally. Add sherry and bring to a boil, scraping up browned bits from the bottom of skillet.
7. Stir in steak marinade and broth and bring to a boil. Reduce heat to medium and simmer until sauce becomes slightly thick, stirring occasionally.
8. Remove from heat and immediately stir in remaining butter, ½ tbsp at a time until sauce becomes smooth. Add salt and black pepper.
9. Divide pork chops on serving plates and top with mushroom sauce. Garnish with garlic chives and serve.

216. PORK STEAKS WITH CREAMY SLAW

24 HOURS | 15 MIN | 4

NUTRITION:
CAL: 55 | FAT: 4 | PROTEIN: 6

INGREDIENTS

- 2 (1-inch thick) pork shoulder steaks
- 1 tsp salt
- ½ tsp freshly ground black pepper
- 1 tsp vegetable oil
- For Creamy Slaw:
- ½ small, purple cabbage head, cored and thinly sliced
- ¼ tsp fine sea salt
- ½ tsp freshly ground black pepper
- 2 tbsps olive oil
- 2 tbsps mayonnaise
- Fresh juice of 1 lemon
- 1 tsp Dijon mustard

DIRECTIONS

1. Preheat a sous vide water bath to 160°F.
2. For pork steaks: season pork steaks evenly with salt and black pepper.
3. Divide pork steaks into two cooking pouches. Seal pouches tightly after removing the Cover the sous vide bath with plastic wrap to minimize water evaporation. Add water intermittently to keep the water level up.
4. Cook for 20-24 hours.
5. For slaw: in a large bowl, place cabbage, sea salt, and black pepper and toss to coat well.
6. In a small bowl, add remaining slaw ingredients and beat until well combined. Pour mustard mixture over cabbage and toss to coat well.
7. Remove pouches from the sous vide bath and open carefully. Remove pork steaks from pouches and pat dry with paper towels.
8. In a cast iron skillet, heat oil over medium heat and sear pork steaks for 1 minute on each side.
9. Cut each steak into 2 pieces of equal size. Divide pork pieces onto serving plates and serve alongside creamy slaw.

6. BEEF AND LAMB

217. LAMB SHANK COOKED IN RED WINE

48 HOURS | 10 MIN | 4

NUTRITION:
CAL: 235 | FAT: 15 | PROTEIN: 16

INGREDIENTS
- 1 lamb shank
- 2 sprigs thyme
- 2 tbsps olive oil
- ½ cup dry red wine
- Salt and pepper to taste

DIRECTIONS
1. Preheat the sous vide water bath to 144 °F.
2. Sprinkle the lamb shank with salt and pepper. Put it into the vacuum bag together with other ingredients and seal it.
3. Set the cooking timer for 48 hours.
4. Serve with mashed potatoes, pouring 3-4 tbsps of cooking juices over before Servings.

218. LAMB CHOPS WITH HONEY MUSTARD SAUCE

3 HOURS | 10 MIN | 4

NUTRITION:
CAL: 324 | FAT: 27 | PROTEIN: 16

INGREDIENTS
- 4 lamb chops
- 4 rosemary sprigs
- 4 tbsps olive oil
- Salt and pepper to taste
- For the sauce
- 4 tbsps Dijon mustard
- 1 tsp liquid honey
- 1 tbsp lemon juice

DIRECTIONS
1. Preheat the sous vide water bath to 145 °F.
2. Season the lamb chops with salt and pepper.
3. Put the lamb into the bag; add 2 tbsps of olive oil, and 1 rosemary sprig on each chop.
4. Remove the air and cook for 3 hours.
5. When the time is up, preheat the remaining 2 tbsps of olive oil in a cast-iron skillet, and sear the chops over high heat for about 30 seconds on each side until golden.
6. Whisk the mustard with the liquid honey and lemon juice, then pour the sauce over the chops and serve.

219. LAMB SHANK WITH WINE SAUCE AND ROSEMARY

12 HOURS | 10 MIN | 4

NUTRITION:
CAL: 235 | FAT: 15 | PROTEIN: 16

INGREDIENTS
- 1 lamb shank
- 2 sprigs rosemary
- 2 tbsps olive oil
- ½ cup dry red wine
- Salt and pepper to taste

DIRECTIONS
1. Preheat the sous vide water bath to 144 °F.
2. Sprinkle the lamb shank with salt and pepper. Put the lamb, rosemary, and olive oil into the vacuum bag and seal it.
3. Set the cooking timer for 12 hours.
4. When the time is up, carefully open the bag and pour the cooking juices into a pan.
5. Bring the sauces to a boil and remove the scums from the top of the liquid with a spoon.
6. Add the red wine and simmer until the liquid reduces.
7. Pour the sauce over the lamb and serve.

220. BEEF BURGERS

1 HOUR | 10 MIN | 1

NUTRITION:
CAL: 344 | FAT: 31 | PROTEIN: 29

INGREDIENTS

- ½ lb minced beef
- 2 buns for hamburgers
- 2 slices cheddar cheese
- 8 slices marinated cucumbers
- 2 tbsps Dijon mustard
- 2 tbsps ketchup
- Salt and pepper to taste

DIRECTIONS

1. Preheat the sous vide water bath to 137 °F.
2. Shape the minced beef into 2 patties, seasoning them with salt and pepper to taste.
3. Put them into a plastic bag, removing as much air as possible.
4. Seal it and set the cooking time for 1 hour.
5. While the patties are cooking, toast the buns.
6. Remove the patties from the bag, dry them, and roast on high heat for about 20-30 seconds on each side.
7. Assemble the burgers with cheddar slices, mustard, ketchup, and sliced marinated cucumbers; serve.

221. BEEF TENDERLOIN

2 HOURS | 10 MIN | 1

NUTRITION:
CAL: 294 | FAT: 28 | PROTEIN: 24

INGREDIENTS

- 1 beef tenderloin
- 2 garlic cloves, minced
- ½ tbsp dried rosemary
- ½ tbsp dried thyme
- 1 tbsp olive oil
- Salt and pepper to taste

DIRECTIONS

1. Preheat the sous vide water bath to 133 °F.
2. Season the meat with salt and pepper to taste. Then grease it with the olive oil on both sides and add the herbs.
3. Carefully place the meat into the vacuum bag.
4. Seal the bag and set the cooking time for 2 hours.
5. Remove the meat from the bag and dry it, setting aside the oily herbs and garlic mixture from the bag.
6. Heat the olive oil in a skillet and roast the cooked piece of meat for about 1 minute on each side.
7. Serve hot, garnished

222. LAMB AND CUCUMBER MIX

1.4 HOURS | 10 MIN | 4

NUTRITION:
CAL: 447 | FAT: 27 | PROTEIN: 29

INGREDIENTS

- 2 lbs lamb stew meat, roughly cubed
- 2 tbsps olive oil
- 1 cup cucumbers, cubed
- 1 tsp cumin, ground
- ¼ cup beef stock
- 4 garlic cloves, minced
- A pinch of salt and black pepper
- 1 tbsp cilantro, chopped

DIRECTIONS

1. In a large sous vide bag mix the lamb with the oil, cucumber and the other Ingredients, seal the bag, cook in the water oven at 180 °F for 1 hour and 30 minutes, divide the mix between plates and serve.

223. BEEF STROGANOFF

1 HOUR | 20 MIN | 2

NUTRITION:
CAL: 724 | FAT: 69 | PROTEIN: 19

INGREDIENTS

- 1½ lbs beef loin
- 6 tbsps unsalted butter
- 1 cup button mushrooms, chopped
- 1 onion, finely chopped
- 3 tbsps all-purpose flour
- 1 cup beef broth
- 2 tbsps dry white wine
- 1 cup sour cream
- rosemary sprigs

DIRECTIONS

1. Preheat the sous vide water bath to 136 ºF.
2. Season the steaks with salt and pepper and place them in the vacuum bag, putting a piece of butter and rosemary sprigs on top of each steak.
3. Seal the bag and cook the steaks in the preheated water bath for 1 hour.
4. In the meantime, heat 2 tbsps of butter in a skillet and sauté the chopped onion until translucent.
5. Add the mushrooms, salt, and pepper to taste, and cook until the liquid evaporates. Set aside.
6. Sear the steaks in 1 tbsp of butter. Set aside.
7. Add 2 tbsps of butter and flour to the pan, mix it well with a spoon, and then add the stock, wine, and cooked mushrooms.
8. Cook until the sauce thickens. Stir in the sour cream and serve the sauce with the chopped steak over mashed potatoes

224. LAMB WITH BASIL CHIMICHURRI

2 HOURS | 10 MIN | 4

NUTRITION:
CAL: 134 | FAT: 9 | PROTEIN: 15

INGREDIENTS

Lamb chops

- 12 oz lamb, frenched
- ½ tsp pepper
- 1 tsp salt
- 2 cloves garlic, crushed

Basil chimichurri

- ¼ tsp pepper
- ¼ tsp salt
- 3 tbsps red wine vinegar
- ½ tbsp olive oil
- 1 tsp red chili flakes
- 2 cloves garlic, minced
- 1 onion, diced
- 1 cup fresh basil, finely chopped

DIRECTIONS

1. Set the temperature on your Sous Vide appliance to 133ºF. Season the lamb with pepper and salt, then vacuum seal it together with the crushed garlic and cook for 2 hours.
2. Meanwhile, combine all basil chimichurri ingredients in a bowl and mix well. Season as desired, then cover and refrigerate to allow the flavors to blend together.
3. Remove the lamb chops from the vacuum-sealed bag after 2 hours of cooking, and then dry using a paper towel.
4. Sear with a scalding hot well-oiled pan, and then slice between the bones.
5. Top liberally with the basil chimichurri sauce. Enjoy!

225. GROUND LAMB AND CARROTS MIX

1 HOUR | 10 MIN | 4

NUTRITION:
CAL: 479| FAT: 27 | PROTEIN: 29

INGREDIENTS

- 2 lbs lamb stew meat, ground
- 1 tbsp balsamic vinegar
- 1 red onion, sliced
- 2 tbsps olive oil
- 3 carrots, peeled and grated
- 1 parsnip, peeled and sliced
- ¼ cup red wine
- 1 tbsp chives, chopped
- A pinch of salt and black pepper

DIRECTIONS

1. In a large sous vide bag, mix the lamb with the vinegar, onion and the other Ingredients, seal the bag, submerge in the water oven, cook at 175 °F for 1 hour, divide the mix into bowls and serve.

226. LAMB AND CAPERS

1 HOUR | 10 MIN | 4

NUTRITION:
CAL: 450 | FAT: 27 | PROTEIN: 29

INGREDIENTS

- 2 lbs lamb stew meat, cubed
- 1 red onion, sliced
- 2 tbsps capers, drained
- Juice of 1 lemon
- ½ tsp chili pepper
- 1 green bell pepper, cut into strips
- 2 tbsps olive oil
- ½ tsp red pepper flakes, crushed
- A pinch of salt and black pepper
- 1 tbsp cilantro, chopped

DIRECTIONS

1. In a large sous vide bag, mix the lamb with the onion, capers and the other Ingredients, seal the bag, submerge in the water bath, cook at 180 °F for 1 hour and 10 minutes, divide the mix between plate sand serve.

227. ORANGE LAMB

1 HOUR | 10 MIN | 4

NUTRITION:
CAL: 446 | FAT: 26| PROTEIN: 29

INGREDIENTS

- 2 lbs lamb chops
- 2 tbsps olive oil
- Juice of 2 oranges
- 2 tbsps orange zest, grated
- ½ tsp turmeric powder
- A pinch of salt and black pepper
- 1 tbsp chives, chopped

DIRECTIONS

1. In a large sous vide bag, mix the lamb chops with the oil, orange juice and the other Ingredients, seal the bag, submerge in the water bath, cook at 180 °F for 1 hour, divide between plates and serve.

228. BEEF AND SPICY ZUCCHINIS

1 HOUR | 10 MIN | 4

NUTRITION:
CAL: 355 | FAT: 24 | PROTEIN: 32

INGREDIENTS

- 2 lbs beef stew meat, cubed
- 2 zucchinis, cubed
- 1 tsp chili powder
- ½ tsp hot paprika
- 1 red onion, sliced
- 2 tbsps avocado oil
- ¼ cup beef stock
- A pinch of salt and black pepper
- 1 tsp cayenne pepper
- 1 tbsp chives, chopped

DIRECTIONS

1. In a large sous vide bag, mix the beef with the zucchinis, chili powder and the other Ingredients, seal the bag, cook in the water bath at 175 ºF for 1 hour and 10 minutes, divide mix between plates and serve.

229. PORK WITH TOMATOES AND POTATOES

1 HOUR | 10 MIN | 4

NUTRITION:
CAL: 357 | FAT: 12 | PROTEIN: 48

INGREDIENTS

- 2 lbs pork stew meat, roughly cubed
- 1 cup cherry tomatoes, halved
- ½ lb gold potatoes, peeled and cut into wedges
- 1 tsp sweet paprika
- Juice of 1 lime
- 1 red onion, chopped
- 2 tbsps avocado oil
- 3 garlic cloves, minced
- 1 tbsp chives, chopped

DIRECTIONS

1. In a large sous vide bag, mix the pork with the tomatoes, potatoes and the other Ingredients, seal the bag, submerge in the water bath, cook at 180 ºF for 1 hour and 40 minutes, divide the mix between plates and serve.

230. LAMB AND SAVOY CABBAGE MIX

1 HOUR | 10 MIN | 4

NUTRITION:
CAL: 442 | FAT: 27 | PROTEIN: 29

INGREDIENTS

- 2 lbs lamb shoulder, cubed
- 2 tbsps olive oil
- 1 cup Savoy cabbage, shredded
- 1 tbsp balsamic vinegar
- 2 spring onions, chopped
- A pinch of salt and black pepper
- Juice of 1 lime
- 1 tbsp chives, chopped

DIRECTIONS

1. In a large sous vide bag, mix the lamb with the cabbage, oil and the other Ingredients, seal the bag, submerge in the water bath, cook at 180 ºF for 1 hour and 20 minutes, divide everything between plates and serve.

231. BEEF WITH CARROTS AND CABBAGE

1.5 HOUR | **10 MIN** | **4**

NUTRITION:
CAL: 388 | FAT: 28 | PROTEIN: 32

INGREDIENTS

- 2 lbs beef stew meat, roughly cubed
- 2 tbsps olive oil
- 2 carrots, peeled and sliced
- 1 cup red cabbage, shredded
- Juice of 1 lime
- 2 tbsps balsamic vinegar
- 1 red onion, chopped
- A pinch of salt and black pepper
- ½ tsp cumin, ground
- 1 tbsp chives, chopped

DIRECTIONS

1. In a sous vide bag, mix the beef with the oil, carrots and the other ingredients, seal the bag, submerge in the water oven and cook at 186 °F for 1 hour and 30 minutes.
2. Divide the mix into bowls and serve.

232. BEEF AND BEETS

1.5 HOUR | **10 MIN** | **4**

NUTRITION:
CAL: 388 | FAT: 28 | PROTEIN: 32

INGREDIENTS

- 2 lbs beef stew meat, cubed
- 2 beets, peeled and cut into wedges
- 1 red onion, chopped
- 2 tbsps balsamic vinegar
- 2 tbsps olive oil
- 2 garlic cloves, minced
- A pinch of salt and black pepper
- ½ tsp chili powder
- 1 tbsp cilantro, chopped

DIRECTIONS

1. In a large sous vide bag, mix the beef with the beets, onion and the other ingredients, seal the bag, submerge in the water bath, cook at 180 °F for 1 hour and 35 minutes, divide everything between plates and serve.

233. LAMB AND BROCCOLI

1.5 HOUR | **10 MIN** | **4**

NUTRITION:
CAL: 442 | FAT: 27 | PROTEIN: 29

INGREDIENTS

- 2 lbs lamb chops
- 2 spring onions, chopped
- 1 cup broccoli florets
- 2 tbsps olive oil
- 2 tbsps lime zest, grated
- Juice of ½ lime
- 1 tbsp chives, chopped
- A pinch of salt and black pepper
- 1 tbsp cilantro, chopped

DIRECTIONS

1. In a large sous vide bag, mix the lamb chops with the spring onions, broccoli and the other Ingredients, seal the bag, cook in the water bath at 175 °F for 1 hour and 30 minutes, divide the mix between plates and serve.

234. LAMB AND RADISH MIX

1.5 HOUR | 10 MIN | 4

NUTRITION:
CAL: 445 | FAT: 27 | PROTEIN: 28

INGREDIENTS

- 2 lbs lamb shoulder, cubed
- 1 cup radishes, halved
- 2 tbsps avocado oil
- 1 tbsp lemon juice
- 1 tbsp lemon zest, grated
- 2 spring onions, chopped
- ½ tsp rosemary, dried
- ¼ cup beef stock
- 2 garlic cloves, minced
- Salt and black pepper to the taste

DIRECTIONS

1. In a large sous vide bag, mix the lamb with the radishes, oil and the other Ingredients, seal the bag, cook in the water oven at 175 °F for 1 hour and 30 minutes, divide everything between plates and serve.

235. CITRUS LAMB MIX

1.5 HOUR | 10 MIN | 6

NUTRITION:
CAL: 295 | FAT: 16 | PROTEIN: 19

INGREDIENTS

- 2 lbs lamb chops
- Juice of 1 orange
- Juice of 1 lime
- 1 tsp nutmeg, ground
- 2 spring onions, chopped
- ½ tsp chili powder
- 1 tbsp olive oil
- 2 garlic cloves, minced
- A pinch of salt and black pepper
- 1 tbsp chives, chopped

DIRECTIONS

1. In a large sous vide bag, mix the lamb chops with the orange juice, lime juice and the other ingredients, seal the bag, submerge in the water bath, cook at 180 °F for 1 hour and 30 minutes, divide between plates and serve with a side salad.

236. BEEF TENDERLOIN WITH LEMON PARSLEY BUTTER

4 HOURS | 15 MIN | 4

NUTRITION:
CAL: 352 | FAT: 36 | PROTEIN: 19

INGREDIENTS

- 1½-lb center cut beef tenderloin, trimmed
- salt and freshly cracked black pepper, to taste
- 4 thyme sprigs
- 7 tbsps unsalted butter, softened and divided
- 1 garlic clove, minced
- 2 tbsps fresh parsley leaves, chopped

DIRECTIONS

1. Preheat a sous vide water bath to 140°F.
2. With a sharp knife, cut tenderloin into 4 6-oz portions. Place each portion onto a cutting board, cut-side down and flatten gently with your hand until the portion reaches 2-inch thickness. Season tenderloin generously with salt and black pepper.
3. Place beef tenderloin and thyme sprigs in a cooking pouch. Seal pouch tightly after removing the excess air. Place pouch in sous vide bath and set the cooking time for a minimum of 1 hour and a maximum time of 4 hours.
4. While tenderloin cooks, combine 6 tbsps of butter, garlic, parsley, lemon zest, lemon juice, salt, and black pepper in a bowl. Set aside.

- 1 tsp fresh lemon zest
- 1 tsp fresh lemon juice
- 1 tbsp vegetable oil

5. Remove pouch from the sous vide bath and open carefully. Remove tenderloin pieces from pouch and pat dry with paper towels.
6. In a heavy-bottomed 12-inch skillet, heat oil and remaining butter over high heat and sear tenderloin pieces for 1 minute on each side.
7. Divide tenderloin pieces onto servings plates. Top with parsley butter and serve immediately.

237. SANTA MARIA TRI-TIP

2 HOURS | 10 MIN | 6

NUTRITION:
CAL: 556 | FAT: 35 | PROTEIN: 58

INGREDIENTS

- 1½ tbsps garlic salt with dried parsley
- 1 tbsp freshly ground black pepper
- 2½-lb (2-inch-thick) tri-tip
- 1 tsp liquid smoke
- 1 tbsp olive oil

DIRECTIONS

1. Preheat a sous vide water bath to 135°F.
2. In a bowl, combine garlic salt and black pepper. Sprinkle tri-tip with garlic salt mixture generously.
3. Place tri-tip, liquid smoke, and oil in a cooking pouch. Seal pouch tightly after removing the excess air. Place pouch in sous vide bath and set the cooking time for 2 hours.
4. Preheat grill to high heat.
5. Remove pouch from the sous vide bath and open carefully. Remove tri-tip from pouch and pat dry with paper towels.
6. Grill tri-tip for 1 minute on each side.
7. Remove from grill and cut into desired slices. Serve immediately.

238. MARINATED TRI-TIP

4 HOURS | 15 MIN | 4

NUTRITION:
CAL: 676 | FAT: 42 | PROTEIN: 69

INGREDIENTS

- 3 tbsps low-sodium soy sauce
- 1 tbsp honey
- 1 tbsp red miso
- 1-2 tsps chili paste with fermented soy bean
- 1 tsp onion powder
- 1 tsp garlic powder
- 1 tsp ginger powder
- 1 tsp sesame oil (optional
- 3-lb tri-tip roast

DIRECTIONS

1. Preheat a sous vide water bath to 135°F.
2. Mix all ingredients in a large bowl except tri-tip. Add tri-tip and coat generously with mixture.
3. Place tri-tip in a cooking pouch. Seal pouch tightly after removing the excess air. Place pouch in sous vide bath and set the cooking time for 4 hours.
4. Preheat grill to high heat.
5. Remove pouch from the sous vide bath and open carefully. Remove tri-tip from pouch and pat dry with paper towels.
6. Grill tri-tip for 1 minute on each side.
7. Remove from grill and cut into desired slices. Serve immediately.

239. SMOKEY BRISKET

24 HOURS | 10 MIN | 4

NUTRITION:
CAL: 439 | FAT: 20 | PROTEIN: 58

INGREDIENTS

- 2½-lb grass-fed beef brisket
- ½ tbsp salt
- 2 tsps ground black pepper

DIRECTIONS

1. Preheat a sous vide water bath to 135ºF.
2. Season brisket with salt and black pepper generously.
3. Place brisket in a cooking pouch. Seal pouch tightly after removing the excess air. Place pouch in sous vide bath and set the cooking time for 24 hours. Cover the sous vide bath with plastic wrap to minimize water evaporation. Add water intermittently to keep the water level up.
4. Remove pouch from the sous vide bath and open carefully. Remove brisket from pouch and pat dry completely with paper towels. Season brisket once again with salt and black pepper.
5. Heat a cast iron skillet over medium-high heat and sear brisket for 2-3 minutes on each side.
6. Remove from heat and transfer to a cutting board for 5-10 minutes. Cut into desired slices and serve.

240. TERIYAKI BEEF RIBS

48 HOURS | 20 MIN | 8

NUTRITION:
CAL: 592 | FAT: 44 | PROTEIN: 29

INGREDIENTS

For Ribs

- 3-4-lb beef ribs, cut into three portions
- ½ cup sugar
- ½ cup salt
- Vegetable oil, as required
- For Teriyaki Glaze:
- 1 cup mirin
- 2/3 cup sake
- ½ cup dark soy sauce
- For Chili Oil:
- 3 tbsps vegetable oil
- 4 tbsps garlic, chopped
- 4 tbsps fresh ginger, grated
- 1 green chili, finely chopped

DIRECTIONS

1. In a large bowl of water, dissolve sugar and salt. Add beef ribs and set aside for 1-2 hours. Remove ribs from brine and pat dry with paper towels.
2. Preheat a sous vide water bath to 132ºF.
3. Divide ribs into two large cooking pouches. Seal pouches tightly after removing the excess air. Place pouches in sous vide bath and set the cooking time for 48 hours. Cover the sous vide bath with plastic wrap to minimize water evaporation. Add water intermittently to keep the water level up.
4. For teriyaki glaze: while ribs cook, add mirin, sake, and soy sauce to a pan and bring to a boil. Reduce heat and simmer for 10 minutes, stirring occasionally.
5. For chili oil: in another pan, add oil, garlic, ginger, and green chili over low heat and cook until fragrant.
6. Remove pouches from the sous vide bath and open carefully. Remove ribs from pouch and pat dry with paper towels.
7. In a cast iron skillet, heat oil over medium-high heat and sear ribs for 1 minute on each side.
8. Place ribs on a servings platter and top with glaze and chili oil. Serve immediately.

241. FILET MIGNON

47 HOURS | 15 MIN | 4

NUTRITION:
CAL: 275 | FAT: 14 | PROTEIN: 36

INGREDIENTS

- 4 (1-inch-thick) filet mignons
- salt and freshly ground black pepper, to taste
- olive oil, as required
- minced garlic clove, to taste
- chopped fresh thyme, to taste
- 1 tbsp butter

DIRECTIONS

1. Preheat a sous vide water bath to 129ºF.
2. Season steaks evenly with salt and pepper.
3. Divide steaks, olive oil, garlic, and thyme into two cooking pouches. Seal pouches tightly after removing the excess air. Place pouches in sous vide bath and set the cooking time for 45 minutes.
4. Remove pouches from the sous vide bath and open carefully. Remove steaks from pouches and pat dry with paper towels.
5. In a non-stick pan, melt butter over medium-high heat and sear steaks until browned.

242. CRUSTED PRIME RIB ROAST

10 HOURS | 15 MIN | 6

NUTRITION:
CAL: 612 | FAT: 40 | PROTEIN: 59

INGREDIENTS

For Rib Roast:
- ½ tbsp garlic powder
- ¼ tbsp ancho Chile powder
- 3-4 lb prime rib roast
- Salt and freshly ground black pepper, to taste
- 4 fresh thyme sprigs
- 2 fresh rosemary sprigs

For Crust:
- 8 garlic cloves, peeled and root cut off
- 4 fresh thyme sprigs
- 4 fresh rosemary sprigs
- 2-4 tbsps olive oil

DIRECTIONS

1. Preheat a sous vide water bath to 131ºF.
2. In a small bowl, mix together garlic powder, ancho Chile powder, salt, and black pepper. Coat prime rib roast generously with spice mixture.
3. Place roast and herb sprigs in a cooking pouch. Seal pouch tightly after removing the excess air. Place pouch in sous vide bath and set the cooking time for a minimum of 5 and no more than 10 hours. Longer cooking times will be required for Dijon more tender results.
4. Preheat oven to 400ºF.
5. For crust: place garlic cloves and herb sprigs on a square of tinfoil and drizzle with olive oil. Fold the tin foil around the garlic mixture to make a sealed pouch. Bake for 30 minutes.
6. Remove from oven and mash roasted garlic into a paste with a fork. Set aside.
7. Preheat oven to 450ºF.
8. Remove pouch from the sous vide bath and open carefully. Remove roast from pouch and pat dry with paper towels.
9. Coat roast evenly with garlic paste. Arrange roast in a roasting pan and bake for 5 minutes, then serve.

243. BEEF CHUCK ROAST

48 HOURS | 15 MIN | 4

NUTRITION:
CAL: 422 | FAT: 15 | PROTEIN: 72

INGREDIENTS

- 3-4-lb chuck roast
- Olive oil, as required
- 4 garlic cloves, minced
- Salt and freshly ground black pepper, to taste
- Butter, as required

DIRECTIONS

1. Preheat a sous vide water bath to 132ºF.
2. Coat roast evenly with olive oil and garlic.
3. Place roast in a cooking pouch. Seal pouch tightly after removing the excess air. Place pouch in sous vide bath and set the cooking time for 36-48 hours. Cover the sous vide bath with plastic wrap to minimize water evaporation. Add water intermittently to keep the water level up.

4. Remove pouch from the sous vide bath and open carefully. Remove roast from pouch, reserve cooking liquid. Pat roast dry with paper towels and season evenly with salt and black pepper.

5. Heat a cast iron pan over high heat and sear roast until browned completely. Transfer roast to a cutting board.

6. In the same pan as used for roast, add reserved cooking liquid and scrape the browned bits from the pan. Add butter and cook until sauce reaches desired consistency.

7. Cut roast into strips and serve with the sauce topping.

244. BEEF MASALA

10 HOURS | 15 MIN | 4

NUTRITION:
CAL: 455 | FAT: 27 | PROTEIN: 34

INGREDIENTS

- 2 lbs beef, cut into 2-inch cubes
- 1-2 tbsps meat curry masala seasoning, divided
- Salt, to taste
- 3 tsps ginger garlic paste
- 2 tbsps almonds, boiled and skinned
- 2 tbsps thick coconut milk
- 1 onion, chopped
- 1 cup plain yogurt
- 1/2 cup tomato puree
- Oil, as required

DIRECTIONS

1. Preheat a sous vide water bath to 180°F.
2. Rub beef evenly with a little of the curry masala and salt.
3. Place roast in a cooking pouch. Seal pouch tightly after removing the excess air. Place pouch in sous vide bath and set the cooking time for 10 hours.
4. Meanwhile in a food processor, add garlic ginger paste, almonds, and coconut milk and pulse until a paste is formed.
5. Remove pouch from the sous vide bath and open carefully. Remove beef from pouch, reserve cooking liquid.
6. Heat oil in a pan and sauté onion until light golden. Add paste and sauté for 5 minutes. Add remaining masala powder and sauté for 2 minutes. Slowly add yogurt and stir to combine. Add tomato puree and stir for a few minutes more.
7. Add beef along with reserved cooking liquid and bring to a boil. Reduce heat and simmer for 5 minutes. Stir in salt and remove from heat.
8. Serve hot.

245. BEEF BOURGUIGNON

25 HOURS | 25 MIN | 4

NUTRITION:
CAL: 669 | FAT: 41 | PROTEIN: 43

INGREDIENTS

For Beef:

- 2 lbs beef, cubed
- Vegetable oil, as required
- ¼ cup small bacon, cubed
- 1 bottle nice burgundy wine
- 1 tbsp butter, divided
- 1-lb mushrooms, chopped roughly
- 20 pearl onions
- 2 celery stalks, finely chopped
- 2 carrots, peeled and finely chopped
- 1 white onion, finely chopped
- 2 garlic cloves, mashed

DIRECTIONS

1. In a wide cast iron pan, heat enough vegetable oil to cover the bottom of the pan and cook bacon cubes until just browning. Add beef and sear until browned completely. Transfer beef and bacon to a bowl, reserve Fat in a separate small bowl.

2. Add some wine and scrape the brown bits from bottom and sides of the pan. Cook until a thick glaze is formed. Move glaze to a small bowl and set aside to cool.

3. In the same pan as used for glaze, melt ½ tbsp of butter over medium-high heat. Add mushrooms and cook for 5 mins. Cover and cook for 1-2 minutes. Transfer mushrooms to a bowl.

4. Add more wine to the now-empty pan and scrape the brown Bits from bottom and sides of the pan. Cook until a thick glaze Is formed. Add glaze to the bowl of reserved glaze and set aside to cool.

5. Melt remaining ½ tbsp of butter over medium-high heat in the same pan. Add pearl onions and cook for 5 minutes. Transfer the onions into the bowl of mushrooms.

6. Add some wine to the pan and scrape the brown bits from bottom and sides. Cook until a thick glaze is formed. Transfer glaze into the bowl of reserved glaze and set aside to cool.

7. For wine reduction: In the same pan, cook reserved bacon Fat over medium-high heat and add celery, carrot, and white onion for 7-10 minutes. Add 3¾ cups of wine, garlic, bay leaf, some cooked bacon, and reserved glaze and cook for 30 mins,

- 1 bay leaf
- Sugar, to taste
- ½ tbsp all-purpose flour
- ½ tbsp cold water
- Salt and freshly ground black pepper, to taste
- 1 rosemary sprig
- Chopped fresh parsley, for garnishing

For Mashed Potatoes:

- 2 russet potatoes, peeled and cubed
- 3 tbsps heavy cream
- Butter, as required
- Salt, to taste

stirring occasionally.

8. Strain wine reduction through a fine strainer. Return strained sauce to the pan and bring to a gentle boil.
9. In a small bowl, dissolve flour into cold water. Add flour mixture to strained wine reduction and cook for 3 minutes. Remove from heat and stir in sugar, salt, and black pepper. Set aside to cool.
10. Preheat a sous vide water bath to 180°F.
11. Place beef, bacon, mushrooms, pearl onions, rosemary sprigs, and wine reduction in a large cooking pouch. Seal pouch tightly after removing the excess air. Place pouch in sous vide bath and set the cooking time for 24 hours. Cover the sous vide bath with plastic wrap to minimize water evaporation.
12. Add water intermittently to keep the water level up.
13. For mashed potatoes: cook potatoes in a pan of boiling water for 10 minutes.
14. Remove from heat and drain potatoes. Return potatoes to the pan. Add heavy cream and some butter and mash until well combined. Season with salt.
15. Remove pouch from the sous vide bath and open carefully.
16. Remove beef, mushrooms, and pearl onions from pouch, reserve the cooking liquid in a pan. Discard rosemary sprigs.
17. Place pan with reserved liquid over stove and cook for 5-10 minutes or until desired thickness of sauce is reached. Remove from heat and stir in beef, mushrooms, and pearl onions. Serve with mashed potatoes.

246. CORNED BEEF AND CABBAGE

48 HOURS | 15 MIN | 6

NUTRITION:
CAL: 796 | FAT: 59 | PROTEIN: 54

INGREDIENTS

- 4 lbs corned beef
- 6 bacon slices, cut into ½-inch strips
- 1 head cabbage, cut into ½-inch strips
- 2 cups chicken broth
- ½ cup champagne vinegar

DIRECTIONS

1. Preheat a sous vide water bath to 134°F.
2. Place corned beef in a cooking pouch. Seal pouch tightly after removing the excess air. Place pouch in sous vide bath and set the cooking time for 48 hours. Cover the sous vide bath with plastic wrap to minimize water evaporation. Add water intermittently to keep the water level up.
3. Heat a skillet over medium heat and cook bacon until crisp. Remove bacon fat, leaving only 1-2 tbsps in the skillet.
4. Stir in cabbage and increase heat to medium high. Cook for 5 minutes. Add chicken broth and vinegar and cook until cabbage becomes tender.
5. Remove pouch from the sous vide bath and open carefully. Remove corned beef from pouch and cut into ½-¾-inch slices.
6. Transfer cabbage mixture onto servings plate. Top with corned beef slices and serve.

247. BACON WRAPPED FILET WITH HORSERADISH CREAM

6 HOURS | 20 MIN | 8

NUTRITION:
CAL: 949 | FAT: 75 | PROTEIN: 61

INGREDIENTS

For Beef Tenderloin:

- 6-lb beef tenderloin
- transglutaminase, as required
- thin bacon strips, as required
- fresh thyme sprigs, as required
- vegetable oil, as required
- for horseradish cream:
- 1 cup heavy cream
- ¼ cup prepared horseradish, drained well
- 2 tbsps coarse grain mustard
- 1 tbsp Dijon mustard
- Salt and freshly ground black pepper, to taste

DIRECTIONS

1. Preheat a sous vide water bath to 131°F.
2. Carefully remove silver skin from tenderloin then remove all Fats. Cut tenderloin into steaks of the desired size.
3. Arrange a parchment paper on a cutting board. Place bacon strips on parchment paper and dust with the transglutaminase.
4. Arrange 1 tenderloin filet over dusted side of 1 bacon strip. Roll the bacon strip over the filet to wrap and press firmly to adhere. Repeat with remaining fillets. Arrange 1 thyme sprig over each wrapped fillet and sprinkle with salt.
5. Place each filet in an individual cooking pouch. Seal pouches tightly after removing the excess air. Place pouches in sous vide bath and set the cooking time for 2-6 hours.
6. For horseradish cream: in a bowl, add heavy cream and beat with a mixer until thick but not too stiff. Fold in remaining horseradish cream Ingredients.
7. Remove pouches from the sous vide bath and open carefully. Remove fillets from pouches and pat dry with paper towels.
8. Heat a cast iron skillet over high heat and sear each fillet until browned on both sides.
9. Serve immediately alongside horseradish cream.

248. BEEF CARNITAS

24 HOURS | 20 MIN | 4

NUTRITION:
CAL: 332 | FAT: 14 | PROTEIN: 47

INGREDIENTS

For Beef Tenderloin:

- 1 tsp dried oregano
- 2 tsps garlic powder
- 1 tsp onion powder
- 1 tsp ground cumin
- ¼ tsp ground cloves
- ¼ tsp ground allspice
- 2-lb chuck roast
- Salt and freshly ground black pepper, to taste

For Sauce:

- 2 tangerines, seeded and chopped
- 2-3 chipotle peppers in adobo sauce
- 1 tbsp honey
- 1 tbsp oregano leaves
- ½ cup cooking liquid from chuck rust

For servings:

- Corn tortillas
- Avocado, peeled, pitted, and cut into slices

DIRECTIONS

1. Preheat a sous vide water bath to 156°F.
2. For carnitas: in a small bowl, combine oregano and spices. Season roast with salt and pepper lightly and then coat with spice mixture.
3. Place roast in a cooking pouch. Seal pouch tightly after removing the excess air. Place pouch in sous vide bath and set the cooking time for 18-24 hours. Cover the sous vide bath with plastic wrap to minimize water evaporation. Add water intermittently to keep the water level up.
4. Remove pouch from the sous vide bath and open carefully. Remove roast legs from pouch, reserve ½ cup of cooking liquid.
5. For sauce: in a pan, add all sauce ingredients except cooking liquid and bring to a gentle boil. Cook for 10 minutes, stirring occasionally. Remove from heat and stir in reserved cooking liquid.
6. Shred beef with two forks and set aside.
7. Arrange tortillas on servings plates. Place shredded beef on each tortilla. Top with sauce and avocados and serve.

249. CUBAN SHREDDED BEEF

24 HOURS | 20 MIN | 4

NUTRITION:
CAL: 332 | FAT: 14 | PROTEIN: 44

INGREDIENTS

- 2-lb center-cut chuck eye roast
- salt and freshly ground black peppor, to taste
- 4 tbsps canola oil, divided
- 1 onion, thinly sliced
- 2 garlic cloves, minced
- 2 tsps ground cumin
- ½ tsp red pepper flakes, crushed
- ½ cup orange juice
- 2 tbsps fresh lime juice

DIRECTIONS

1. Preheat a sous vide water bath to 140°F.
2. Season chuck roast evenly with salt and pepper.
3. Place roast in a cooking pouch. Seal pouch tightly after removing the excess air. Place pouch in sous vide bath and set the cooking time for 24 hours. Cover the sous vide bath with plastic wrap to minimize water evaporation. Add water intermittently to keep the water level up.
4. Remove pouch from the sous vide bath and open carefully. Remove roast legs from pouch and transfer to a cutting board. Shred roast into bite-sized pieces with two forks.
5. In a large skillet, heat 2 tbsps of oil over medium-high heat and cook onion for 5 minutes, stirring occasionally.
6. Add garlic and spices and cook for 2 minutes. Stir in both juices and cook for 2 minutes. Stir in salt and black pepper and transfer to a bowl.
7. In the same skillet, heat remaining oil and cook shredded beef until browned and crisp, stirring occasionally.
8. Stir in cooked onion mixture, salt, and pepper and serve.

250. BEEF MEATBALLS

2 HOURS | 20 MIN | 4

NUTRITION:
CAL: 555 | FAT: 38 | PROTEIN: 43

INGREDIENTS

- 1 lb 85% lean ground beef
- ½ lb ground sausage
- ½ cup Parmesan cheese, grated freshly
- ½ cup onion, finely chopped
- 1/3 cup quick-cooking oats
- 1 large egg, beaten lightly
- ¼ cup milk
- ½ tsp garlic powder
- ¾ tsp salt
- ¼ tsp freshly ground black pepper
- Olive oil, as required
- Pasta sauce, as required

DIRECTIONS

1. Combine all ingredients except oil and pasta sauce in a bowl. Make 30-36 equal-sized meatballs from mixture. Arrange meatballs onto baking sheet lined with parchment paper in a single layer. Freeze meatballs on sheet for 1-2 hours or until very firm.
2. Preheat a sous vide water bath to 144°F.
3. Place meatballs in a cooking pouch. Seal pouch tightly after removing the excess air. Place pouch in sous vide bath and set the cooking time for 2 hours.
4. Remove pouch from the sous vide bath and open carefully. Remove meatballs from pouch and pat dry with paper towels.
5. Heat oil in a skillet and sear meatballs for 1-2 minutes.
6. Add meatballs to a large bowl with the pasta sauce and toss to coat.
7. Serve immediately.

251. HAMBURGER PATTIES

4 HOURS | 20 MIN | 4

NUTRITION:
CAL: 488 | FAT: 26 | PROTEIN: 36

INGREDIENTS

- 2 lbs fresh ground beef
- salt and freshly ground black pepper, to taste
- 1 tbsp vegetable oil
- 4 cheese slices
- 4 soft hamburger buns, toasted lightly
- Hamburger toppings, as desired

DIRECTIONS

1. Preheat a sous vide water bath to 138°F.
2. Divide beef into 4 equal-sized portions. Make patties that are slightly wider than the buns from each portion. Season each patty generously with salt and black pepper.
3. Divide patties into four cooking pouches. Seal pouches tightly after removing the excess air. Place pouches in sous vide bath and set the cooking time for 4 hours.
4. Remove pouches from the sous vide bath and open carefully. Remove patties from pouches and pat dry with paper towels. Season each patty with salt and black pepper and set aside at room temperature for 10 minutes.
5. In a large cast iron skillet, heat oil over high heat and cook patties for 1 minute. Flip patties and place a cheese slice over each patty. Cook for 45-60 seconds.
6. Place 1 patty over each prepared bun. Top with desired topping and serve immediately.

252. SUMMER SAUSAGE

3 HOURS | 20 MIN | 4

NUTRITION:
CAL: 248 | FAT: 17 | PROTEIN: 21

INGREDIENTS

- 1 lb grass-fed, 85% lean ground beef
- 1/3 tsp celery juice powder
- 1 tsp Braggs organic sprinkle seasoning, ground to a powder consistency
- 1 tsp mustard seeds
- ½ tsp mustard powder
- ½ tsp onion powder
- ½ tsp garlic powder
- ½ tsp hot paprika
- 1/8 tsp ground coriander
- 2 tsps canning salt
- ½ tsp freshly ground black pepper
- Sausage casings

DIRECTIONS

1. Add all ingredients to a bowl and combine.
2. Place beef mixture in a cooking pouch and refrigerate for 3-4 days.
3. Preheat a sous vide water bath to 160°F.
4. Place non-edible, fibrous casing in a bowl of warm water for 30 minutes.
5. Place beef mixture tightly into casing by rolling and pinprick any air pockets. After filling casing, tie off with a knot.
6. Place sausage in a cooking pouch. Seal pouch tightly after removing the excess air. Place pouch in sous vide bath and set the cooking time for 3 hours.
7. Remove pouch from the sous vide bath and open carefully. Remove sausage from pouch. Untie the knot at the end of sausage stick and pat dry with paper towels. You can preserve this sausage in freezer

253. CHUCK ROAST WITH MUSHROOM GRAVY

48 HOURS | 20 MIN | 4

NUTRITION:
CAL: 378 | FAT: 18 | PROTEIN: 50

INGREDIENTS

For Gravy:

- 2 cups water
- 1½ cups apple juice
- ½ cup soy sauce
- 2 tbsps mirin
- 1 tbsp cider vinegar
- 1 tbsp sesame oil
- 1 onion, chopped
- 1 carrot, peeled and chopped
- 2 garlic cloves, minced
- Salt and freshly ground black pepper, to taste
- ¼ cup red wine

For Chuck roast:

- 2-lb (2-inch-thick beef chuck roast, trimmed and cut into pieces
- Butter, as required

For Mushrooms:

- Butter, as required
- 12-oz mushrooms

DIRECTIONS

1. Preheat a sous vide water bath to 160°F.
2. For gravy: add all gravy ingredients except wine to a pan and cook over medium heat for 15 minutes. Strain the gravy through a strainer and set aside to cool.
3. Place roast pieces and ½ of the gravy in a cooking pouch. Seal pouch tightly after removing the excess air. Place pouch in sous vide bath and set the cooking time for 24-48 hours. Cover the sous vide bath with plastic wrap to minimize water evaporation. Add water intermittently to keep the water level up.
4. Transfer remaining gravy to a pan over high heat. Stir in wine and cook until gravy reduces by half.
5. In another pan, melt butter and sauté mushrooms until tender. Transfer mushrooms to the pan of gravy.
6. Remove pouch from the sous vide bath and open carefully. Remove roast pieces from pouch and pat dry with paper towels.
7. In a cast iron skillet, melt butter and sear roast pieces for 1 minute on each side.
8. Serve roast pieces with the mushroom gravy.

254. LONDON BROIL

8 HOURS | 10 MIN | 4

NUTRITION:
CAL: 526 | FAT: 31 | PROTEIN: 62

INGREDIENTS

- 2-3-lb London broil, trimmed
- 3 tbsp Worcestershire sauce
- Seasoning of your choice
- 2 tbsp Butter

DIRECTIONS

1. Coat meat evenly with Worcestershire sauce then season one side of meat with seasoning.
2. Place meat in a cooking pouch. Seal pouch tightly after removing the excess air. Refrigerate for 1 day.
3. Preheat a sous vide water bath to 133°F.
4. Place pouch in sous vide bath and set the cooking time for 6-8 hours.
5. Remove pouch from the sous vide bath and open carefully. Remove meat from pouch and pat dry with paper towels.
6. In a cast iron skillet, melt butter and sear meat for 1 minute on each side.
7. Cut into desired slices and serve.

255. HERB CRUSTED SIRLOIN

8 HOURS | 10 MIN | 4

NUTRITION:
CAL: 526 | FAT: 31 | PROTEIN: 62

INGREDIENTS

For Sirloin Roast:

- ½ tbsp garlic powder
- ½ tbsp paprika powder
- ¼ tbsp ancho Chile powder
- 3-4-lb sirloin roast
- 2 rosemary sprigs
- 2 thyme sprigs

For Crust:

- 8 garlic cloves
- 2-4 tbsps sweet marjoram
- 4 thyme springs
- 4 rosemary sprigs
- 2-4 tbsps olive oil

DIRECTIONS

1. Preheat a sous vide water bath to 131ºF.
2. For sirloin roast: in a bowl, mix together garlic, paprika, and ancho Chile powder. Rub sirloin roast generously with spice mixture.
3. Place sirloin roast and herbs sprigs in a cooking pouch. Seal pouch tightly after removing the excess air. Place pouch in sous vide bath and set the cooking time for 12-48 hours. Cover the sous vide bath with plastic wrap to minimize water evaporation. Add water intermittently to keep the water level up.
4. Preheat oven to 450ºF.
5. For crust: add all crust ingredients to a food processor and pulse until a thick paste is formed.
6. Remove pouch from the sous vide bath and open carefully. Remove sirloin roast from pouch and pat dry with paper towels.
7. Evenly coat sirloin roast with paste and arrange on a roasting pan. Roast for 5 minutes.
8. Remove sirloin roast from oven and keep on a cutting board for 5-10 minutes before slicing. Cut into slices of the desired size and serve. Serve with mashed potatoes, a side salad, or mixed vegetables.

256. FLANK STEAK WITH CHIMICHURRI SAUCE

36 HOURS | 20 MIN | 4

NUTRITION:
CAL: 432 | FAT: 36 | PROTEIN: 24

INGREDIENTS

For Steak:

- 2-lb flank steak
- Salt and freshly ground black pepper, to taste
- For Chimichurri Sauce:
- ¼ medium red onion, chopped
- 3 garlic cloves, chopped
- 2 cups fresh parsley leaves
- ½ cup fresh mint leaves
- 2 tsps fresh lemon zest
- ½ cup olive oil
- 2 tbsps fresh lemon juice
- 1 tbsp white vinegar
- 1/3 tsp red pepper flakes
- Salt, to taste

DIRECTIONS

1. Preheat a sous vide water bath to 134ºF.
2. Season flank steak evenly with salt and black pepper.
3. Place flank steak in a cooking pouch. Seal pouch tightly after removing the excess air. Place pouch in sous vide bath and set the cooking time for 30-36 hours. Cover the sous vide bath with plastic wrap to minimize water evaporation. Add water intermittently to keep the water level up.
4. Preheat the grill to high heat.
5. For Chimichurri Sauce: add all sauce ingredients to a food processor and pulse until smooth.
6. Remove pouch from the sous vide bath and open carefully. Remove steak from pouch and pat dry with paper towels.
7. Grill flank steak for 45 seconds on each side. Remove flank steak from grill and set aside for 5 minutes before slicing.
8. Cut into ½-inch slices, across the grain. Serve with a topping of chimichurri sauce.

257. ROSEMARY SEASONED FLANK STEAK

12 HOURS | 15 MIN | 4

NUTRITION:
CAL: 237 | FAT: 12 | PROTEIN: 30

INGREDIENTS

- 1¼ lb flank steak
- ½ tsp dried rosemary
- ¼ tbsp garlic powder
- ¼ tsp onion powder
- ½ tsp salt
- ¼ tsp ground black pepper
- Olive oil, for drizzling
- 2 scallion tops, sliced on the bias
- Coarse sea salt, to taste

DIRECTIONS

1. Preheat a sous vide water bath to 130ºF.
2. Place flank steak in a cooking pouch. Seal pouch tightly after removing the excess air. Place pouch in sous vide bath and set the cooking time for 12 hours.
3. Preheat grill to high heat.
4. In a coffee grinder, mix together rosemary, garlic powder, onion powder, salt, and black pepper and grind to a fine powder.
5. Remove pouch from the sous vide bath and open carefully. Remove steak from pouch and pat dry with paper towels.
6. Rub steak evenly with rosemary mixture. Grill the steak for 2-3 minutes on each side. Remove flank steak from grill and set aside for 5 minutes before slicing. Cut into thin slices, across the grain.
7. Drizzle steak slices with olive oil and garnish with scallion tops. Sprinkle with coarse sea salt and serve immediately.

258. BEEF BRISKET

72 HOURS | 15 MIN | 4

NUTRITION:
CAL: 527 | FAT: 24 | PROTEIN: 69

INGREDIENTS

- 1 tsp dried oregano, crushed
- 2 tbsps ground coriander
- 2 tbsps ground cumin
- 1 tsp ground cinnamon
- 2 tbsp garlic powder
- 2 tbsps paprika
- 1 tsp chipotle powder
- 1 tsp freshly ground black pepper
- 3-4 lbs beef brisket
- 1 tbsp liquid smoke
- salt, to taste

DIRECTIONS

1. In a bowl, mix together the oregano, coriander, spices and black pepper. Generously coat brisket with spice mixture.
2. Into a cooking pouch, add the brisket and the liquid smoke. Seal pouch tightly after squeezing out excess air, and refrigerate for at least 2 days.
3. Preheat a sous vide water bath to 135ºF.
4. Place pouch in sous vide bath and set the cooking time for between 1 and 3 days. Grass fed or younger, more tender cuts of meat will require less cooking time to become tender. Cook your cut of meat until it reaches desired level of tenderness.
5. Preheat the grill to a high heat.
6. Remove pouch from sous vide bath and carefully open it. Remove brisket from pouch. With paper towels, pat brisket completely dry.
7. Generously season brisket with salt.
8. Grill brisket for 1-2 minutes per side. Remove from the grill and keep aside for 5 minutes to rest.
9. Cut into 1¼-inch thick slices and serve.

259. MEATLOAF WITH CHIPOTLE GLAZE

4 HOURS | 15 MIN | 4

NUTRITION:
CAL: 423 | FAT: 25 | PROTEIN: 19

INGREDIENTS

For Meatloaf:

- 2 tbsps olive oil
- 1 red bell pepper, seeded and chopped
- ½ yellow onion, chopped

DIRECTIONS

1. Preheat a sous vide water bath to 140ºF.
2. For the meatloaf:
3. in a skillet, heat the olive oil over a medium heat.
4. Add bell pepper and onion, and sauté for 4-5 minutes. Remove from heat and keep

- 2 eggs
- ¼ cup heavy cream
- ¼ cup breadcrumbs
- 1 tbsp soy sauce
- ½ tsp paprika
- pinch of cayenne pepper
- ¼ tsp garlic powder
- 1 tsp salt
- ½ tsp freshly ground black pepper
- 1 lb ground beef
- ½ lb Italian sausage, casing removed
- 1 tbsp canola oil

For Glaze:
- ½ cup honey
- 2 tbsps canola oil
- 1 tbsp Dijon mustard
- 1 tbsp chipotle in adobo sauce, pureed
- 1 tsp salt

5. Into a large bowl, add the cooled onion mixture, egg, cream, breadcrumbs, soy sauce, spices, salt and black pepper, and mix until well-combined.
6. Add the beef and sausage and, using your hands, knead until well-combined, then shape beef mixture into a loaf.
7. Place the meatloaf into a cooking pouch, and seal tightly after squeezing out the excess air.
8. Place pouch in sous vide bath and set the cooking time for 2-4 hours.
9. While the meatloaf is cooking:
10. For the glaze:
11. in a bowl, add all glaze ingredients and beat until well-combined.
12. Just before the end of the sous vide cooking period:
13. Preheat broiler to a high setting and place a rack into the top position of the oven.
14. Remove pouch from sous vide bath and carefully open it. Remove meatloaf from pouch. With paper towels, pat meatloaf completely dry.
15. In a cast iron skillet, heat the canola oil over a high heat.
16. Add the meatloaf and cook for 1-2 minutes per side, or until browned completely.
17. Remove from heat and coat the top of the meatloaf evenly with the glaze.
18. Broil for 1-2 minutes.

260. STANDING RIB ROAST

36 HOURS | 15 MIN | 8

NUTRITION:
CAL: 897 | FAT: 57 | PROTEIN: 86

INGREDIENTS

- 1 x 3-rib standing rib roast (6-8 lbs prime rib roast)
- 1-2 oz dried morel mushrooms
- salt and freshly cracked black pepper, to taste
- 3 oz garlic-infused olive oil

DIRECTIONS

1. Preheat a sous vide water bath to 130°F.
2. Into a cooking pouch, add rib roast and mushrooms. Seal pouch tightly after squeezing out the excess air. Place pouch in sous vide bath and set the cooking time for at least 24 and up to 36 hours.
3. Remove pouch from sous vide bath and carefully open it. Transfer rib roast onto a cutting board, reserve mushroom and cooking liquid into a bowl. With paper towels, pat rib roast completely dry.
4. Rub rib roast with salt and black pepper evenly.
5. Heat cast iron pan to medium high heat and place the rib roast in, Fat cap down. Sear for 1-2 minutes per side (or until browned on all sides.
6. Meanwhile, season reserved mushroom mixture with garlic oil, a little salt, and black pepper.
7. Transfer rib roast onto a cutting board, bone side down.
8. Carefully, remove rib bones and cut rib roast into ½-inch-thick slices across the grain.
9. Serve immediately with mushroom mixture.

261. BEST PRIME RIB ROAST

72 HOURS | 15 MIN | 12

NUTRITION:
CAL: 997 | FAT: 64 | PROTEIN: 97

INGREDIENTS

- 1 x 10-lb prime rib roast
- prime rib spice rub, to taste
- dried rosemary, to taste
- dried thyme, to taste
- onion powder, to taste
- garlic powder, to taste
- salt and freshly ground black pepper, to taste

DIRECTIONS

1. Preheat a sous vide water bath to 135°F.
2. Carefully, cut individual ribs from the roast.
3. In a bowl, mix together spice rub, dried herbs, spices, salt and black pepper.
4. Generously coat roast with spice mixture.
5. Lightly coat ribs with spice mixture.
6. Into a cooking pouch, add the roast. In another cooking pouch, place ribs. Seal pouches tightly after squeezing out the excess air. Place pouches in sous vide bath. Each pouch will cook for a different time to allow for maximum tenderness for each cut of meat.
7. After 5-10 hours, remove roast from sous vide bath and serve. Grass fed or younger, more tender beef will only take 5 hours, while other cuts may take up to 10 hours to become truly tender.
8. The cuts of ribs can remain in the sous vide bath for up to 72 hours before being removed and served.

262. KOREAN SHORT RIBS

4 HOURS | 15 MIN | 4

NUTRITION:
CAL: 777 | FAT: 36 | PROTEIN: 24

INGREDIENTS

For Barbecue Sauce:

- 1 scallion, finely chopped
- 6 garlic cloves, crushed
- 1 tbsp fresh ginger, grated
- 1½ cups soy sauce
- 1½ cups brown sugar
- ½ cup mirin
- ½ cup water plus 2 tbsps water, divided
- 3 tbsps chili paste
- 2 tbsps rice wine vinegar
- 1 tbsp sesame oil
- 1 tsp black pepper, freshly ground
- 2 tbsps cornstarch
- 2 tbsps water

For Ribs:

- 4 x 8-oz boneless beef short ribs
- ½ tsp salt
- ½ tsp black pepper, freshly ground

DIRECTIONS

1. Preheat a sous vide water bath to 130°F.
2. For the barbecue sauce:
3. in a small bowl, dissolve the cornstarch into 2 tbsps of water. Keep aside.
4. In a large pan, mix together remaining sauce ingredients and bring to a boil and cook for 5-7 minutes, stirring occasionally.
5. Slowly add cornstarch mixture, beating continuously.
6. Reduce heat to medium and cook for 3-4 minutes.
7. Remove from heat and keep aside.
8. For the ribs:
9. lightly season ribs with salt and black pepper.
10. Into a cooking pouch, add 1 short rib and 2 tbsps of barbecue sauce and toss to coat.
11. Repeat with remaining ribs in separate cooking pouches, and reserve remaining sauce.
12. Seal pouches tightly after squeezing out the excess air. Place pouches in sous vide bath and set the cooking time for 4 hours.
13. Remove pouches from sous vide bath and carefully open them. Remove ribs from pouches. With paper towels, pat ribs completely dry.
14. Heat a cast iron grill pan over high heat, and sear ribs for 10-15 seconds.
15. Remove ribs from pan and keep aside for 5-10 minutes to rest.
16. Cut into thin slices and serve immediately with reserved barbecue sauce.

263. TERIYAKI BEEF CUBES

55 MIN | 10 MIN | 2

NUTRITION:
CAL: 280 | FAT: 21 | PROTEIN: 25

INGREDIENTS

- 2 fillet mignon steaks
- ½ cup teriyaki sauce (extra 6 tbsps
- 2 tbsps soy sauce
- 2 tsps fresh chilis, chopped
- 1½ tbsps sesame seeds, toasted
- Rice noodles
- 2 tbsps sesame oil
- 1 tbsp scallion for garnishing, finely chopped

DIRECTIONS

1. Preheat a sous vide water bath to 134°F
2. Slice the steaks into small portions and put them in a zipper bag
3. Add ½ a cup of teriyaki sauce to the bag. Seal using the immersion method, submerge and cook for 1 hour.
4. Add the soy sauce and chopped chilis in a small bowl
5. Add the sesame seeds in another bowl
6. After 50 minutes of cooking, start cooking the rice noodles according to the package's instructions
7. Once done, drain the noodles and put them on a servings platter
8. Take the bag out from the water and remove the beef. Discard the marinade
9. Take a large skillet and put it over a high heat. Add your sesame oil and allow the oil to heat up.
10. Add the beef and 6 tbsps of teriyaki sauce, and cook for 5 seconds
11. Transfer the cooked beef to your servings platter and garnish with toasted sesame seeds and scallions
12. Serve with the prepped chili-soy dip

264. WILLY CHEESESTEAK

1 HOUR | 1 MIN | 4

NUTRITION:
CAL: 374 | FAT: 29 | PROTEIN: 23

INGREDIENTS

- 1 red bell pepper, thinly sliced
- 1 yellow bell pepper, thinly sliced
- ½ white onion, thinly sliced
- 2 tbsps olive oil
- salt and black pepper as needed
- 1 lb. cooked skirt steak, thinly sliced
- 4 soft hoagie rolls
- 8 slices of Provolone cheese

DIRECTIONS

1. Preheat a sous vide water bath to 185°F
2. Add the bell peppers, onion and olive oil in a heavy-duty zip bag
3. Season the mixture with salt and pepper
4. Seal the bag using the immersion method and submerge and cook for 1 hour.
5. At the 55-minute mark, put the cooked steak in another zip bag and submerge it
6. Allow both to cook for 5-minutes more and take them out
7. Preheat your oven to 400°F
8. Slice the hoagie rolls in half and top them with cheese
9. Place them in the oven and bake for 2 minutes
10. Add the pepper, steak and onions, then serve!

265. ROSEMARY GARLIC LAMB CHOPS

2.5 HOURS | 5 MIN | 4

NUTRITION:
CAL: 251 | FAT: 21 | PROTEIN: 16

INGREDIENTS

- 4 lamb chops

DIRECTIONS

1. Fill and preheat a sous vide water bath to 140° F.

- 1 tbsp butter
- 1 tsp fresh thyme
- 1 tsp fresh rosemary
- 2 garlic cloves
- Pepper
- Salt

2. Season lamb chops with pepper and salt.
3. Sprinkle lamb chops with garlic, thyme, and rosemary.
4. Add butter to the zip-lock bag then place lamb chops into the bag.
5. Remove all air from the bag before sealing.
6. Place bag in hot water bath and cook for 2 1/2 hours.
7. Once it done then sear it on high heat until lightly brown.
8. Serve and enjoy.

266. LAMB CHOPS WITH BASIL CHIMICHURRI

2 HOURS | 10 MIN | 4

NUTRITION:
CAL: 363| FAT: 37 | PROTEIN: 7

INGREDIENTS

- 2 racks of lamb, drenched
- 2 garlic cloves, crushed
- Pepper
- Salt

For basil Chimichurri:

- 3 tbsp red wine vinegar
- 1/2 cup olive oil
- 1 tsp red chili flakes
- 2 garlic cloves, minced
- 1 shallot, diced
- 1 cup fresh basil, chopped
- 1/4 tsp pepper
- 1/4 tsp sea salt

DIRECTIONS

1. Fill and preheat a sous vide water bath to 132ºF.
2. Season lamb with pepper and salt.
3. Place lamb in a large zip-lock bag with garlic and remove all air from the bag before sealing.
4. Place bag into the hot water bath and cook for 2 hours.
5. Add all chimichurri ingredients to the bowl and mix well. Place in refrigerator for minutes.
6. Remove lamb from bag and pat dry with paper towel.
7. Sear lamb in hot oil. Sliced lamb between the bones.
8. Place seared lamb chops on serving dish and top with chimichurri. Serve and enjoy.

267. GARLIC BUTTER LAMB CHOPS

2 HOURS | 10 MIN | 4

NUTRITION:
CAL: 278 | FAT: 23 | PROTEIN: 16

INGREDIENTS

- 4 lamb chops
- 1/2 tsp onion powder
- 1 garlic clove, minced
- 2 tbsp butter
- 1 tsp dried rosemary
- Pepper
- Salt

DIRECTIONS

1. Fill and preheat a sous vide water bath to 140º F.
2. Season chops with rosemary, pepper, and salt.
3. Place lamb chops into the zip-lock bag and remove all air from the bag before sealing.
4. Place bag in hot water bath and cook for 2 hours.
5. Remove lamb chops from bag and pat dry with paper towel.
6. In a microwave-safe bowl, add butter and microwave until butter is melted. Make sure butter doesn't burn it.
7. Add onion powder and garlic into the melted butter and stir well.
8. Baste lamb chops with butter mixture and sear until golden brown. Serve and enjoy.

268. SIMPLE RACK OF LAMB

2 HOURS | 5 MIN | 4

NUTRITION:
CAL: 676 | FAT: 55 | PROTEIN: 35

INGREDIENTS

- 2 lbs. rack of lamb
- 2 tbsp butter
- 2 tbsp canola oil
- Black pepper
- Salt

DIRECTIONS

1. Fill and preheat a sous vide water bath to 140° F.
2. Season lamb with pepper and salt and place in large zip-lock bag.
3. Remove all air from the bag before sealing.
4. Place bag in hot water bath and cook for 2 hours.
5. Remove lamb from bag and pat dry with paper towels.
6. Heat canola oil in a pan over medium heat.
7. Spread butter over lamb and sear lamb in hot oil until lightly brown. Serve and enjoy.

269. HERB GARLIC LAMB CHOPS

2 HOURS | 10 MIN | 4

NUTRITION:
CAL: 288 FAT: 27 | PROTEIN: 18

INGREDIENTS

- 4 lamb chops, bone in
- 2 tbsp butter
- 8 black peppercorns
- 1 tsp fresh oregano
- 1 tbsp fresh parsley
- 1 bay leaf
- 4 fresh thyme sprigs
- 2 tsp garlic, sliced
- Sea salt

DIRECTIONS

1. Fill and preheat a sous vide water bath to 132° F.
2. Add lamb, butter, peppercorns, herbs, and garlic into the large zip-lock bag and remove all the air from the bag before sealing.
3. Place bag into the hot water bath and cook for 2 hours.
4. Remove lamb chops from bag and pat dry with paper towels.
5. Heat pans over high heat and sear lamb chops for 30 seconds on each side.

270. MEATBALLS

3 HOURS | 9 MIN | 10

NUTRITION:
CAL: 182 FAT: 12 | PROTEIN: 17

INGREDIENTS

- 2 lbs ground beef
- 4 to 6 oz milk
- ½ tsp pepper
- 1 shallot minced
- 2 tbsps dried oregano
- 6 tbsps grated parmesan cheese
- ½ cup dried breadcrumbs
- 1 tsp salt, or to taste
- 2 large eggs, beaten
- 1/3 cup chopped parsley
- 2 tbsps garlic powder

DIRECTIONS

1. Add all the ingredients into a large bowl and mix with your hands until just incorporated. Do not mix for long, as the meat will tend to get tough.
2. Make 1-inch balls of the mixture. Place on a tray and freeze until firm.
3. Preheat a sous vide water bath to 135°F.
4. Transfer the meatballs into 1 or 2 large vacuum-seal pouches or Ziploc bags.
5. Vacuum seal the pouches.
6. Immerse the pouches in the water bath. Set the timer for 3 hours.
7. When the timer goes off, remove pouch from the water bath. Set aside to cool.
8. Open the pouch and transfer into a bowl.
9. Serve with a dip of your choice.

- Dip of your choice, to serve
- A little oil to seas (optional)

10. If you want to sear the meatballs: Place a non-stick pan over medium heat and add a bit of oil. When the oil is heated, add meatballs and cook until browned.
11. Serve.

271. BONELESS STRIP STEAK

2.5 HOURS | 30 MIN | 2

NUTRITION:
CAL: 481 | FAT: 36 | PROTEIN: 42

INGREDIENTS

- 1 14-16-oz boneless strip steak, 1½–2 inches thick
- ¼ tsp garlic powder
- ¼ tsp onion powder
- 1 tsp salt, plus more
- ¼ tsp freshly ground black pepper, plus more
- 3 sprigs rosemary
- 3 sprigs thyme
- 1 tbsp grape seed or other neutral oil

DIRECTIONS

1. Preheat a sous vide water bath to 130°F for a medium-rare steak.
2. Mix garlic powder, onion powder, 1 tsp salt, ¼ tsp pepper in a bowl.
3. Rub the mixture all over all 4 sides of the steak. Smack the sprigs of herbs against a cutting board.
4. Place the steak in the bag you're going to use to sous vide, along with the sprigs of herbs, and seal the bag.
5. Place the bag in your preheated water. Set timer for 2 hours and 30 minutes.
6. When the steak is ready, allow it to rest for 15 minutes.
7. Take the steak out of the bag and let it rest for a few more minutes.
8. While it's resting, season it with salt and pepper to taste.
9. Heat a skittle (ideally cast iron) on high heat. When it gets really hot, pour in the oil and put in the steak. Let the steak sear for 1 to 2 minutes total, flipping it on all four sides. The steak should form a very nice crust on all sides.
10. Serve immediately.

272. HANGER STEAK

2.5 HOURS | 15 MIN | 4

NUTRITION:
CAL: 588 | FAT: 52 | PROTEIN: 25

INGREDIENTS

- 4 (8 oz.) pieces of hanger steak
- Freshly ground black pepper
- 12 sprigs thyme
- 2 garlic cloves
- 2 shallots, peeled and thinly sliced
- 2 tbsp high-smoke point oil

DIRECTIONS

1. Preheat your sous vide water bath to 130°F for a medium-rare steak.
2. Season the steak with salt and pepper to taste.
3. Place the steak in the bag you're going to use to sous vide along with the sprigs of thyme, garlic and shallots. Divide the herbs garlic, and shallots among the 4 steaks places thyme sprigs, and shallots slices on both sides, and seal the bag.
4. Place the bag in your preheated water and set the timer for 4 hours.
5. When the steak is ready, allow it to rest for a few minutes.
6. While it's resting, heat a skittle (ideally cast iron) on high heat. When it gets really hot, pour in the oil and put in the steak. Let the steak sear for 1 minute per side. Should form a nice crust on both sides. Serve.

273. KOREAN KALBI SHORT RIBS

2.5 HOURS | 15 MIN | 4

NUTRITION:
CAL: 588 | FAT: 52 | PROTEIN: 25

INGREDIENTS

- 16 Korean Style crosscut beef short ribs

Marinade:

- 2 tbsp sesame oil
- 2 tbsp brown sugar
- 1 ½ tsp chili flakes
- 1 tbsp chopped garlic
- ½ cup soy sauce
- ¼ cup chopped green onions
- ¼ cup orange juice

DIRECTIONS

1. Heat a pan on medium-high heat and add in the sesame oil and garlic. Allow the garlic to cook for 2 minutes then take the pan off the heat. Add the rest of the marinade ingredients to the pan while it's still warm and stir the mixture until well combined.
2. Place the ribs in a baking dish and pour in the marinade. Place the dish in the refrigerator, covered for 1 hr. Turn the meat every 15 min.
3. Preheat your sous vide water bath to 138°F
4. Save the marinade for later.
5. Place the steak in the bag you're going to use to sous. Seal the bag.
6. Place the bag in your preheated water and set the timer for 2 hours 30 minutes.
7. While the meat is cooking, put the marinade in a put and allow it to come to a boil. Allow the sauce to cook for 15 to 20 minutes until it starts to reduce a little.
8. When the ribs are almost done, preheat your broiler.
9. When the steaks are cooked, use a brush to coat them with the marinade.
10. Place the ribs on an aluminum foil rimmed baking sheet or pan.
11. Put the baking sheet under the broiler and allow the meat to cook for 1 to 2 minutes per side. You just want the sauce to caramelize and then serve.

274. SPICE RUBBED SHORT RIBS

48 HOURS | 10 MIN | 6

NUTRITION:
CAL: 694 | FAT: 59 | PROTEIN: 37

INGREDIENTS

- 1 tbsp ground cumin
- 1 tbsp ancho chili powder
- 1/4 tsp ground cloves
- 1 tsp salt
- 1 tsp freshly ground black pepper
- 3 lbs. beef short ribs

DIRECTIONS

1. Preheat your sous vide water bath to 140°F
2. Combine the spices in a bowl. Coat the beef ribs with the spice rub.
3. Place the steak in the bag or bags you're going to use to sous vide and seal the bag or bags.
4. Place the bag in your preheated water and set the timer for 48 hours.
5. When the ribs are almost ready preheat your broiler
6. Place the cooked ribs on an aluminum foil rimmed baking sheet or pan. Broil for about 5 minutes, until you see the edges char. Serve.

275. ROAST BEEF

24 HOURS | 15 MIN | 6

NUTRITION:
CAL: 262 | FAT: 8 | PROTEIN: 43

INGREDIENTS

- 3 ½ lb. beef roast
- 2 cloves garlic minced
- 1 tbsp rosemary minced

DIRECTIONS

1. Preheat your sous vide water bath to 136°F
2. Combine all the ingredients, except for the beef and Worcestershire sauce in a bowl.
3. Rub the Worcestershire sauce all over the beef then coat the beef with the spice mixture.

- ½ tbsp Worcestershire sauce
- 1 tsp smoked paprika
- ½ tsp mustard powder
- ½ tsp onion powder
- 2 ½ tsp salt
- ½ tsp pepper

4. Place the beef in the bag you're going to use to sous vide and seal the bag.
5. Place the bag in your preheated water and set the timer for 24 hours.
6. When the beef is almost ready, preheat your oven to 350°F.
7. Place the cooked roast on a boiler pan.
8. Place the roast in the oven and allow it cook for 15 minutes.

276. BEEF SHOGAYAKI

12 HOURS | 10 MIN | 3

NUTRITION:
CAL: 162 | FAT: 20 | PROTEIN: 12

INGREDIENTS

- 18 oz. beef stew meat
- 3 tbsp soy sauce
- 3 tbsp mirin
- 3 tbsp water
- 1 thumb-sized piece ginger grated
- 1 tbsp high-smoke point oil

DIRECTIONS

1. Preheat your sous vide water bath to 140°F
2. Mix together soy, water, ginger, and mirin in a bowl. Add the beef, and toss it in the mixture to coat.
3. Place the beef in the bag you're going to use to sous vide along with the sauce and seal the bag.
4. Place the bag in your preheated water and set the timer for 12 hours.
5. When the beef is ready, heat a skittle (ideally cast iron) on high heat.
6. When it gets really hot, pour in the oil and put in the beef. Let the steak sear for 1 minute, flipping halfway through. The steak should form a nice crust on both sides.

277. TUSCAN RIBEYE STEAK

30 MIN | 11 MIN | 4

NUTRITION:
CAL: 322 | FAT: 29 | PROTEIN: 16

INGREDIENTS

- 4 tbsp olive oil
- 2 tbsp finely chopped garlic
- 1 tbsp ground black pepper
- 1 tbsp ground fennel
- 2 tbsp chopped anchovies
- 2 tbsp chopped parsley
- 1 tbsp chopped rosemary
- 12 oz. natural boneless rib eye steaks
- 2 tbsp olive oil

DIRECTIONS

1. Preheat your sous vide water bath to 168°F
2. Heat a skillet on medium heat and add in the olive oil and garlic. Allow the garlic to cook until it browns, about 4 min. Then put in the anchovies, rosemary, fennel, parsley, and black pepper. Take the skillet off the heat.
3. Season the rib eyes with a little salt. Coat both sides of the steaks with the rosemary mixture.
4. Rub the Worcestershire sauce all over the beef then coat the beef with the spice mixture.
5. Place each steak in its own bag and seal the bags.
6. Place the bag in your preheated water and set the timer for 30 min.
7. When the steaks are ready heat a skittle (ideally cast iron) on high heat and get the skillet really hot. Place a little oil in the skillet
8. Place the cooked steaks in the skillet. Sear for about 1 min. per side.
9. Serve the steaks immediately.

278. BURGERS

1 HOUR | 6 MIN | 2

NUTRITION:
CAL: 282 | FAT: 20 | PROTEIN: 24

INGREDIENTS

- 10 oz. freshly ground beef
- 2 hamburger buns
- 2 slices american cheese
- salt
- pepper
- condiments and toppings of choice

DIRECTIONS

1. Preheat your sous vide water bath to 137ºF
2. Use your hands to form the burgers into 2 equal sized 1-inch-thick patties.
3. Place the patties in the bag you're going to use to sous vide and seal the bag.
4. Place the bag in your preheated water and set the timer for 1 hour.
5. When the patties are ready, heat a skittle (ideally cast iron) on high heat.
6. When it gets really hot, put in the patties. Let the patties sear for 1 minute, flipping halfway through. When you flip the burgers, top with cheese slices, so the cheese melts.
7. Serve on buns with the condiments of your choice.

279. SMOKED BRISQUET

38 HOURS | 2 MIN | 10

NUTRITION:
CAL: 351 | FAT: 16 | PROTEIN: 48

INGREDIENTS

- 2 oz. coarsely ground black peppercorns
- 2 ¼ oz. salt
- ¼ oz. pink salt
- 1, 5 lb. flat-cut or point-cut brisket
- ¼ tsp liquid smoke

DIRECTIONS

1. Mix together the different salts and pepper in a bowl. Coat the brisket with about 2/3 of the mixture. Then cut the brisket in half crosswise.
2. Place the 2 briskets in 2 bags, put in 4 drops of liquid smoke in each bag, and seal the bags.
3. Allow the bags to marinate in your refrigerator for 2 to 3 hours
4. Preheat your sous vide water bath to 155ºF
5. Place the bag in your preheated water and set the timer for 36 hours.
6. When the brisket is almost ready, move one of your oven racks to the lower-middle position. Preheat your oven to 300ºF.
7. Use a paper towel to pat the cooked brisket dry. Coat the brisket with the remaining seasoning mixture.
8. Put a wire rack on a baking sheet and place the brisket on top of it with the fat side up. Place the brisket in the oven for about 2 hours. The brisket is done when a dark bark forms on the outside
9. Place the brisket on a cutting board and use aluminum foil to tent it. Allow the brisket to rest for 30 min. Set the internal temperature between 145ºF and 165ºF.
10. Cut the brisket against the grain into desired size pieces and serve.

7. GOURMET RECIPES

280. BISON RUMP ROAST

14 HOURS | 15 MIN | 4

NUTRITION:
CAL: 417 | FAT: 24 | PROTEIN: 45

INGREDIENTS

- 1 x 2-lb, 2-inch-thick bison rump roast
- 2 tsps dry steak rub (your choice)

DIRECTIONS

1. Preheat your sous vide water bath to 130°F.
2. Rub bison roast with steak rub evenly.
3. Into a cooking pouch, add bison roast. Seal pouch tightly after squeezing out the excess air. Place pouch in sous vide bath and set the cooking time for 12-14 hours.
4. Remove pouch from sous vide bath and carefully open it. Remove bison roast from pouch, reserving some liquid. With paper towels, pat bison roast completely dry.
5. Heat a cast iron grill pan over high heat, and sear bison roast for 1 minute per side.
6. Remove bison roast from pan and keep aside for 5-10 minutes to rest.
7. Cut into thin slices and serve immediately with reserved cooking liquid.

281. LEMON SHRIMP AND AVOCADO BOWLS

20 MIN | 10 MIN | 4

NUTRITION:
CAL: 206 | FAT: 11 | PROTEIN: 23

INGREDIENTS

- 1-lb shrimp, peeled and deveined
- Juice of ½ lemon
- 1 avocado, peeled, pitted and cubed
- 1 cup baby spinach
- A pinch of salt and black pepper to the taste
- 2 tbsps ghee, melted

DIRECTIONS

1. In a sous vide bag, mix the shrimp with the lemon juice and the other ingredients, toss, seal the bag, put it into your sous vide water bath and cook everything at 126 °F for 20 minutes.
2. Divide into bowls and serve for lunch

282. MUSTARD SALMON STEAK

25 MIN | 10 MIN | 4

NUTRITION:
CAL: 251 | FAT: 10 | PROTEIN: 33

INGREDIENTS

- 4 salmon steaks, bones removed
- 2 tbsps mustard
- salt and black pepper to the taste
- 1 tbsp lemon juice
- 1 tsp chives, chopped
- 2 tbsps olive oil

DIRECTIONS

1. In a bowl, mix the salmon with the mustard and the other ingredients, and toss well.
2. Transfer the salmon steaks to sous vide bags, seal them, submerge in your sous vide water bath and cook at 130 °F for 25 minutes.
3. Divide steaks between plates and serve with a side salad.

283. BBQ COD MIX

30 MIN | 10 MIN | 2

NUTRITION:
CAL: 246 | FAT: 9 | PROTEIN: 36

INGREDIENTS

- 1-lb cod fillets, boneless
- 2 tbsp chives, chopped
- ½ tsp coriander, ground
- 1 tbsp olive oil
- 1 tbsps BBQ sauce
- 1 tbsp lime juice
- A pinch of salt and black pepper

DIRECTIONS

1. In a bowl, mix the cod with the BBQ sauce and the other ingredients, toss gently and transfer to a sous vide bag.
2. Seal the bag, introduce in the preheated water oven and cook at 140 °F for 30 minutes.
3. Divide between plates and serve.

284. CALAMARI, SALMON AND SHRIMP BOWLS

50 MIN | 10 MIN | 4

NUTRITION:
CAL: 246 | FAT: 9 | PROTEIN: 36

INGREDIENTS

- 1-lb cod fillets, boneless
- 2 tbsp chives, chopped
- ½ tsp coriander, ground
- 1 tbsp olive oil
- 1 tbsps BBQ sauce
- 1 tbsp lime juice
- A pinch of salt and black pepper

DIRECTIONS

1. In a bowl, mix the cod with the BBQ sauce and the other ingredients, toss gently and transfer to a sous vide bag.
2. Seal the bag, introduce in the preheated water oven and cook at 140 °F for 30 minutes.
3. Divide between plates and serve

285. MUSTARD SALMON MIX

35 MIN | 10 MIN | 4

NUTRITION:
CAL: 201 | FAT: 13 | PROTEIN: 23

INGREDIENTS

- 1-lb salmon fillets, boneless and roughly cubed
- 2 tbsps mustard
- 1 cup baby spinach
- 1 cup baby kale
- salt and black pepper to the taste
- 1 tbsp homemade mayonnaise
- juice of 1 lemon
- zest of 1 lemon, grated
- 2 scallions, chopped
- 2 tbsps capers, chopped
- 2 tbsps olive oil

DIRECTIONS

1. In a sous vide bag, combine the salmon with the spinach, mustard and the other ingredients, seal the bag, submerge in the water oven and cook at 170°F for 35 minutes.
2. Divide into bowls serve.

286. BALSAMIC CALAMARI AND TOMATOES

🍲 30 MIN ⏱ 10 MIN 🍴 2

NUTRITION:
CAL: 133 | FAT: 6 | PROTEIN: 12

INGREDIENTS

- 1 cup calamari rings
- ½ cup tomato sauce
- 1 cup cherry tomatoes, halved
- 1 tsp chili powder
- 4 scallions, chopped
- ½ tsp balsamic vinegar
- A pinch of salt and black pepper

DIRECTIONS

1. In a sous vide bag, mix the calamari rings with the tomatoes and the other ingredients, toss, seal the bag, submerge in the water bath and cook at 170 ºF for 30 minutes.
2. Divide into bowls and serve.

286. MUSTARD SALMON MIX

🍲 35 MIN ⏱ 10 MIN 🍴 4

NUTRITION:
CAL: 201 | FAT: 13 | PROTEIN: 23

INGREDIENTS

- 1-lb salmon fillets, boneless and roughly cubed
- 2 tbsps mustard
- 1 cup baby spinach
- 1 cup baby kale
- salt and black pepper to the taste
- 1 tbsp homemade mayonnaise
- juice of 1 lemon
- zest of 1 lemon, grated
- 2 scallions, chopped
- 2 tbsps capers, chopped
- 2 tbsps olive oil

DIRECTIONS

1. In a sous vide bag, combine the salmon with the spinach, mustard and the other ingredients, seal the bag, submerge in the water oven and cook at 170ºF for 35 minutes.
2. Divide into bowls serve.

287. CREAMY CALAMARI

🍲 30 MIN ⏱ 10 MIN 🍴 2

NUTRITION:
CAL: 676 | FAT: 53 | PROTEIN: 26

INGREDIENTS

- 2 cups calamari rings
- 1 cup heavy cream
- 1 cup baby spinach
- 1 cup cherry tomatoes, halved
- 1 cup corn
- 2 tbsps olive oil
- salt and black pepper to taste
- 2 tbsps chives, chopped

DIRECTIONS

1. In a sous vide bag, mix the calamari rings with the spinach, cream and the other ingredients, seal the bag, cook in the water bath at 180 ºF for 30 minutes,
2. Divide into bowls and serve.

288. LIME LOBSTER

30 MIN | 10 MIN | 2

NUTRITION: CAL: 196 | FAT: 12 | PROTEIN: 20

INGREDIENTS

- 2 lobster tails
- 6 tbsps butter, melted
- 1 tsp sweet paprika
- ½ tsp turmeric powder
- Juice of 1 lime
- salt and black pepper to the taste

DIRECTIONS

1. In a sous vide bag, combine the lobster with the melted butter and the other ingredients, toss, seal the bag, introduce in the preheated sous vide water bath and cook at 140 ºF for 30 minutes.
2. Divide the lobster tails and lime sauce between plates and serve.

289. CHICKEN, SHRIMP AND RICE

1 HOUR | 10 MIN | 4

NUTRITION: CAL: 393 | FAT: 10 | PROTEIN: 59

INGREDIENTS

- 1-lb chicken breast, skinless, boneless and cubed
- 1-lb shrimp, peeled and deveined
- 1 cup wild rice
- 2 cups chicken stock
- 1 cup cherry tomatoes, halved
- ½ tsp chili powder
- 1 tbsp Creole seasoning
- Salt and black pepper to the taste
- 1 green bell pepper, chopped
- 2 spring onions, chopped
- 3 garlic cloves, minced
- 1 tbsp chives, chopped

DIRECTIONS

1. In a sous vide bag, mix the chicken with the shrimp, rice and the other ingredients, seal the bag, submerge in the sous vide water bath and cook at 180 ºF for 1 hour.
2. Divide into bowls and serve.

290. VANILLA AND BUTTER SHRIMP

30 MIN | 10 MIN | 2

NUTRITION: CAL: 342 | FAT: 15 | PROTEIN: 45

INGREDIENTS

- 1-lb shrimp, peeled and deveined
- ½ tsp vanilla extract
- ¼ tsp sweet paprika
- A pinch of salt and black pepper
- 1 cup cherry tomatoes, halved
- 2 tbsps butter, melted
- 1 tbsp chives, chopped

DIRECTIONS

1. In a sous vide bag combine the shrimp with the vanilla, butter and the other ingredients, seal, introduce in the preheated sous vide water bath and cook at 136 ºF for 30 minutes.
2. Divide into bowls and serve.

291. PORK AND BLUEBERRIES MIX

2 HOURS | 10 MIN | 2

NUTRITION:
CAL: 657 | FAT: 28 | PROTEIN: 93

INGREDIENTS

- 2 lbs pork roast, sliced
- 1 tbsp olive oil
- salt and black pepper to the taste
- 1 tbsp cinnamon powder
- A pinch of cayenne pepper
- 1 tsp cumin, ground
- 1 tsp fennel seeds, crushed
- 2 tbsps soy sauce
- ½ cup blueberries
- 2 tbsps stevia
- ½ tsp chili sauce
- 1 tbsps chive, chopped

DIRECTIONS

1. In a sous vide bag, mix the roast with the oil, cinnamon and the other ingredients, seal the bag, cook in the sous vide water bath at 180 °F for 2 hours.
2. Divide between plates and serve.

292. BBQ AND PAPRIKA RIBS

2 HOURS | 10 MIN | 4

NUTRITION:
CAL: 465 | FAT: 22 | PROTEIN: 46

INGREDIENTS

- 2 lbs baby back pork ribs
- 2 tbsps olive oil
- 1 cup BBQ sauce
- Salt and black pepper to the taste
- 2 tbsps sweet paprika
- 2 tbsps cumin, ground
- 2 tbsps garlic powder
- 1 tbsp chives, chopped

DIRECTIONS

1. In a sous vide bag, mix the ribs with the oil, sauce and the other ingredients, toss, seal the bag, submerge in the sous vide water bath and cook at 180 °F for 2 hours.
2. Divide between plates and serve them with a side salad.

293. SALMON GRAVLAX

1 HOUR | 30 MIN | 4

NUTRITION:
CAL: 292 | FAT: 11 | PROTEIN: 44

INGREDIENTS

- 8 salmon fillets
- 4 tbsp sugar
- 4 tbsp salt

DIRECTIONS

1. Preheat your sous vide water bath to 104 °F.
2. In a small bowl, mix the sugar with salt.
3. Season the salmon with the mixture and set aside for half an hour.
4. Rinse the salmon fillets and place them into the vacuum bag.
5. Seal it, setting the timer for 1 hour.
6. Serve immediately with toasted bread and cream cheese.

294. HERBED PORK AND SUN-DRIED TOMATOES

2 HOURS | 10 MIN | 4

NUTRITION:
CAL: 595 | FAT: 40 | PROTEIN: 60

INGREDIENTS

- 2 lbs pork roast, sliced
- 1 cup sun-dried tomatoes, chopped
- 2 tbsps olive oil
- Juice of 1 lime
- 1 tbsp mustard
- Zest of 1 lime, grated
- ½ tsp cloves, crushed
- 1 tsp oregano, dried
- 1 tsp coriander, ground
- 1 tsp thyme, chopped
- 1 tbsp chives, chopped

DIRECTIONS

1. In a large sous vide bag, combine the roast with the tomatoes, oil and the other ingredients, seal the bag, submerge in the sous vide water bath and cook at 180 ºF for 2 hours
2. Divide between plates and serve right away.

295. BUTTERY PORK TENDERLOIN

2 HOURS | 10 MIN | 4

NUTRITION:
CAL: 348 | FAT: 17 | PROTEIN: 46

INGREDIENTS

- 2 lbs pork tenderloin, sliced
- ½ tsp turmeric powder
- 1 tsp chili powder
- Juice of 1 lime
- 1 and ½ tbsps Italian seasoning
- salt and black pepper to the taste
- 2 tbsps butter, melted

DIRECTIONS

1. In a sous vide bag, combine the pork with the melted butter and the other ingredients, seal the bag, introduce it in the preheated sous vide water oven and cook at 135 ºF for 2 hours.
2. Divide between plates and serve with a side salad.

296. SALMON TERIYAKI

1 HOUR | 30 MIN | 4

NUTRITION:
CAL: 299 | FAT: 14 | PROTEIN: 44

INGREDIENTS

- 8 salmon fillets
- 8 tbsp Teriyaki sauce

DIRECTIONS

1. Preheat your sous vide water bath to 104 ºF.
2. Evenly cover the salmon fillets with the Teriyaki sauce set aside for half an hour.
3. Place the fillets in the vacuum bag.
4. Seal it, setting the timer for 1 hour.
5. Serve immediately with steamed white rice.

297. GARLIC AND NUTMEG PORK

2 HOURS | 10 MIN | 4

NUTRITION:
CAL: 595 | FAT: 40| PROTEIN: 61

INGREDIENTS

- 2 lbs pork roast, sliced
- 4 garlic cloves, minced
- 1 tsp nutmeg, ground
- 2 tbsps olive oil
- juice of 1 lime
- salt and black pepper to the taste
- 1 tsp rosemary, dried
- 2 bay leaves
- 1 tbsp cilantro, chopped

DIRECTIONS

1. In a sous vide bag, combine the pork with the garlic, nutmeg and the other ingredients, seal, introduce them into your preheated sous vide water bath and cook at 180 °F for 2 hours.
2. Divide between plates and serve.

298. GINGER SALMON

30 MIN | 40 MIN | 2

NUTRITION:
CAL: 218 | FAT: 10| PROTEIN: 21

INGREDIENTS

- 2 salmon fillets
- 2 tbsp soy sauce
- 1 tbsp liquid honey
- 1 tbsp sesame oil
- 1 tbsp ginger root, minced
- Chili pepper to taste

DIRECTIONS

1. Put all ingredients into the vacuum bag and set aside for 1 hour to marinate.
2. In the meantime, preheat the sous vide water bath to 125 °F.
3. Seal the bag and set the timer for 30 minutes.
4. When the time is up, you can serve salmon immediately, or sear it on both sides in a cast iron skillet until it browns a bit and then serve over rice, pouring the juices from the bag over the rice.

299. SALMON IN ORANGE & BUTTER SAUCE

30 MIN | 10 MIN | 2

NUTRITION:
CAL: 308 | FAT: 22| PROTEIN: 25

INGREDIENTS

For the salmon:

- 2 salmon steaks
- Salt to taste
- 1 tbsp olive oil

For the butter sauce:

- 1 cup water
- 1 shallot, finely chopped
- 1/3 cup freshly squeezed orange juice
- 1 tbsp lemon juice
- A pinch of salt and sugar
- 2 tbsp butter

DIRECTIONS

1. Rub the fish with salt and put it into the vacuum bag together with olive oil.
2. Preheat the sous vide water bath to 115 °F.
3. Seal the bag and set the timer for 25 minutes.
4. In the meantime, cook the butter sauce.
5. In a small saucepan, combine water, juices, chopped shallot, salt and pepper. Bring to boil and simmer over medium heat until the amount of liquid is reduced to about 4 tbsp
6. Mix in the butter, pour over the salmon and serve.

300. ORIENTAL SOY & GINGER FISH

20 MIN | 10 MIN | 2

NUTRITION:
CAL: 192 | FAT: 11 | PROTEIN: 23

INGREDIENTS

- 2 medium cod fillets
- 1/3 cup sugar free soy sauce
- 2 tbsp peanut oil
- 2 tbsp sesame oil
- 2 tbsp ginger root, grated
- 2 garlic cloves, minced

DIRECTIONS

1. In a small pan, sauté ginger and garlic in peanut oil until lightly golden.
2. Preheat the sous vide water bath to 135 °F.
3. Put the fish, the sautéed ginger and garlic and the rest of the ingredients in the vacuum bag.
4. Seal the bag and set the timer for 20 minutes.

301. COD IN HOLLANDAISE SAUCE

20 MIN | 10 MIN | 2

NUTRITION:
CAL: 170 | FAT: 11 | PROTEIN: 20

INGREDIENTS

- 2 medium cod fillets
- 2 tbsp olive oil
- salt and pepper to taste
- Sous Vide Hollandaise sauce

DIRECTIONS

1. Preheat the water bath to 135 °F.
2. Rub the cod fillets with salt and pepper and put the fish and olive oil into the vacuum bag.
3. Seal the bag and set the timer for 20 minutes.
4. Serve with the Sous Vide Hollandaise sauce

302. COD IN LEMON AND CAPERS SAUCE

30 MIN | 30 MIN | 2

NUTRITION:
CAL: 170 | FAT: 11 | PROTEIN: 20

INGREDIENTS

- 2 medium cod fillets
- 2 tbsp olive oil
- Salt and pepper to taste
- 2 tbsp lemon juice
- 2 tbsp marinated capers
- 4 garlic cloves, coarsely chopped

DIRECTIONS

1. Rub the cod fillets with salt, pepper and lemon juice, put the fish into the vacuum bag and set aside for 30 minutes to marinate.
2. Preheat the sous vide water bath to 135 °F.
3. Add the capers, olive oil and garlic cloves to the vacuum bag.
4. Seal the bag and set the timer for 30 minutes.

303. SPICY COBBLER

30 MIN | 30 MIN | 2

NUTRITION:
CAL: 175 | FAT: 13 | PROTEIN: 21

INGREDIENTS

- 2 medium cobbler fillets
- 2 tbsp unsalted butter, softened
- 2 garlic cloves, minced
- 1 tsp red chili paste
- 1 tbsp fresh lemon juice
- A pinch of salt

DIRECTIONS

1. In a small bowl, combine the softened butter with garlic, chili paste, salt and lemon juice.
2. Rub the cobbler fillets with the butter mixture and set aside.
3. In the meantime, preheat the sous vide water bath to 145 °F.
4. Seal the bag and set the timer for 30 minutes.

304. BLUE CHEESE FISH

20 MIN | 10 MIN | 2

NUTRITION:
CAL: 180 | FAT: 18 | PROTEIN: 21

INGREDIENTS

- 2 medium fish fillets of your choice (salmon, cod, trout or other)
- 2 tbsp olive oil
- salt and pepper to taste
- Sous Vide Blue Cheese sauce

DIRECTIONS

1. Preheat the sous vide water bath to 135 °F.
2. Rub the fish fillets with salt and pepper and put the fish and olive oil into the vacuum bag.
3. Seal the bag and set the timer for 20 minutes.
4. Serve with the Sous Vide Blue Cheese sauce.

305. TROUT IN WHITE WINE

40 MIN | 10 MIN | 2

NUTRITION:
CAL: 775 | FAT: 59 | PROTEIN: 34

INGREDIENTS

For the fish:

- 2 medium trout fillets
- 2 tbsp olive oil
- Salt and pepper to taste

For the sauce:

- 1 cup dry white wine
- 1 cup heavy cream
- 1 onion, chopped
- salt and pepper to taste
- 1 tsp lemon juice

DIRECTIONS

1. Preheat the sous vide water bath to 120 °F.
2. Rub the trout fillets with salt and pepper and put the fish and olive oil into the vacuum bag.
3. Seal the bag and set the timer for 30 minutes.
4. In the meantime, prepare the wine sauce.
5. Combine the wine, chopped onion, salt and pepper in a pan and reduce over medium hit.
6. Mix in the heavy cream.
7. Serve the trout fillets with the sauce, sprinkled with lemon juice.

306. TROUT WITH PESTO & LEMON JUICE

30 MIN | 10 MIN | 2

NUTRITION:
CAL: 432 | FAT: 29 | PROTEIN: 35

INGREDIENTS

- 2 medium fish fillets of your choice (salmon, cod, trout or other)
- 2 tbsp olive oil
- Salt and pepper to taste
- 4 tbsp Pesto sauce
- 2 tbsp lemon juice

DIRECTIONS

1. Preheat the sous vide water bath to 135 °F.
2. Rub the trout fillets with salt, pepper and pesto sauce, and put the fish and olive oil into the vacuum bag.
3. Seal the bag and set the timer for 30 minutes.
4. Serve sprinkled with lemon juice.

307. SEA BASS

30 MIN | 10 MIN | 2

NUTRITION:
CAL: 190 | FAT: 12 | PROTEIN: 21

INGREDIENTS

- 2 medium sea bass fillets
- 1 tbsp olive oil
- Salt and pepper to taste
- 1 tbsp lime juice

DIRECTIONS

1. Preheat the sous vide water bath to 135 ºF.
2. Rub the sea bass fillets with salt, pepper and olive oil, and put the fish into the vacuum bag.
3. Seal the bag and set the timer for 30 minutes.
4. Serve sprinkled with lime juice.

308. GARLIC & HERBS COD

30 MIN | 10 MIN | 2

NUTRITION:
CAL: 130 | FAT: 7 | PROTEIN: 20

INGREDIENTS

- 2 medium cod fillets
- 2 garlic cloves, minced
- 1 tbsp fresh rosemary, chopped
- 1 tbsp fresh thyme, chopped
- 2 tbsp unsalted butter
- 1 tbsp olive oil
- Juice of 1 lemon

DIRECTIONS

1. Preheat the sous vide water bath to 135 ºF.
2. Rub the cod fillets with salt and pepper, and put them into the vacuum bag adding rosemary, thyme, butter, minced garlic and lemon juice.
3. Seal the bag and set the timer for 30 minutes.
4. When the time is up, sear the fish in a cast iron skillet in 1 tbsp olive oil on both sides and serve over white rice.

309. COCONUT CREAM SEA BASS

30 MIN | 10 MIN | 2

NUTRITION:
CAL: 241 | FAT: 19 | PROTEIN: 22

INGREDIENTS

- For the fish
- 2 medium cod fillets
- 2 tbsp coconut milk
- Salt and pepper to taste
- For the sauce
- ½ cup coconut milk
- ½ cup chicken broth
- ½ tsp white sugar
- 1 tsp lime juice
- 2 slices ginger root
- Chopped cilantro for serving

DIRECTIONS

1. Preheat the sous vide water bath to 135 ºF.
2. Rub the sea bass fillets with salt, pepper, and coconut milk and put them into the vacuum bag.
3. Seal the bag and set the timer for 30 minutes.
4. While the fish is cooking, make the sauce.
5. Combine the chicken broth and coconut milk in a pan, and simmer for about 10 minutes over the medium heat.
6. Add the lime juice, sugar and ginger root, mix well and take the sauce off the heat. Close the pan with the lid and set aside for a couple of minutes.
7. Put the fish in bowls, pour the sauce over and serve topped with the freshly chopped cilantro.

310. THAI TOM YUM FISH

30 MIN | 10 MIN | 2

NUTRITION:
CAL: 130 | FAT: 6 | PROTEIN: 21

INGREDIENTS

- 2 medium fish fillets (any white fish of your choice)
- 2 tbsp Tom Yum paste
- Fresh cilantro for serving
- 1 tbsp lime juice for serving

DIRECTIONS

1. Preheat the sous vide water bath to 135 °F.
2. Rub the fillets with the Tom Yum paste, and put them into the vacuum bag.
3. Seal the bag and set the timer for 30 minutes.
4. Serve over white rice sprinkled with lime juice and topped with freshly chopped cilantro.

311. BUTTER SHRIMPS

30 MIN | 10 MIN | 2

NUTRITION:
CAL: 107 | FAT: 7 | PROTEIN: 12

INGREDIENTS

- 16 shrimps, peeled and deveined
- 1 shallot, minced
- 1 tbsp unsalted butter, melted
- 2 tsp thyme
- 1 tsp lemon zest, grated

DIRECTIONS

1. Preheat the sous vide water bath to 125 °F.
2. Put all ingredients in the vacuum bag.
3. Seal the bag, put it into the water bath and set the timer for 25 minutes.
4. Serve immediately as an appetizer or tossed with penne pasta.

312. GARLIC SHRIMPS

25 MIN | 10 MIN | 2

NUTRITION:
CAL: 107 | FAT: 7| PROTEIN: 12

INGREDIENTS

- 16 shrimps, peeled and deveined
- 1 shallot, minced
- 1 tbsp unsalted butter, melted
- 2 garlic cloves, minced

DIRECTIONS

1. Preheat the sous vide water bath to 125 °F.
2. Put all ingredients in the vacuum bag.
3. Seal the bag, put it into the water bath and set the timer for 25 minutes.
4. Serve immediately as an appetizer or tossed with penne pasta.

313. SHRIMPS CAJUN

25 MIN | 10 MIN | 2

NUTRITION:
CAL: 112 | FAT: 10 | PROTEIN: 12

INGREDIENTS

- 16 shrimps, peeled and deveined
- 1 shallot, minced
- 1 tbsp unsalted butter, melted
- 1 tbsp Cajun seasoning
- 2 garlic cloves, minced
- 1 tbsp lemon juice
- Freshly ground black pepper to taste
- 4 tbsp freshly chopped parsley

DIRECTIONS

1. Preheat the sous vide water bath to 125 °F.
2. Put all ingredients except parsley into the vacuum bag.
3. Seal the bag, put it into the water bath and set the timer for 25 minutes.
4. Serve immediately as an appetizer garnished with the chopped parsley.

314. ORIENTAL SHRIMP SALAD

30 MIN | 10 MIN | 2

NUTRITION:
CAL: 130 | FAT: 6 | PROTEIN: 21

INGREDIENTS

For the shrimps:
- 16 shrimps, peeled and deveined
- 1 tbsp coconut oil
- 2 garlic cloves, minced
- salt and pepper to taste

For the salad:
- ½ cup sliced shallot
- ½ cup chopped parsley

For the dressing:
- ½ cup mayo
- 4 tbsp lime juice
- 1 tsp ginger powder
- 1 tsp curry powder

DIRECTIONS

1. Preheat the sous vide water bath to 125 °F.
2. Put shrimp ingredients into the vacuum bag.
3. Seal the bag, put it into the water bath and set the timer for 25 minutes.
4. In the meantime, cook the dressing. Whisk the dressing ingredients together in a bowl.
5. When the shrimps are ready, let them cool down and mix in the dressing, chopped parsley and sliced shallot.

315. BUTTER SCALLOPS

30 MIN | 10 MIN | 4

NUTRITION:
CAL: 160 | FAT: 9 | PROTEIN: 15

INGREDIENTS

- 16 scallops
- salt and pepper to taste
- 1 tbsp olive oil
- 1 tbsp butter
- Sous Vide Hollandaise sauce

DIRECTIONS

1. Preheat the sous vide water bath to 125 °F.
2. Remove the muscles from scallops and sprinkle them with salt and pepper.
3. Put the scallops into the vacuum bag, add olive oil.
4. Seal the bag, put it into the water bath and set the timer for 30 minutes.
5. When the scallops are ready, dry them with a paper towel and sear in 1 tbsp butter until golden on both sides.
6. Serve with hollandaise sauce.

316. LOBSTER PROVENCAL

1 HOUR | 10 MIN | 4

NUTRITION:
CAL: 345 | FAT: 28 | PROTEIN: 21

INGREDIENTS

- 4 lobster tails
- 10 tbsp butter
- 2 tbsp Provencal herbs
- salt and pepper to taste
- 4 tbsp lemon juice for serving

DIRECTIONS

1. Preheat the sous vide water bath to 135 °F.
2. Remove the shell from the lobster tails; sprinkle them with salt and pepper, season evenly with herbs.
3. Put the tails into the vacuum bag, add butter and seal the bag.
4. Set the timer for 1 hour.
5. Drizzle the cooked lobster tails with the cooking liquid, sprinkle each with 1 tbsp lemon juice and serve.

317. SHRIMP PENNE

25 MIN | 10 MIN | 4

NUTRITION:
CAL: 227 | FAT: 9 | PROTEIN: 14

INGREDIENTS

- 16 shrimps, peeled and deveined
- 1 tbsp lemon zest
- 3 tbsp lemon juice
- salt and pepper to taste
- 2 tbsp butter
- cooked penne pasta for 4 persons

DIRECTIONS

1. Preheat the sous vide water bath to 125 °F.
2. Put the shrimps into the vacuum bag, add butter and salt and pepper to taste.
3. Seal the bag, put it into the water bath and set the timer for 25 minutes.
4. Carefully pour the cooked shrimps together with all cooking liquid into a medium pot.
5. Add the lemon juice, lemon zest and 2 cups dry white wine to the pot.
6. Simmer the mixture until it thickens, pour the sauce over the cooked penne and serve.

318. BLUE CHEESE LOBSTER TAILS

1 HOUR | 10 MIN | 4

NUTRITION:
CAL: 3450 | FAT: 28 | PROTEIN: 21

INGREDIENTS

- 4 lobster tails, shells removed
- 10 tbsp butter
- salt and pepper to taste
- Sous Vide Blue Cheese sauce for serving

DIRECTIONS

1. Preheat the sous vide water bath to 135 °F.
2. Sprinkle the lobster tails with salt and pepper.
3. Put the tails into the vacuum bag and add the butter.
4. Seal the bag and set the timer for 1 hour.
5. Drizzle the cooked lobster tails with the cooking liquid and serve with Sous Vide Blue Cheese sauce.

319. LOBSTER ROLL

1 HOUR | 10 MIN | 4

NUTRITION:
CAL: 310 | FAT: 16 | PROTEIN: 14

INGREDIENTS

- 2 lobster tails, shells removed
- 2 tbsp butter
- salt and pepper to taste
- 4 tbsp mayo
- 1 tbsp lemon juice
- 4 big salad leaves
- 4 hot dog buns

DIRECTIONS

1. Preheat the sous vide water bath to 135 °F.
2. Sprinkle the lobster tails with salt and pepper.
3. Put the tails into the vacuum bag and add the butter.
4. Seal the bag and set the timer for 1 hour.
5. When the time is up, carefully removing the cooked lobster tails, let them cool down a bit and chop them into bite-size pieces.
6. Mix the lobster pieces with mayo, sprinkle with lemon juice.
7. Put 1 big salad leave into each hot dog bun, lay the lobster mayo mixture on each leave and serve.

320. LOBSTER CAJUN SPAGHETTI

1 HOUR | 10 MIN | 4

NUTRITION:
CAL: 320 | FAT: 7 | PROTEIN: 19

INGREDIENTS

- 2 lobster tails, shell removed

DIRECTIONS

1. Preheat the sous vide water bath to 135 °F.

INGREDIENTS

- 1 shallot, minced
- 1 tbsp unsalted butter, melted
- 1 tbsp Cajun seasoning
- 2 garlic cloves, minced
- 4 tbsp lemon juice
- 1 tbsp lemon zest
- salt and pepper to taste
- 2 cups dry white wine
- 4 tbsp freshly chopped parsley
- Cooked spaghetti (for 4 persons)

2. Season the lobster tails with Cajun, salt and pepper, and put into the vacuum bag. Add shallots and butter.
3. Seal the bag, put it into the water bath and set the timer for 1 hour.
4. Carefully chop the cooked lobster tails into bite-size pieces and pour them together with all cooking liquid into a medium pot.
5. Add the lemon juice, lemon zest and 2 cups dry white wine to the pot.
6. Simmer the mixture until it thickens, pour the sauce over the cooked penne and serve with chopped fresh parsley.

321. AROMATIC SHRIMPS

30 MIN | 10 MIN | 2

NUTRITION:
CAL: 285 | FAT: 9 | PROTEIN: 45

INGREDIENTS

- 1-lb large shrimps, peeled and deveined
- 1 tsp olive oil
- any aromatics of your choice
- salt to taste
- 2 tbsp lemon juice (optional)

DIRECTIONS

1. Preheat the sous vide water bath to 125 °F.
2. Season the shrimps with salt and put into the vacuum bag.
3. Add 1 tsp olive oil and aromatics.
4. Seal the bag, put it into the water bath and set the timer for 30 minutes.
5. Serve with any sauce of your choice or sprinkled with lemon juice.

322. DRUNKEN MUSSELS

15 MIN | 10 MIN | 2

NUTRITION:
CAL: 678 | FAT: 32 | PROTEIN: 49

INGREDIENTS

- 2 lbs mussels in their shells
- 1 cup dry white wine
- 2 garlic cloves, chopped
- 4 tbsp butter
- salt to taste

DIRECTIONS

1. Preheat the sous vide water bath to 194 °F.
2. Season the mussels with salt and put into the vacuum bag.
3. Reduce the air in the bag to 30% (70% of vacuum) otherwise the shell won't open.
4. Add dry white wine, garlic cloves and butter
5. Seal the bag, put it into the water bath and set the timer for 15 minutes.
6. Serve sprinkled with lemon juice.

323. GARLIC SQUID

2 HOURS | 10 MIN | 2

NUTRITION:
CAL: 184 | FAT: 11 | PROTEIN: 19

INGREDIENTS

- 4 small clean squids
- 2 garlic cloves, chopped
- 2 tbsp olive oil
- Salt and pepper to taste

DIRECTIONS

1. Preheat the sous vide water bath to 140 °F.
2. Season the squid with salt and put into the vacuum bag.
3. Add olive oil and chopped garlic
4. Seal the bag, put it into the water bath and cook for 2 hours.
5. Serve sprinkled with lemon juice.

324. HONG KONG STYLE SQUID WITH TERIYAKI SAUCE

2 HOURS | 10 MIN | 2

NUTRITION:
CAL: 294 | FAT: 20 | PROTEIN: 18

INGREDIENTS

- 4 small clean squids
- 2 garlic cloves, chopped
- 4 tbsp olive oil
- 4 tbsp Teriyaki sauce
- 1 tbsp sesame seeds
- Salt and pepper to taste

DIRECTIONS

1. Preheat the sous vide water bath to 140 °F.
2. Season the squid with salt and put into the vacuum bag.
3. Add 2 tbsp olive oil and chopped garlic
4. Seal the bag, put it into the water bath and cook for 2 hours.
5. Preheat 2 tbsp olive oil in the skillet, pour the Teriyaki sauce and sear the squids on medium to high heat from both sides until brown.
6. Serve sprinkled with sesame seeds.

325. POACHED HALIBUT

30 MIN | 10 MIN | 2

NUTRITION:
CAL: 687 | FAT: 32 | PROTEIN: 49

INGREDIENTS

- 2 lbs mussels in their shells
- 1 cup dry white wine
- 2 garlic cloves, chopped
- 4 tbsp butter
- Salt to taste

DIRECTIONS

1. Preheat the sous vide water bath to 132°F.
2. Sprinkle the fish fillets with salt and sugar. Place aside minutes.
3. Place the halibut fillets into separate sous vide bags. Add dry white wine.
4. Vacuum seal the bags and submerge in water.
5. Cook the fish 30 minutes.
6. Finishing steps:
7. Make the sauce; simmer white wine and chicken stock in a saucepan until reduced by half.
8. Add the butter and whisk until sauce-like consistency. Season to taste.
9. Remove the fish from the bags and arrange on a plate.
10. Drizzle with sauce and sprinkle with chives.
11. Serve.

326. PUMPKIN SHRIMP

35 MIN | 6 MIN | 4

NUTRITION:
CAL: 185 | FAT: 14 | PROTEIN: 7

INGREDIENTS

- 8 large raw shrimps, peeled and de-veined
- 1 tbsp butter
- Salt and pepper as needed

For Soup:

- 1 lb. pumpkin
- 4 tbsps lime juice
- 2 yellow onions, chopped
- 1-2 small red chilies, finely chopped
- 1 stem of lemon grass, white part only, chopped

DIRECTIONS

1. Prepare your sous vide water bath to 122°F
2. Add the shrimps into your Sous Vide bag with the butter
3. Sprinkle salt and pepper in and seal the bag using the immersion method and cook for 15-35 minutes
4. Peel the pumpkin and remove the seeds. Cut the flesh into 1-inch chunks
5. Add the onion, lemon grass, chili, shrimp paste, sugar and ½ the coconut milk into a food processor. Mix them well
6. Add the onion puree, remaining coconut milk, tamarind paste and water into a separate pot
7. Put the pumpkin to this pot and bring to a boil
8. Once the boiling point is reached, lower down the heat and simmer for 10 minutes

- 1 tsp shrimp paste
- 1 tsp sugar
- 1½ cups coconut milk
- 1 tsp tamarind paste
- 1 cup water
- ½ cup coconut cream
- 1 tbsp fish sauce
- 2 tbsps fresh Thai basil, chopped

9. Remove the shrimps from the bag and add them to the soup
10. Add in the coconut cream, fish sauce, lime juice and basil, stir them well.
11. Serve!

327. PAN TOMATO ESPELETTE SHRIMP

25 MIN | 15 MIN | 2

NUTRITION:
CAL: 341 | FAT: 14 | PROTEIN: 49

INGREDIENTS

- 1 lb. shrimps, peeled and de-veined
- 1 tbsp olive oil
- ¾ tsp Piment d'Espelette*
- salt as needed
- ½ loaf of bread cut up into 1½ inch slices
- 1 garlic clove, halved
- 2 tomatoes, 1 sliced horizontally, the other sliced into wedges
- Flaky sea salt as needed

DIRECTIONS

1. Prepare your sous vide water bath to 122°F
2. Take a large-sized bowl and put the shrimps in it along with the olive oil, a pinch of salt and the Piment d'Espelette
3. Whisk it well and transfer the mixture to a large-sized heavy-duty zip bag. Seal the bag using the immersion method
4. Submerge the bag underwater and cook for 25 minutes
5. Place a grill pan over a medium-high heat for 5 minutes before the shrimps are done
6. Carefully arrange the bread slices in a single layer in your pan and toast them on both sides
7. Once toasted, remove the bread and rub one side of the slices with the garlic clove
8. Rub the tomato halves over your toast as well and divide them between your serving plates
9. Once cooked, remove the bag and drain the liquid
10. Return the grill pan to a medium-high heat and add the shrimp a single layer
11. Sear for 10 seconds and divide the shrimps among the tomato bread
12. Drizzle the olive oil over your shrimps
13. Sprinkle some salt over and serve with the tomato wedges!

328. ASIAN STYLE SALMON

30 MIN | 10 MIN | 4

NUTRITION:
CAL: 314 | FAT: 18 | PROTEIN: 32

INGREDIENTS

- 4, 5oz. salmon fillets
- 2 tbsps rice wine
- 2 tbsps sweet rice wine
- 2 tbsps miso paste

DIRECTIONS

1. Preheat your sous vide water bath to 105°F.
2. Combine rice wine, sweet rice wine, miso paste, Sriracha, and butter in a bowl.
3. Spread the miso paste over salmon.
4. Place the salmon into sous vide bags and vacuum seal.
5. Submerge in water and cook 30 minutes.

- 1 tbsp Sriracha
- 2 tbsp unsalted butter
- 1 tbsp vegetable oil
- 2 spring onions, chopped
- 1 tbsp toasted sesame seeds

6. Finishing steps:
7. Remove the salmon from bag.
8. Heat vegetable oil in a large skillet.
9. Sear salmon on both sides, 1 minute per side.
10. Serve on a plate. Top with chopped spring onion and sesame seeds.

329. PERFECT SCALLOPS IN CITRUS SAUCE

30 MIN | 15 MIN | 4

NUTRITION:
CAL: 583 | FAT: 30 | PROTEIN: 40

INGREDIENTS
- 2 lb. scallops, cleaned
- 2 lemons (1 quartered, 1 zested and juiced)
- 2 tbsps ghee
- 2 shallots, chopped
- ¼ cup pink grapefruit juice
- ¼ cup orange juice
- 2 tbsps acacia honey
- Salt and pepper, to taste

DIRECTIONS
1. Preheat your sous vide water bath to 122°F.
2. Rinse scallops and drain.
3. Season scallops with salt and pepper. Divide scallops between two sous vide bags.
4. Place 2 quarters lemon in each bag and vacuum seal.
5. Cook the scallops 30 minutes.
6. Finishing steps:
7. Make the sauce; heat ghee in a saucepan.
8. Add the chopped shallots and cook until tender 4 minutes.
9. Remove the scallops from the bag and sear on both sides in a lightly greased skillet.
10. Remove the scallops from the skillet.
11. Deglaze the pan with orange juice. Pour in pink grapefruit juice and lemon juice.
12. Add shallots and lemon zest. Simmer until half reduces the sauce. Stir in honey and simmer until thickened.
13. Serve scallops with sauce.

330. SALMON WITH YOGURT DILL SAUCE

20 MIN | 10 MIN | 2

NUTRITION:
CAL: 284 | FAT: 17 | PROTEIN: 26

INGREDIENTS
- 2 salmon fillets
- ½ tsp salt
- ½ tsp pepper
- 2-4 sprigs fresh dill for sauce:
- 1 cup plain Greek yogurt
- 1 tbsp fresh dill, minced
- Juice of 1 lemon

DIRECTIONS
1. Season salmon with salt and pepper. Seal into the bag with dill. Refrigerate ½ hour.
2. Preheat your sous vide water bath to 140°F. Place salmon into the water bath and cook 20 minutes.
3. Meanwhile, prepare the sauce. Combine all sauce ingredients and season to taste.
4. When salmon is cooked, arrange on a plate and top with sauce.

331. HADDOCK ON VEGETABLE SAUCE

70 MIN | 10 MIN | 4

NUTRITION:
CAL: 233 | FAT: 14 | PROTEIN: 19

INGREDIENTS

- 4, 6oz. haddock fillets

Marinade:

- 1 pinch curry
- 1 pinch brown sugar
- 1 pinch fine sea salt
- 5 tbsps olive oil
- 1 sprig thyme, chopped
- 1 tsp lemon juice

Vegetables:

- 1 pinch chili powder
- 1 cucumber
- 3 carrots
- 1 leek, chopped
- 1 tbsp olive oil
- 3 bell peppers, red, yellow, and green
- 1 sweet potato

DIRECTIONS

1. Preheat your sous vide water bath to 130°F.
2. In a sous vide bag combine marinade ingredients.
3. Add haddock fillets and shake to coat the fish
4. Vacuum seal the bag and cook 30 minutes.
5. In a separate sous vide bag, combine all vegetables, with seasonings, and olive oil. Vacuum seal the bag and cook the veggies in sous vide at 185°F 40 minutes.
6. Finishing steps:
7. Open the bags carefully.
8. Heat some olive oil in a large skillet. Cook the fish fillets 2 minutes per side.
9. Serve fish with vegetables.

332. LOBSTER RISOTTO

1 HOUR | 40 MIN | 2

NUTRITION:
CAL: 421 | FAT: 26 | PROTEIN: 20

INGREDIENTS

- 1 lobster, claws and tail separated from the carapace
- 1 carrot, coarsely chopped
- 1 stalk celery, coarsely chopped
- 1 onion, coarsely chopped
- 2 cloves garlic
- 2 sprigs thyme
- 1 bay leaf
- 1 tsp salt
- 1 tsp pepper
- 2 tbsps white wine
- ¼ cup butter
- 1 cup arborio rice
- ¼ cup grated Parmesan

DIRECTIONS

1. Preheat your sous vide water bath to 140°F. Seal lobster tail and claws into a bag. Place in water bath and cook 1 hour. Transfer to an ice bath once cooked.
2. While the lobster is cooking, make the stock. Place the carapace in a pot with the carrot, celery, onion, garlic, thyme, bay leaf, and salt and pepper. Add about 6 cups water. Bring to a boil and simmer 1 hour. Liquid should reduce by half. Strain solids. Stir in wine.
3. When the stock is finished, make the risotto. Melt the butter in a pot. Add rice and toast for about 2 minutes. Pour in ¼ cup of stock. Stir until the liquid is mostly absorbed. Continue adding the stock ¼ cup at a time until you have added 3 cups of stock.
4. Shell lobster and chop into bite-size pieces. Stir into risotto along with Parmesan and pepper to taste. Serve.

333. SOLE MEUNIERE

30 MIN | 30 MIN | 2

NUTRITION:
CAL: 403 | FAT: 25 | PROTEIN: 41

INGREDIENTS

- 4 sole fillets
- 1 tsp salt
- 1 tsp pepper
- ¼ cup butter
- Juice of 1 lemon
- ¼ cup fresh parsley, chopped

DIRECTIONS

1. Preheat your sous vide water bath to 140°F.
2. Season fish with salt and pepper. Seal into the bag and place in water bath. Cook 30 minutes.
3. While fish is cooking, prepare the sauce. Melt butter over low heat and cook until golden brown, being careful not to brown. Remove from heat and stir in lemon juice.
4. Remove fish to the plate and pour sauce over. Top with parsley.

334. SAN FRANCISCO CIOPPINO

30 MIN | 30 MIN | 2

NUTRITION:
CAL: 403 | FAT: 25 | PROTEIN: 41

INGREDIENTS

- 1-lb shrimp, shelled
- 1-lb clams, scrubbed
- 1-lb scallops, trimmed if necessary
- 1-lb halibut fillet, cut into 1-inch pieces
- 1 tbsp olive oil
- 1 onion, chopped
- 1 stalk celery, chopped
- 4 cloves garlic, minced
- 1 can (28 oz) whole tomatoes, crushed
- 1 cup clam juice
- 1 cup chicken broth
- 1 cup white wine
- ¼ cup fresh basil, chopped
- ¼ cup fresh parsley, chopped
- Crusty bread, preferably sourdough, for serving

DIRECTIONS

1. Preheat your sous vide water bath to 140°F. Seal shrimp, clams, scallops, and halibut into separate bags and place in water bath. Remove scallops and clams after 20 minutes and halibut and shrimp after 45 minutes.
2. Meanwhile, prepare the soup. Heat olive oil in the pan. Add onion and celery and cook until onion is translucent, then add garlic. Add tomatoes, clam juice, chicken broth, white wine, and bay leaf and cook until reduced by 1/3.
3. Stir in basil, parsley, and seafood until heated through. Serve with crusty bread.

335. HOME-CURED GRAVLAX

1 HOUR | 20 MIN | 2

NUTRITION:
CAL: 645 | FAT: 16 | PROTEIN: 64

INGREDIENTS

- 1 ½ lb thinly-sliced salmon fillet
- ¼ cup salt
- ¼ cup sugar
- 2 tbsps pepper
- 2 tbsps dried dill
- Crackers or toast for serving

DIRECTIONS

1. Preheat your sous vide water bath to 105°F.
2. Mix together salt, sugar, pepper, and dill. Spread all over salmon.
3. Seal salmon into the bag, being sure to vacuum-tightly, and place in water bath. Cook 1 hour. Transfer to ice bath.
4. Slice thinly and serve on crackers or toast.

336. LINGUINE WITH CLAM SAUCE

1 HOUR | 20 MIN | 2

NUTRITION:
CAL: 340 | FAT: 13 | PROTEIN: 18

INGREDIENTS

- 2 dozen clams, cleaned
- 2 tbsps butter
- 1 tbsp flour
- 3 garlic cloves, minced
- ¼ cup white wine
- 1 tsp pepper
- ¼ cup fresh basil, chopped
- Cooked linguine for serving

DIRECTIONS

1. Preheat your sous vide water bath to 180°F.
2. Seal clams into the bag. Place in water bath and cook 15 minutes.
3. Meanwhile, prepare the sauce. Melt butter in a pan. Add garlic and stir. Add flour and cook until bubbling subsides. Pour in wine, stirring rapidly, until sauce thickens. When clams are cooked, add to sauce along with cooking liquid. Stir in basil.
4. Serve clam sauce on top of cooked linguine.

337. SHRIMP SCAMPI

40 MIN | 10 MIN | 2

NUTRITION:
CAL: 640 | FAT: 28| PROTEIN: 52

INGREDIENTS

- 1-lb shrimp, shelled
- ¼ cup butter
- 3 cloves garlic, minced
- ½ cup white wine
- ¼ cup fresh parsley, chopped
- Juice of half a lemon
- ½ tsp salt
- 1 tsp pepper
- Cooked pasta for serving

DIRECTIONS

1. Preheat your sous vide water bath to 140° F. Seal shrimp into the bag. Place in water bath and cook 30 minutes.
2. Meanwhile, prepare the sauce. Melt butter in pan. Add garlic and cook 30 seconds. Add white wine and lemon juice and cook until reduced by half. When shrimp is cooked, add to pan along with cooking juices. Stir in parsley. Season with salt and pepper.
3. Serve on top of cooked pasta.

338. LAZY MAN'S LOBSTER

1 HOUR | 20 MIN | 1

NUTRITION:
CAL: 603 | FAT: 47 | PROTEIN: 25

INGREDIENTS

- Tail and claws of 1 lobster
- 2 tbsps butter
- 1 clove garlic, minced
- ½ tbsp fresh thyme, minced
- ¼ cup sherry
- ½ tsp salt
- ½ tsp pepper
- ¼ cup heavy cream
- Toast for serving

DIRECTIONS

1. Preheat your sous vide water bath to 140°F. Seal lobster into the bag. Place in water bath and cook 1 hour.
2. Meanwhile, prepare the sauce. Melt butter in a pan. Add garlic and thyme and cook 30 seconds. Add sherry and bring to a boil. Remove from heat and stir in cream. Season with salt and pepper.
3. When lobster is cooked, remove the shell and stir into sauce. Serve with toast.

339. WHOLE RED SNAPPER

1 HOUR | 20 MIN | 1

NUTRITION:
CAL: 314 | FAT: 24 | PROTEIN: 21

INGREDIENTS

- 1 small red snapper, cleaned and gutted
- 1 tsp salt
- 1 tsp pepper
- 4 garlic cloves, crushed
- 2 sprigs rosemary
- 1 lemon, cut into wedges
- 2 tbsps butter, cut into pats

DIRECTIONS

1. Preheat your sous vide water bath to 140°F.
2. Season the fish all over with salt and pepper. Stuff the center of the fish with garlic, rosemary, half the lemon, and butter.
3. Seal into a bag and place in water bath. Cook 60 minutes. Serve with remaining lemon wedges.

340. SWORDFISH PICCATA

30 MIN | 20 MIN | 2

NUTRITION:
CAL: 455 | FAT: 37 | PROTEIN: 26

INGREDIENTS

- 2 swordfish steaks
- 1 tsp salt
- 1 tsp pepper
- 2 tbsps olive oil
- ¼ cup butter
- 2 cloves garlic, minced
- 2 tbsps lemon juice
- 2 tbsps capers, with juice
- 2 tbsps fresh basil, chopped

DIRECTIONS

1. Preheat your sous vide water bath to 140°F.
2. Season swordfish with salt and pepper. Seal into the bag. Place in water bath and cook 30 minutes.
3. Meanwhile, prepare the sauce. Melt butter with olive oil. Add garlic and cook 30 seconds. Stir in lemon juice and capers with juice, then add basil.
4. When swordfish is cooked, transfer to plate. Serve topped with sauce.

341. SOLE FISH WITH BACON

25 MIN | 10 MIN | 2

NUTRITION:
CAL: 228 | FAT: 11 | PROTEIN: 25

INGREDIENTS

- 2, 5oz. sole fish fillets
- 2 tbsps olive oil
- 2 slices bacon
- ½ tbsp lemon juice
- Salt and pepper, to taste

DIRECTIONS

1. Preheat the sous vide water bath to 132°F.
2. Cook the bacon in a non-stick skillet and cook bacon until crispy.
3. Remove the bacon and place aside.
4. Season fish fillets with salt, pepper, and lemon juice. Brush the fish with olive oil.
5. Place the fish in a sous vide bag. Top the fish with the bacon. Vacuum seal the bag.
6. Submerge in a water bath and cook 25 minutes.
7. Finishing steps:
8. Remove the fish from the bag.
9. Serve while warm.

342. TERIYAKI SALMON

15 MIN | 15 MIN | 2

NUTRITION:
CAL: 320 | FAT: 12 | PROTEIN: 39

INGREDIENTS

- 2 (5 oz.) skinless salmon fillets
- ½ cup plus 1 tsp teriyaki sauce
- 4 oz. Chinese egg noodles
- 1 tbsp sesame oil
- 2 tsps soy sauce
- 2 tsps thinly sliced scallions, plus 4 (1-inch) pieces scallion greens, for serving
- 1-inch fresh ginger, peeled and sliced into thin strips
- 4 oz. lettuce, chopped
- 1/8 small red onion, thinly sliced
- 1 tbsp Japanese roasted sesame dressing
- 1 tbsp sesame seeds, toasted

DIRECTIONS

1. Divide ½ cup teriyaki sauce between 2 zip-lock bags.
2. Place 1 salmon fillet in each bag and seal bags using water immersion method.
3. Do not place salmon fillets, but place aside to marinate at room temperature for 15 minutes.
4. Meanwhile, preheat the sous vide water bath to 131ºF.
5. Place the bags in a water bath and cook for 15 minutes.
6. While salmon is cooking, prepare egg noodles according to package instructions.
7. Drain well, return to cooking pot and stir in sesame oil and soy sauce, reserving one tsp
8. Divide pasta between serving plates.
9. Prepare the dipping sauce; combine scallions, ginger, remaining teriyaki sauce and one tsp soy sauce.
10. Also, prepare the salad by combining lettuce and onion with one tbsp roasted sesame dressing.
11. Finishing steps:
12. When the timer goes off, remove salmon from the water bath, reserving cooking liquid.
13. Top the pasta with salmon fillets and drizzle all with reserved cooking liquid.
14. Garnish salmon with sesame seeds and serve with prepared salad and dipping sauce.

343. CRUSTED TUNA FISH

25 MIN | 10 MIN | 4

NUTRITION:
CAL: 262 | FAT: 15 | PROTEIN: 30

INGREDIENTS

- 4, 5oz. tuna fillets
- 3 tbsps all-purpose flour
- 3 tbsps ground almonds
- ½ tbsp butter
- Marinade:
- 1 pinch chili powder
- 1 pinch salt
- 1 pinch black pepper
- 5 tbsps vegetable oil
- 2 tsps lemon juice

DIRECTIONS

1. Preheat the sous vide water bath to 132ºF.
2. Combine the marinade ingredients in a sous vide bag.
3. Add the tuna and vacuum seal.
4. Submerge in a water bath and cook 25 minutes.
5. Finishing steps:
6. Remove the fish from sous vide bag. Pat dries the fish.
7. In a bowl, combine all-purpose flour and almonds. Sprinkle with a pinch of salt.
8. Heat the butter in a large skillet.
9. Coat the tuna with the flour-nut mixture and fry in butter until golden brown.
10. Serve warm.

344. SOUS VIDE LOBSTER WITH TARRAGON

1 HOUR | 10 MIN | 4

NUTRITION:
CAL: 415 | FAT: 36 | PROTEIN: 23

INGREDIENTS

- 1 lb. lobster tail, cleaned
- ¾ cup butter, cubed
- 2 sprigs tarragon
- 1 lime, cut into wedges
- salt, to taste

DIRECTIONS

1. Preheat the sous vide water bath to 134°F.
2. In a sous vide bag, combine lobster tail, cubed butter, tarragon, and salt.
3. Vacuum seal the bag.
4. Submerge the bag in a water bath and cook 1 hour.
5. Finishing steps:
6. Remove the bag from the water bath.
7. Open carefully and transfer the lobster onto a plate.
8. Drizzle the lobster tail with cooking/butter sauce.
9. Serve with lime wedges.

345. CRAB ZUCCHINI ROULADE WITH MOUSSE

10 MIN | 20 MIN | 4

NUTRITION:
CAL: 235 | FAT: 15 | PROTEIN: 23

INGREDIENTS

- 3 lb. crab legs and claws
- 2 tbsps olive oil
- 1 medium zucchini
- salt and pepper, to taste

Moose
- 1 avocado, peeled, pitted
- 1 tbsp Worcestershire sauce
- 2 tbsps crème Fraiche
- 2 tbsps fresh lime juice
- salt, to taste

DIRECTIONS

1. Preheat the sous vide water bath to 185°F.
2. Place the claws and legs in a sous vide bag and vacuum seal.
3. Submerge the bag with content in a water bath. Cook the crab 10 minutes.
4. Finishing steps:
5. Slice the zucchini with a vegetable peeler. This way you will have some skinny strips.
6. Remove the crab from the water bath and crack the shell.
7. Flake the meat and transfer into a bowl. Add olive oil, salt, and pepper, and stir to bind gently.
8. Make the mousse; in a food blender, blend the avocado and crème Fraiche until smooth.
9. Stir in the remaining ingredients and spoon the mixture into piping bag.
10. Arrange the zucchini slices on aluminum foil and fill with the crab meat.
11. Roll up the zucchinis and crab into a log and refrigerate 30 minutes.
12. To serve; cut the roulade into four pieces. Serve onto a plate with some avocado mousse.
13. Enjoy.

346. HERBED PRAWNS

25 MIN | 20 MIN | 4

NUTRITION:
CAL: 657 | FAT: 54 | PROTEIN: 14

INGREDIENTS

Prawns:
- 12 large prawns, cleaned
- 3 tbsps olive oil
- 1 cup basil, chopped
- ½ cup parsley, chopped
- ½ cup dill, chopped
- 1 large organic lemon, sliced
- 2 chili peppers, seeded, chopped

Pasta:
- 1 cup pine nuts
- ¾ cup basil
- ¾ cup parsley
- ¼ cup dill
- ½ cup olive oil
- 2 cloves garlic
- salt and pepper, to taste
- 1 lb. spaghetti, cooked

DIRECTIONS

1. Preheat the sous vide water bath to 134°F.
2. In a bowl, combine all ingredients. Toss to coat the prawns with olive oil and herbs.
3. Transfer the coated prawns into sous vide cooking bag, and top with lemon slices. Vacuum seal the bag.
4. Submerge the prawns in the water bath and cook the prawns 25 minutes.
5. Finishing steps:
6. While the prawns are cooking, make the pesto. In a food blender, blend pine nuts, basil, parsley, dill, and garlic until just smooth. Set the blender to run on low and stream in the oil. Mix 2 minutes.
7. Toss the spaghetti with pesto.
8. Open the bag and spread the prawns over the spaghetti.
9. Serve.

347. CORIANDER-GARLIC SQUIDS

2 HOURS | 20 MIN | 4

NUTRITION:
CAL: 486 | FAT: 43 | PROTEIN: 21

INGREDIENTS

- 4 (4oz.) squids, cleaned
- ¼ cup olive oil
- ¼ cup chopped coriander
- 4 cloves garlic, minced
- 2 chili peppers, chopped
- 2 tsps minced ginger
- ¼ cup vegetable oil
- 1 lemon, cut into wedges
- salt and pepper, to taste

DIRECTIONS

1. Preheat the sous vide water bath to 136°F.
2. Place the squids and 2 tbsps olive oil in a sous vide bags. Season to taste and vacuum seal the bag.
3. Submerge in water and cook 2 hours.
4. Finishing steps:
5. Heat remaining olive oil in a skillet. Add garlic, chili pepper, and ginger and cook 1 minute. Add half the coriander and stir well. Remove from the heat.
6. Remove the squids from the bag.
7. Heat vegetable oil in a skillet, until sizzling hot. Add the squid and cook 30 seconds per side.
8. Transfer the squids onto a plate. Top with garlic-coriander mixture and sprinkle with the remaining coriander.
9. Serve with lemon.

348. ELK STEAK

2 HOURS | 10 MIN | 4

NUTRITION:
CAL: 240 | FAT: 8 | PROTEIN: 37

INGREDIENTS

For Steaks:

- 4 elk steaks
- sea salt, to taste
- bacon Fat, as required
- For Brussels Sprouts:
- 3-4 cups brussels sprouts, trimmed
- 1-2 tbsps coconut oil
- sea salt, to taste
- 1-2 tbsps balsamic vinegar

DIRECTIONS

1. Preheat the sous vide water bath to 130ºF.
2. Season steaks evenly with salt.
3. Into a cooking pouch, add the steaks. Seal pouch tightly after squeezing out the excess air. Place pouch in sous vide bath and set the cooking time for 1-2 hours.
4. Preheat the oven to 400ºF.
5. For the Brussels sprouts: In a pan of boiling water, cook Brussels sprouts for 3 minutes.
6. Drain well and immediately plunge into a large bowl of ice water to cool.
7. After cooling, cut Brussels sprouts in half.
8. Arrange Brussels sprout onto a baking sheet. Top with some coconut oil and sprinkle with salt.
9. Place baking sheet in oven and bake for 2 minutes.
10. Remove baking sheet from oven and toss sprouts well.
11. Bake for a further 20 minutes, tossing once midway.
12. Remove sprouts from oven and transfer into a bowl with the vinegar and toss to coat.
13. Remove steak pouch from sous vide bath and carefully open it. Remove steaks from pouch. With paper towels, pat steaks completely dry.
14. In a cast iron skillet, heat bacon Fat and sear steaks for 1 minute per side.
15. Serve steaks alongside Brussels sprouts.

349. LAMB STEAKS

6 HOURS | 10 MIN | 4

NUTRITION:
CAL: 668 | FAT: 58 | PROTEIN: 35

INGREDIENTS

- 4, 7-oz lamb leg steaks
- 2/3 cup olive oil, divided as ½ cup and the remaining oil
- 4 garlic cloves, crushed
- 1 sprig thyme
- 1 sprig rosemary
- 1 bay leaf

DIRECTIONS

1. In a large bowl, mix together ½ cup of oil, garlic, the herbs and the bay leaf.
2. Add steaks to bowl and coat generously with mixture.
3. Refrigerate for 1-4 hours.
4. Preheat the sous vide water bath to 144ºF.
5. Into a cooking pouch, add steaks and remaining oil. Seal pouch tightly after squeezing out the excess air. Place pouch in sous vide bath and set the cooking time for 6 hours.
6. Remove pouch from sous vide bath and carefully open it. Remove steaks from pouch. With paper towels, pat steaks completely dry.
7. Heat a cast iron skillet over high heat, and sear steaks until browned from both sides.
8. Serve immediately.

350. LAMB SWEETBREADS

45 MIN | 15 MIN | 4

NUTRITION:
CAL: 347 | FAT: 17 | PROTEIN: 23

INGREDIENTS

- 4 cups milk, divided
- 10 oz lamb sweetbreads
- 3 ½ oz soft flour
- 1-oz dried rosemary, crushed
- salt and freshly ground black pepper, to taste
- oil, as required

DIRECTIONS

1. Into a large bowl, add 2 cups of milk and the lamb sweetbreads, and allow to soak for 8 hours.
2. Preheat the sous vide water bath to 144ºF.
3. Drain lamb sweetbreads.
4. Into a large pan, add 4 cups of water and bring to a boil.
5. Add lamb sweetbreads and cook for 10 seconds.
6. Remove lamb sweetbreads from boiling water and immediately plunge into a large bowl of ice water to cool.
7. After cooling, peel off any excess sinew.
8. Into a cooking pouch, add lamb sweetbreads and the remaining 2 cups of milk. Seal pouch tightly after squeezing out the excess air. Place pouch in sous vide bath and set the cooking time for 40 minutes.
9. Remove pouch from sous vide bath and carefully open it. Remove lamb sweetbreads from pouch. With paper towels, pat lamb sweetbreads completely dry.
10. In a bowl, mix together the flour, rosemary, salt and black pepper.
11. Roll lamb sweetbreads evenly with flour mixture.
12. In a cast iron pan, heat some oil and fry and pan fry lamb sweetbreads until crisp.
13. Serve immediately.

351. VENISON STEAKS

36 HOURS | 20 MIN | 4

NUTRITION:
CAL: 264 | FAT: 12 | PROTEIN: 40

INGREDIENTS

For Steaks:

- 1-lb venison blade steak
- 2 shallots, roughly chopped
- 6 cloves garlic, roughly chopped
- 3 chili peppers, seeded and roughly chopped
- salt and freshly ground black pepper, to taste
- 1 tbsp avocado oil

For Gravy:

- reserved cooking liquid mixture
- 2 tbsps butter
- 1 tsp all-purpose flour
- 1 cup beef broth
- For Garnish:
- black mustard blossoms
- micro green herbs
- red amaranth

DIRECTIONS

1. For the steak:
2. To a large bowl, add the steak, shallots, garlic, chili peppers, salt, and pepper, and deplete toss to coat well.
3. Refrigerate for at least 30 minutes.
4. Preheat the sous vide water bath to 137ºF.
5. Into a cooking pouch, add steak mixture. Seal pouch tightly after squeezing out the excess air. Place pouch in sous vide bath and place a weight over pouch. Set the cooking time for 36 hours.
6. Remove pouch from sous vide bath and carefully open it. Remove steak from pouch, reserving cooking liquid mixture. With paper towels, pat steak completely dry and set aside to rest briefly.
7. In a skillet, heat 1 tbsp of avocado oil and sear steak for 1 minute per side.
8. Transfer steak onto a plate and keep aside.
9. For the gravy:
10. In in a food processor, add the reserved cooking liquid mixture and pulse until a smooth paste is formed.
11. In a heavy-bottomed pan, melt butter. Stir in flour and paste cook until browned slightly, stirring continuously.
12. Reduce heat and stir in paste and broth. Bring to a boil and remove from heat.
13. Cut steak into desired slices and decorate with favorite garnish.
14. Serve with gravy.

352. RABBIT LEGS

⏲ 4 HOURS   ⏱ 10 MIN   🍴 2

NUTRITION:
CAL: 130 | FAT: 15 | PROTEIN: 8

INGREDIENTS

- 2 rabbit legs
- 1 tsp salt
- ½ tsp freshly ground black pepper
- 1 sprig rosemary
- 2 tbsps olive oil

DIRECTIONS

1. Preheat the sous vide water bath to 145°F.
2. Season rabbit legs with salt and pepper.
3. Into a cooking pouch, add the rabbit legs, rosemary and olive oil. Seal pouch tightly after squeezing out the excess air. Place pouch in sous vide bath and set the cooking time for 4 hours.
4. Preheat broiler to high. Line a rimmed baking sheet with a piece of foil.
5. Remove pouch from sous vide bath and carefully open it. Remove rabbit legs from pouch. With paper towels, pat rabbit legs completely dry.
6. Arrange rabbit legs onto prepare baking sheet. Broil for 5 minutes.
7. Serve immediately.

353. OSSO BUCO

⏲ 72 HOURS   ⏱ 20 MIN   🍴 2

NUTRITION:
CAL: 257 | FAT: 15 | PROTEIN: 28

INGREDIENTS

- 2 veal shanks
- salt and freshly ground black pepper, to taste
- flour, as required
- olive oil, as required
- butter, as required
- 1 onion, chopped
- 2 oz pancetta, chopped
- 1 glass dry white wine
- ½ cup concentrated veal broth
- 2 tsps tomato paste
- For Gremolata:
- fresh flat leaf parsley, as required
- 1 fresh sprig rosemary
- 2 fresh sage leaves
- fresh lemon zest, as required
- 1 garlic clove

DIRECTIONS

1. Preheat the sous vide water bath to 143°F.
2. With a sharp knife, make 1-inch cuts in the around the shanks.
3. With paper towels, pat shanks and season with salt and black pepper.
4. Dust each shank with flour evenly.
5. In a frying pan, heat olive oil and sear shanks until browned from both sides.
6. Transfer shanks onto a plate. Discard most of the oil from the pan.
7. In the same pan, melt butter and sauté onion until translucent.
8. Add pancetta and sauté until slightly golden.
9. Stir in wine and cook until half the wine is absorbed.
10. Stir in veal broth and tomato paste, then remove from heat.
11. Into a large cooking ouch, place shanks and wine mixture. Seal pouch tightly after squeezing out the excess air. Place pouch in sous vide bath and set the cooking time for 72 hours.
12. Meanwhile for gremolata:
13. in a food processor, add all ingredients listed under gremolata piece above, and pulse until minced finely.
14. Remove pouch from sous vide bath and carefully open it. Remove shanks from pouch.
15. Transfer shanks with mixture onto serving platter. Top with gremolata and serve.

354. RABBIT LOIN

4 HOURS | 20 MIN | 6

NUTRITION:
CAL: 413 | FAT: 23 | PROTEIN: 55

INGREDIENTS

- 6 tbsps olive oil, divided 4 + 2
- 1-oz fresh flat leaf parsley, chopped
- ½ oz fresh dill, chopped
- 2 tbsps Dijon mustard
- 1 tsp apple cider vinegar
- 1 tsp garlic, minced
- ½ tsp freshly ground black pepper
- ¼ tsp ground ginger
- pinch of salt
- 4, 8-oz rabbit loins

DIRECTIONS

1. Preheat the sous vide water bath to 150°F.
2. Into a bowl, add all ingredients except 2 tbsps of oil and the rabbit loins. Mix well.
3. Add rabbit loins and coat generously with mixture.
4. In 4 separate cooking pouches, divide rabbit loins with marinade. Seal pouches tightly after squeezing out the excess air. Place pouches in sous vide bath and set the cooking time for 4 hours.
5. Remove pouches from sous vide bath and open them. Remove rabbit loins from pouches. With paper towels, pat rabbit loins completely dry.
6. In a skillet, heat remaining oil and sear the loins until golden brown from both sides.

355. FOIE GRAS

20 MIN | 10 MIN | 2

NUTRITION:
CAL: 125 | FAT: 15 | PROTEIN: 6

INGREDIENTS

- Foie gras, cut into 1¼-inch pieces across lobe *
- Sea salt, to taste

DIRECTIONS

1. Preheat the sous vide water bath to 137°F.
2. Into a cooking pouch, add foie gras. Seal pouch tightly after squeezing out the excess air. Place pouch in sous vide bath and set the cooking time for 15-20 minutes.
3. Remove pouch from sous vide bath and carefully open it. Remove foie gras from pouch. With paper towels, pat foie gras completely dry.
4. Season with salt and serve immediately.

356. CURED SALMON

1 HOUR | 8 MIN | 2

NUTRITION:
CAL: 306 | FAT: 10 | PROTEIN: 36

INGREDIENTS

- 2 salmon fillets (6 oz each)
- 8 tbsps sugar
- 8 tbsps salt
- 2 tsps smoke flavor powder (optional)

DIRECTIONS

1. Take 2 bowls and place a fillet in each bowl.
2. Divide the sugar, salt and smoke flavor powder among the bowls. Mix well. Set aside for 30 minutes.
3. Rinse the fillets in water.
4. Place in a large Ziploc bag. Vacuum seal the pouch.
5. Submerge the pouch in the water bath and adjust the timer for 30 minutes.
6. Just before the timer goes off, make an ice water bath by filling a large bowl with water and ice.
7. When done, remove the pouch from the water bath and immerse in the ice water bath. When cooled, remove the pouch from the water bath
8. Remove the fillets from the pouch and serve.

357. FROG LEGS WITH RISOTTO

45 MIN | 25 MIN | 4

NUTRITION:
CAL: 590 | FAT: 37 | PROTEIN: 22

INGREDIENTS

For Frogs Legs:
- 4 lbs frog legs
- ½ cup plus 3 tbsps butter, divided
- 5 chicken broth ice cubes
- 5 fresh thyme sprigs
- 8 garlic cloves, minced
- 2 lemon slices
- 1 bay leaf
- ½ tsp red pepper flakes, crushed
- salt and ground black pepper, to taste
- 3 tbsps grape seed oil

For Risotto:
- 4-6 cups vegetable broth
- 15 oz pure, unsweetened carrot juice
- 3 tbsps grapeseed oil
- 1½ cups rice
- 1 medium onion, minced
- 1 cup chardonnay white wine
- 1 cup bagged frozen carrot/pea mix
- ½ cup mascarpone cheese

DIRECTIONS

1. Preheat the sous vide water bath to 135°F.
2. With a sharp knife, cut between the doubled frog legs to separate into two.
3. Into a cooking pouch, add frog leg pieces, ½ cup of butter, thyme, garlic, bay leaf, red pepper flakes, salt and black pepper. Seal pouch tightly after squeezing out the excess air. Place pouch in sous vide bath and set the cooking time for 45 minutes.
4. Remove pouch from sous vide bath and carefully open it. Remove frog pieces from pouch. With paper towels, pat frog pieces completely dry.
5. In a large sauté pan, heat oil and remaining butter over medium-high heat, and sear frog pieces until browned slightly.
6. Meanwhile for risotto:
7. In a pan, add broth and carrot juice and bring to a boil. Reduce heat to low and allow to simmer.
8. In a large heavy-bottomed pan, heat oil over medium heat and sauté risotto rice and onion for 2 minutes.
9. Add wine and cook until absorbed, stirring continuously.
10. Add hot broth mixture ½ cup at a time, and cook until absorbed, stirring continuously. (This process will take 15 minutes.)
11. Add carrots/peas and cook for 3 minutes, stirring continuously.
12. Remove from heat and stir in mascarpone cheese, salt and black pepper.
13. Divide risotto onto serving plates. Top with frog meat and serve immediately.

358. OXTAIL OVER VEGETABLE MASH

21 HOURS | 15 MIN | 4

NUTRITION:
CAL: 497 | FAT: 20 | PROTEIN: 33

INGREDIENTS

For Oxtail:
- 8 medium whole onions, unpeeled
- 1 full garlic bulb, unpeeled
- 1 cup white wine
- ½ cup Demerara sugar
- 1/8 tsp ground cloves
- pinch of cayenne pepper
- salt and freshly cracked black pepper, to taste
- 4 lbs oxtail pieces

For Sauce:
- 2 tbsps butter

DIRECTIONS

1. Preheat oven to 392°F and line a baking sheet with a piece of foil.
2. Arrange onions and garlic bulb onto prepared baking sheet.
3. Roast for 50 minutes. After 15 minutes, remove garlic bulb and onions from oven and keep aside.
4. After cooling, squeeze onion pulp and garlic pulp from the skins and retain.
5. Into a small pan, add wine, sugar, cloves, cayenne pepper, salt, black pepper, onion and garlic pulp and bring to a boil. Simmer for 10-15 minutes.
6. With an immersion blender, blend the onion mixture into a thick paste. Remove from heat and keep aside cool completely.
7. Preheat the sous vide water bath to 180°F.
8. Into a cooking pouch, add oxtail pieces and onion puree and freeze for 15 minutes.
9. Remove from freezer and seal pouch tightly after squeezing out the excess air. Place pouch in sous vide bath and set the cooking time for 20 hours.

- 4 medium carrots, peeled and cut into half-moons
- 2 celery sticks, finely chopped
- 1 medium leek, thinly sliced
- 10 closed cup mushrooms, thinly sliced
- 2 tsps English mustard
- 3 cups cooking liquid from oxtail

10. Remove pouch from sous vide bath and carefully open it. Remove oxtail pieces from pouch.
11. Through a sieve, strain cooking liquid into a bowl and refrigerate to cool. (Reserve 4 tbsps of this onion puree separately for the sauce.)
12. After cooling, remove solid Fat from top.
13. Remove meat from bones and, using 2 forks, shred. Remove any large chunks of Fa

For the sauce:

14. In a large pan, melt butter and sauté carrots, celery and leek until tender.
15. Add oxtail meat, mustard, cooking liquid, and onion puree, and bring to a boil.
16. Reduce heat and simmer, covered, for 10-15 minutes.
17. Add mushrooms and simmer for 5 minutes.
18. Stir in cayenne pepper, salt and black pepper, and remove from heat.
19. This oxtail mixture is great served over mashed potatoes. Add wine and cook until absorbed, stirring continuously.
20. Add hot broth mixture ½ cup at a time, and cook until absorbed, stirring continuously. (This process will take 15 minutes.)
21. Add carrots/peas and cook for 3 minutes, stirring continuously.
22. Remove from heat and stir in mascarpone cheese, salt and black pepper. Divide risotto onto serving plates. Top with frog meat and serve immediately.

359. SOUS VIDE MUSHROOMS

30 MIN | 8 MIN | 6

NUTRITION:
CAL: 100 | FAT: 7 | PROTEIN: 6

INGREDIENTS

- 2 lbs mushrooms of your choice
- 4 tbsps olive oil
- 4 tsps minced fresh thyme
- 1 tsp salt or to taste
- 1 tsp freshly ground pepper, or to taste
- 4 tbsps soy sauce
- 2 tbsps vinegar of your choice

DIRECTIONS

1. Preheat the sous vide water bath to 176°F.
2. Place mushrooms in a bowl. Add the other ingredients and stir until well coated.
3. Transfer into a large vacuum-seal pouch or Ziploc bag.
4. Vacuum seal the pouch.
5. Submerge the pouch in the water bath. Set the timer for 30 minutes.
6. When the timer is off, remove bag from the water bath.
7. Set aside to cool.
8. Open the pouch and transfer into a bowl. Serve.

360. SOUS VIDE CORN

30 MIN | 8 MIN | 6

NUTRITION:
CAL: 174 | FAT: 7 | PROTEIN: 4

INGREDIENTS

- 2 ears corn
- salt to taste
- 1 tbsp butter + extra to serve
- handful cilantro, chopped
- 1 or 2 scallions, chopped
- dried red chilies to taste
- 4 or 5 cloves garlic, minced

DIRECTIONS

1. Preheat the sous vide water bath to 183ºF.
2. Add all the ingredients including the aromatics into a vacuum-seal pouch or Ziploc bag. Vacuum seal the pouch.
3. Submerge the pouch in the water bath and fix on the edge of the water bath with clips.
4. Set timer for 30 minutes.
5. Remove corn from the pouch and discard the rest of the ingredients.
6. Brush with more butter and serve.
7. Open the pouch and transfer into a bowl. Serve.

361. TOMATO SUSHI

1 HOUR | 15 MIN | 24

NUTRITION:
CAL: 21 | FAT: 3 | PROTEIN: 2

INGREDIENTS

- 6 Roma tomatoes
- 2 tbsps soy sauce
- 2 cups water
- 6 nori sheets
- ½ tsp salt

For sushi rice:

- 2 cups uncooked glutinous white rice, rinsed
- ½ cup rice vinegar
- ½ tsp salt
- 3 cups water
- 4 tbsps sugar

DIRECTIONS

For tomatoes:

1. Preheat the sous vide water bath to 140ºF.
2. Add 4 nori sheets, soy sauce, water, and salt in a large saucepan over medium heat.
3. Simmer until it has reduced to half its original quantity. Turn off the heat.
4. Cut off a slice from the top of the tomatoes. Make cuts in the shape of an "X" with a paring knife.
5. Place a pan with water over high heat. When it begins to boil, add the tomatoes and let it cook for about 30 to 60 seconds. Remove the tomatoes and place in a bowl filled with ice and water.
6. Peel the tomatoes. Cut each into quarters. Discard the seeds.
7. Place the tomatoes in the nori water. Transfer into a vacuum-seal pouch or Ziploc bag. Vacuum seal the pouch.
8. Submerge the pouch in water bath and adjust the timer for 1 hour.

To make sushi rice:

9. Add vinegar, salt, and sugar into a saucepan over medium heat. Stir frequently until sugar dissolves. Turn off the heat.
10. Add rice and water into a pot over high heat. When it begins to boil, reduce the heat and cover with a lid. Simmer until all liquid is absorbed.
11. Add sugar solution and mix well. Turn off the heat.

To assemble:

12. Cut the remaining nori sheets into 24 strips. Remove the pouch from the water bath.
13. When the rice is cool enough to handle, divide the rice into 24 equal portions and shape into sushi.
14. Place a piece of tomato on each sushi. Wrap the sushi along with the tomato with a nori strip and place on a serving platter.
15. Serve.

362. LEMON-BUTTER SHRIMP

30 MIN | 8 MIN | 8

NUTRITION:
CAL: 174 | FAT: 8 | PROTEIN: 23

INGREDIENTS

- 2 lbs large shrimp, peeled, deveined
- 16 strips (½ inch each) lemon zest
- 4 oz chilled butter, cut into 8 slices
- 1 tsp creole seasoning or to taste + extra to serve
- 6 sprigs fresh thyme

DIRECTIONS

1. Preheat the sous vide water bath to 135°F.
2. Place shrimp in a bowl. Sprinkle creole seasoning on top and toss well.
3. Transfer into a large Ziploc bag or vacuum-seal pouch. Spread the shrimp in a single layer.
4. Use 2 pouches, if required.
5. Scatter lemon zest, butter, and thyme all over the Shrimp and vacuum seal the pouch.
6. Submerge the pouch in water bath and adjust the timer for 30 minutes.
7. When the timer goes off, remove the pouch from the water bath.
8. Transfer the shrimp onto a serving platter.
9. Sprinkle some more creole seasoning and serve.

363. FRESH VEGETABLES CONFIT

2 HOURS | 8 MIN | 12

NUTRITION:
CAL: 717 | FAT: 77 | PROTEIN: 6

INGREDIENTS

- 1 cup peeled pearl onions
- 1 cup peeled garlic cloves
- 4 cups olive oil
- 2 cups halved, deseeded mini peppers

Garnish:

- 10 to 12 oz spreadable goat cheese
- Ciabatta bread slices, as required, toasted
- Salt to taste
- Fresh herbs of your choice

DIRECTIONS

1. Preheat the sous vide water bath to 185°F.
2. Place garlic a Ziploc bag or vacuum-seal pouch. Pour 1½ cups oil into the pouch.
3. Add mini peppers into a second Ziploc bag. Pour 3 cups oil into the pouch.
4. Add pearl onions into a third Ziploc bag. Pour 1½ cups oil into the pouch.
5. Vacuum seal the pouches.
6. Immerse the pouches in water bath and adjust the timer for 1½ hours. When the timer goes off, remove the pouches from the water bath and place in chilled water for 30 minutes.
7. Spread goat cheese over toasted ciabatta slices. Top with vegetables from each pouch. Garnish with fresh herbs and serve

8. DRINKS AND DESSERTS

364. LEMON & BLUEBERRY CRÈME BRULÉE

45 MIN | 10 MIN | 6

NUTRITION:
CAL: 658 | FAT: 48 | PROTEIN: 6

INGREDIENTS

- 6 large egg yolks
- 1 1/3 cup superfine sugar
- 3 cups heavy whipping cream
- Zest of 2 lemons
- 4 tbsps freshly squeezed lemon juice
- 1 tsp vanilla extract
- 1 cup fresh blueberries

DIRECTIONS

1. Preheat the sous vide water bath to 195ºF.
2. Take an electric mixer and mix in egg yolks and sugar until you have a creamy mixture. Set it aside.
3. Take a medium-sized saucepan and place it over medium heat, add the cream and heat it.
4. Add the lemon zest, juice, vanilla and simmer for 4-5 minute over low heat.
5. Remove the cream mixture from heat and allow it to cool. Once cooled, transfer a small amount into egg mixture and mix well.
6. Add in the remaining cream mixture to the egg and stir.
7. Divide the blueberries among six mini mason jars and pour the egg cream mixture evenly over the six jars filled with blueberries.
8. Tightly seal the lid and submerge underwater, cook for 45 minutes.
9. Remove the jars from the water and chill for 5 hours.
10. Caramelize a layer of sugar on top using a blowtorch and serve!

365. BUTTER & SEA SALT RADISH

45 MIN | 15 MIN | 4

NUTRITION:
CAL: 96 | FAT: 9 | PROTEIN: 2

INGREDIENTS

- 1 lb. halved radishes
- 3 tbsps unsalted butter
- 1 tsp sea salt
- ½ tsp freshly ground black pepper

DIRECTIONS

1. Preheat the sous vide water bath to 180ºF.
2. Take a medium-sized resealable bag and add all the listed Ingredients: to the bag
3. Seal it using the immersion method and let it cook underwater for about 45 minutes.
4. Once cooked, remove the bag and transfer the contents to a platter.
5. Serve!

366. BANANA & PEANUT BUTTER FROZEN BITES

30 MIN | 0 MIN | 6

NUTRITION:
CAL: 167 | FAT: 8 | PROTEIN: 4

INGREDIENTS

- 3 bananas
- 3 tbsps peanut butter
- 3 tbsps dark chocolate chips

DIRECTIONS

1. Preheat the sous vide water bath to 140ºF.
2. Slice the bananas into ½ inch slices and add to a resealable bag.
3. Add the peanut butter and dark chocolate chips and seal using the immersion method.
4. Submerge underwater and let it cook for 30 minutes.
5. Stir the contents and chill in popsicle molds
6. Pop out of the molds and serve!

367. PUMPKIN PIE JARS

1 HOUR | 10 MIN | 6

NUTRITION:
CAL: 276 | FAT: 7 | PROTEIN: 8

INGREDIENTS

- 1 large can pumpkin pie filling
- 1 egg + 3 egg yolks
- 2 tbsps flour
- ½ tsp salt
- 1 tbsp pumpkin pie spice
- 1 can evaporated milk
- ½ cup white sugar
- ½ cup brown sugar
- Whipped cream and candied nuts for garnishing

DIRECTIONS

1. Preheat the sous vide water bath to 175°F.
2. Add 1 large can of pumpkin pie filling, 2 tbsps of flour, ½ tsp of salt, 1 tbsp of pumpkin pie spice, 1 egg and 3 egg yolks alongside 1 can of evaporated milk.
3. Whisk them well.
4. Pour the mixture into 6.4-oz jars and seal them tightly.
5. Submerge underwater and cook for 1 hour.
6. Once done, remove the jars and chill for 8 hours.
7. Garnish with whipped cream and candied nuts.
8. Serve.

368. PUMPKIN CRÈME BRULÉE

1 HOUR | 10 MIN | 5

NUTRITION:
CAL: 362 | FAT: 33 | PROTEIN: 15

INGREDIENTS

- 1 cup milk
- 1 cup heavy whipping cream
- 3 whole eggs
- 3 egg yolks
- ½ cup pumpkin puree
- ¼ cup maple syrup
- ½ tsp pumpkin spice
- A pinch of salt
- Granulated sugar

DIRECTIONS

1. Preheat the sous vide water bath to 167°F.
2. Take a large bowl and add the milk, heavy cream, 3 whole eggs, 3 egg yolks, ½ cup of pumpkin puree, ¼ cup of maple syrup, ½ tsp of pumpkin spice and a pinch of salt.
3. Whisk them well and keep whisking until it is combined and smooth.
4. Pour the mixture into 6.4-oz mason jars.
5. Place the lid loosely and cook for 1 hour underwater. Allow them to chill.
6. Spread a thin layer of sugar on top of the custard and caramelize with a blowtorch.
7. Serve!

369. PEACH COBBLER

3 HOURS | 15 MIN | 6

NUTRITION:
CAL: 374 | FAT: 16 | PROTEIN: 3

INGREDIENTS

- 1 cup self-rising flour
- 1 cup granulated sugar
- 1 cup whole milk
- 1 tsp vanilla extract
- 8 tbsps unsalted melted butter
- 2 cups roughly chopped peaches

DIRECTIONS

1. Preheat the sous vide water bath to 195°F.
2. Prepare 6 half-pint canning jars by greasing the jars with melted butter
3. Mix the flour and sugar in a large bowl. Then mix in milk and vanilla.
4. Stir in butter and peaches.
5. Divide the batter between jars and wipe sides, seal gently
6. Submerge underwater and cook for 3 hours.
7. Transfer the jars to a cooling rack, allow them to cool and serve!
8. Serve chilled with a topping of fresh fruit compote.

370. AMARETTO CRÈME BRULÉE

1 HOUR | 30 MIN | 12

NUTRITION:
CAL: 390 | FAT: 31 | PROTEIN: 6

INGREDIENTS

- 12 egg yolks
- ¾ cup sugar
- ½ tsp salt
- 2 oz Amaretto
- 1-quart heavy cream

DIRECTIONS

1. Preheat the sous vide water bath to 181°F.
2. Add the salt, and egg yolks to a bowl and mix them well.
3. Add the Amaretto liqueur to egg mixture and combine them well.
4. Add in the heavy cream and whisk.
5. Then, strain the whole mixture into a bowl through a metal mesh strainer.
6. Allow the mixture to rest. Then fill up the mason jars, making sure that there is ½ inch space on top
7. Gently tighten the lid and submerge underwater.
8. Cook for 1 hour.
9. Chill in your fridge for 2 hours and sprinkle sugar on top. Broil the sugar using a blowtorch!

371. CHEESECAKE

1.5 HOUR | 10 MIN | 6

NUTRITION:
CAL: 308 | FAT: 22 | PROTEIN: 8

INGREDIENTS

- 12 oz. cream cheese at room temperature
- ½ cup sugar
- ¼ cup creole cream cheese
- 2 eggs
- Zest of 1 lemon
- ½ tbsp vanilla extract

DIRECTIONS

1. Preheat the sous vide water bath to 176°F.
2. Take a bowl and add both cream cheeses, and sugar and whisk them well
3. Gradually add the eggs one by one and keep beating until well combined. Add the zest and vanilla and mix well.
4. Pour the cheesecake mixture into 6 different jars of 6 oz and distribute evenly
5. Seal the jars with a lid.
6. Place the jars underwater and let them cook for 90 minutes.
7. Once done, remove from the water bath and chill until they are cooled
8. Serve chilled with a topping of fresh fruit compote.

372. BANANA BREAD

3.5 HOURS | 30 MIN | 9

NUTRITION:
CAL: 335 | FAT: 11 | PROTEIN: 6

INGREDIENTS

- ½ cup butter
- ½ cup brown sugar
- ½ cup white sugar
- 2 eggs
- 1 tsp vanilla
- 1 tsp salt
- 3 tbsps milk

DIRECTIONS

1. Preheat the sous vide water bath to 190°F.
2. Put the butter, white and brown sugar to a warm skillet and mix them well.
3. Remove the heat and allow the mixture to cool, add the egg, vanilla, milk, and sugar.
4. Stir well until the sugar has dissolved.
5. Put the bananas, flour, baking soda, and salt and whisk them well.
6. Transfer the mixture into 4-oz mason jars and gently tighten the lid.
7. Cook for 3 and a ½ hours underwater.

- 3 very ripe mashed bananas
- ½ tsp baking soda
- 2 cups all-purpose flour

8. Open the lid and enjoy!

373. BLUEBERRY CLAFOUTIS

1 HOUR | 5 MIN | 4

NUTRITION:
CAL: 116 | FAT: 11 | PROTEIN: 4

INGREDIENTS

- 1 egg
- ¼ cup heavy cream
- ¼ cup almond flour
- 1 tbsp sugar
- 2 tsps coconut flour
- ¼ tsp baking powder
- ¼ tsp vanilla extract
- ½ cup fresh blueberries
- Granulated sugar for topping 2 cups all-purpose flour

DIRECTIONS

1. Preheat the sous vide water bath to 185°F.
2. Add all the listed ingredients except the blueberries to small mixing bowl and mix well.
3. Grease the mason jars with cooking spray and divide the batter among the jars
4. Top each jar with 2 tbsps of blueberries and lightly seal them.
5. Cook for 1 hour underwater.
6. Once done, remove from the water bath and sprinkle a bit of sugar on top and serve!

374. COCONUT CONGEE & CINNAMON SUGAR

1.5 HOUR | 45 MIN | 6

NUTRITION:
CAL: 332 | FAT: 32 | PROTEIN: 5

INGREDIENTS

- 1 cup short grain rice
- 4 cups water
- 4 cups coconut milk
- 1 cup cinnamon sugar
- 1 tbsp pumpkin pie spice
- A pinch of salt

DIRECTIONS

1. Preheat the sous vide water bath to 190°F.
2. Add the rice, water, coconut milk, sugar and pumpkin pie spice to a resealable bag and seal them using the immersion method.
3. Cook for 1½ hours underwater.
4. Remove the congee (The Sous Vide rice) and season with salt
5. Serve!

375. MINI CHEESECAKES

25 MIN | 45 MIN | 3

NUTRITION:
CAL: 203 | FAT: 12 | PROTEIN: 16

INGREDIENTS

- 3 eggs
- 5 tbsp cottage cheese
- ½ cup cream cheese
- 4 tbsp sugar
- ½ tsp vanilla extract

DIRECTIONS

1. Preheat the sous vide water bath to 175°F.
2. Place all the ingredients in a mixing bowl. Beat with an electric mixer for a few minutes, until soft and smooth. Divide the mixture between 3 mason jars., Seal the jars and submerge the bag in water bath. Set the timer for 25 minutes.
3. Once the timer has stopped, remove the jars. Chill until ready to serve.

376. SALTED CARAMEL ICE CREAM

30 MIN | 60 MIN | 6

NUTRITION:
CAL: 516 | FAT: 30 | PROTEIN: 5

INGREDIENTS

- 1 ½ cup sugar
- 1 ¾ cups heavy cream
- 1 tsp sea salt
- 1 cup whole milk
- 5 egg yolks
- 1 tsp vanilla bean paste
- Pinch of salt
- Tools Required :Ice Cream Maker

DIRECTIONS

1. Preheat the sous vide water bath to 180°F.
2. Heat up 1 cup of sugar in a large-sized nonstick saucepan, making sure to keep stirring it until it begins to melt.
3. Swirl until the sugar has melted and is slightly browned.
4. Whisk in 1 cup of heavy cream and cook until the mixture is smooth.
5. Stir in salt and remove the heat and allow the mixture to cool down.
6. Take a food processor and add the egg yolks, vanilla, ¾ cup of cream, ½ cup of sugar, milk and purée for 30 seconds.
7. Transfer the mixture to a resealable zip bag and seal using the immersion method.
8. Cook for 30 minutes underwater.
9. Stir caramel* into the bag and allow it to chill overnight.
10. Allow the mixture to cool. Churn the mixture in ice cream maker
11. Freeze and serve!

377. SWEET CORN GELATO

30 MIN | 60 MIN | 6

NUTRITION:
CAL: 460 | FAT: 26 | PROTEIN: 10

INGREDIENTS

- 4 ears shucked corn
- 3 cups whole milk
- 1 cup heavy cream
- 1 cup granulated sugar
- 1 tsp salt
- 6 large egg yolks
- ¼ cup crème fraiche

DIRECTIONS

1. Preheat the sous vide water bath to 180°F.
2. Heat up 1 cup of sugar in a large-sized nonstick saucepan, making sure to keep stirring it until it begins to melt.
3. Swirl until the sugar has melted and is slightly browned.
4. Whisk in 1 cup of heavy cream and cook until the mixture is smooth.
5. Stir in salt and remove the heat and allow the mixture to cool down.
6. Take a food processor and add the egg yolks, vanilla, ¾ cup of cream, ½ cup of sugar, milk and purée for 30 seconds.
7. Transfer the mixture to a resealable zip bag and seal using the immersion method.
8. Cook for 30 minutes underwater.
9. Stir caramel* into the bag and allow it to chill overnight.
10. Allow the mixture to cool. Churn the mixture in ice cream maker
11. Freeze and serve!

378. COFFEE BUTTERY BREAD

3 HOURS | 15 MIN | 4

NUTRITION:
CAL: 418 | FAT: 36 | PROTEIN: 6

INGREDIENTS

- 6 oz white bread
- ¾ cup butter
- 6 tbsp coffee
- ½ tsp cinnamon
- 1 tsp brown sugar

DIRECTIONS

1. Preheat the sous vide water bath to 195ºF.
2. Slice the bread into strips and place in a vacuum-sealable bag. Whisk the other Ingredients: in a bowl and pour the mixture over the bread. Release air by the water displacement method, seal and submerge the bag in water bath. Set the timer for 3 hours.
3. Once the timer has stopped, remove the bag. Serve warm.

379. CARROT MUFFINS

3 HOURS | 15 MIN | 4

NUTRITION:
CAL: 424 | FAT: 32 | PROTEIN: 8

INGREDIENTS

- 1 cup flour
- 3 eggs
- ½ cup butter
- ¼ cup heavy cream
- 2 carrots, grated
- 1 tsp lemon juice
- 1 tbsp coconut flour
- ¼ tsp salt
- ½ tsp baking soda

DIRECTIONS

1. Preheat the sous vide water bath to 195ºF.
2. Whisk the wet ingredients in one bowl and combine the dry ones in another. Gently combine the two mixtures together. Divide the mixture between 5 mason jars (Do not fill more than halfway. Use more jars if needed).
3. Seal the jars and submerge in water bath. Set the timer for 3 hours.
4. Once the timer has stopped, remove the jars. Cut into halves and serve.

380. RUM CHERRIES

3 HOURS | 5 MIN | 4

NUTRITION:
CAL: 234 | FAT: 0 | PROTEIN: 0

INGREDIENTS

- 3 cup cherries, pitted
- ¼ cup sugar
- 1 cup rum
- 2 tsp sour cherry
- 1 tsp agar
- 1 tsp lime zest

DIRECTIONS

1. Place all the ingredients in a vacuum-sealable bag.
2. Shake to combine well. Prepare the water bath to 142ºF.
3. Divide between 6 serving glasses.

381. PEACH AND ALMOND YOGURT

1 HOUR | 20 MIN | 4

NUTRITION:
CAL: 99 | FAT: 5 | PROTEIN: 8

INGREDIENTS

- 2 cup whole milk
- 4 oz ground almonds
- 2 tbsp yogurt
- ¼ cup mashed peeled peaches
- ¼ tsp vanilla sugar
- 1 tbsp honey

DIRECTIONS

1. Preheat the sous vide water bath to 110°F. Heat the milk in a saucepan until the temperature reaches 110°F.
2. Stir yogurt, honey, peaches and sugar. Divide the mixture between 4 jars. Seal the jars and immerse in water bath. Cook for 1 hour.
3. Once timer has stopped, remove the jars. Stir in the almonds and serve.

382. ALMOND NECTARINE PIE

3 HOURS | 20 MIN | 6

NUTRITION:
CAL: 374 | FAT: 15 | PROTEIN: 5

INGREDIENTS

- 3 cups nectarines, peeled and diced
- 8 tbsp butter
- 1 cup sugar
- 1 tsp vanilla extract
- 1 tsp almond extract
- 1 cup milk
- 1 cup flour

DIRECTIONS

1. Preheat the sous vide water bath to 194°F. Grease small jars with cooking spray. Gather the nectarines amongst the jars.
2. In a bowl, mix sugar and butter. Add the almond extract, whole milk and vanilla extract, mix well. Stir the self-rising flour and blend until solid. Place the batter into the jars. Seal and submerge the jars in the water bath. Cook for 180 minutes.
3. Once the timer has stopped, remove the jars.
4. Serve.

383. ASIAN-STYLE RICE PUDDING WITH ALMONDS

3 HOURS | 10 MIN | 4

NUTRITION:
CAL: 470 | FAT: 42 | PROTEIN: 6

INGREDIENTS

- 5 tbsp basmati rice
- 2 (14-oz) cans coconut milk
- 3 tbsp sugar
- 5 cardamom pods, crushed
- 3 tbsp cashews, chopped
- Slivered almonds for garnish

DIRECTIONS

1. Preheat the sous vide water bath to 182°F.
2. In a bowl, combine the coconut milk, sugar, and 1 cup water. Pour the rice and mix well. Divide the mixture between the jars. Add a cardamom pod to each pot. Seal and submerge in the bath. Cook for 3 hours.
3. Once the timer has stopped, remove the jars. Allow cooling for 4 hours.
4. Serve and top with cashews and almonds.

384. RASPBERRY LEMON CRÉME BRULÉE

45 MIN | 10 MIN | 4

NUTRITION:
CAL: 371 | FAT: 8 | PROTEIN: 5

INGREDIENTS

- 6 large egg yolks
- 1 1/3 cups sugar

DIRECTIONS

1. Preheat the sous vide water bath to 194°F.
2. In a mixer, combine the egg yolks and sugar until creamy. Set aside. Heat a pot over medium heat and cook the creamy mixture, lemon zest, lemon juice and vanilla. Stir for 4-5 minutes in lower heat.

- 3 cups heavy whipping cream
- Zest of 2 lemons
- 4 tbsp freshly squeezed lemon juice
- 1 tsp vanilla extract
- 1 cup fresh raspberries

3. Remove from the heat and allow cooling. Combine well the egg mix with the creamy blend.
4. Put the raspberries in six mason jars and pour over the mixture. Fill with more raspberries. Seal and submerge the jars in the water bath. Cook for 45 minutes. Once the timer has stopped, remove the jars. Allow chilling for 5 hours. Caramelized the sugar and serve.

385. CINNAMON QUINCE BOURBON

2 HOURS | 10 MIN | 8

NUTRITION:
CAL: 152 | FAT: 1 | PROTEIN: 0

INGREDIENTS
- 2 cups bourbon
- 2 quinces, peeled and sliced
- 1 cinnamon stick

DIRECTIONS
1. Preheat the sous vide water bath to 150°F.
2. Place all the ingredients in a vacuum-sealable bag. Release air by the water displacement method, seal and submerge the bag in water bath. Set the timer for 2 hours. Once the timer has stopped, remove the bag. Strain the bourbon through a cheesecloth.

386. MAPLE & CINNAMON STEEL OATS

3 HOURS | 10 MIN | 2

NUTRITION:
CAL: 247 | FAT: 8 | PROTEIN: 7

INGREDIENTS
- 2 cups almond milk
- ½ cup steel cut oats
- ¼ tsp salt
- Cinnamon and maple syrup for topping

DIRECTIONS
1. Preheat the sous vide water bath to 182°F. Combine all the Ingredients, except the cinnamon and maple syrup and place in a vacuum-sealable bag.
2. Release air by the water displacement method, seal and submerge the bag in the water bath. Cook for 3 hours.
3. Once the timer has stopped, remove the oats and transfer into a serving bowl. Garnish with cinnamon and maple syrup.

387. OATMEAL WITH PRUNES AND APRICOTS

8 HOURS | 10 MIN | 4

NUTRITION:
CAL: 128 | FAT: 5 | PROTEIN: 5

INGREDIENTS
- 2 cups milk
- 2 cups oatmeal
- 3 tbsp chopped prunes
- ¼ cup dried apricots
- 2 tbsp sugar
- 1 tbsp heavy cream
- 1 tbsp butter
- 1 tsp vanilla extract
- ¼ tsp salt

DIRECTIONS
1. Preheat the sous vide water bath to 180°F. Place the oatmeal in a vacuum-sealable bag. Whisk together the remaining ingredients in a bowl and pour over the oats.
2. Stir in the prunes and apricots. Release air by the water displacement method, seal and submerge the bag in water bath.
3. Cook for 8 hours.
4. Once the timer has stopped, remove the bag.

388. GINGERED PEACHES WITH CARDAMOM

1 HOUR | 10 MIN | 4

NUTRITION:
CAL: 65 | FAT: 5 | PROTEIN: 1

INGREDIENTS

- 1-lb peaches, halved
- 1 tbsp butter
- 1 tsp cardamom seeds, freshly ground
- ½ tsp ground ginger
- ½ tsp salt
- Fresh basil, chopped

DIRECTIONS

1. Preheat the sous vide water bath to 182°F. Combine the butter, peaches, ginger, cardamom and salt. Place in a vacuum-sealable bag. Release air by the water displacement method, seal and submerge the bag in the water bath.
2. Cook for 60 minutes. Once the timer has stopped, remove the bag and transfer into a bowl.
3. Garnished with basil and serve.

389. MAPLE POTATO FLAN

1 HOUR | 10 MIN | 6

NUTRITION:
CAL: 311 | FAT: 20 | PROTEIN: 7

INGREDIENTS

- 1 cup milk
- 1 cup heavy whipping cream
- 3 whole eggs
- 3 egg yolks
- ½ cup sweet potatoes puree
- ¼ cup maple syrup
- ½ tsp pumpkin spice
- Sugar for garnish

DIRECTIONS

1. Preheat the sous vide water bath to 168°F
2. Combine the milk, heavy cream, whole eggs, egg yolks, sweet potatoes puree, maple syrup, and pumpkin spice. Mix until smooth. Pour into mason jars. Seal and submerge in the water bath. Cook for 1 hour. Once ready, remove the jars and allow chilling.
3. Sprinkle with sugar, place under broiler until the sugar is caramelized, and serve.

390. HONEY TANGERINES

1 HOUR | 10 MIN | 4

NUTRITION:
CAL: 88 | FAT: 1 | PROTEIN: 1

INGREDIENTS

- 1-lb tangerines
- ¼ cup honey
- ½ tsp salt

DIRECTIONS

1. Preheat the sous vide water bath to 193°F. Slice the tangerines and remove the stems and seeds. Combine the honey, tangerines and salt.
2. Place in a vacuum-sealable bag. Release air by the water displacement method, seal and submerge the bag in the water bath. Cook for 60 minutes.
3. Once the timer has stopped, remove the bag and cool it. Serve.

391. COCONUT BANANA OATROLLS WITH WALNUTS

10 HOUR | 10 MIN | 4

NUTRITION:
CAL: 672 | FAT: 44 | PROTEIN: 16

INGREDIENTS

- 2 cups rolled oats
- 3 cups coconut milk
- 3 cups skimmed milk
- 3 mashed bananas
- 1 tsp vanilla extract
- 1 cup of walnuts, chopped

DIRECTIONS

1. Preheat the sous vide water bath to 182ºF.
2. Combine all the ingredients and place in a vacuum-sealable bag. Release air by the water displacement method, seal and submerge the bag in the water bath. Cook for 9-10 hours. Once the timer has stopped, remove the bags and transfer the oats into serving bowls. Top with walnuts.

392. WHITE CHOCOLATE & BANANA POPSICLES

35 MIN | 10 MIN | 6

NUTRITION:
CAL: 134 | FAT: 8 | PROTEIN: 3

INGREDIENTS

- 3 bananas
- 3 tbsp peanut butter
- 3 tbsp white chocolate chips

DIRECTIONS

1. Preheat the sous vide water bath to 138ºF.
2. Cut the banana in slices. Place them in a vacuum-sealable bag with white chocolate chips and peanut butter. Release air by the water displacement method, seal and submerge the bag in the water bath. Cook for 30 minutes.
3. Once the timer has stopped, remove the bag and transfer into popsicles molds. Allow cooling.
4. Pop-out and serve.

393. PUMPKIN MINI PIES WITH PECANS

1 HOUR | 15 MIN | 6

NUTRITION:
CAL: 247 | FAT: 6 | PROTEIN: 5

INGREDIENTS

- 1 (15-oz) can pumpkin puree
- 1 egg
- 3 egg yolks
- 2 tbsp flour
- ½ tsp salt
- 1 tbsp pumpkin pie spice
- 1 (14-oz) can evaporate milk
- ½ cup white sugar
- ½ cup brown sugar
- Whipped cream
- 4 tbsp pecans, chopped

DIRECTIONS

1. Preheat the sous vide water bath to 175ºF
2. Combine well the butternut squash puree, flour, salt, pumpkin-pie spice, egg, yolks and evaporated milk. Pour into mason jars.
3. Seal and submerge the jars in the water bath. Cook for 1 hour. Once the timer has stopped, remove the jars and allow chilling 8 hours. Top with whipped cream and pecans.

394. VANILLA CHEESECAKE

1.5 HOURS | 15 MIN | 6

NUTRITION:
CAL: 328 | FAT: 25 | PROTEIN: 7

INGREDIENTS

- 12 oz cream cheese, at room temperature
- ½ cup sugar
- ¼ cup mascarpone, at room temperature
- 2 eggs
- Zest of 1 lemon
- ½ tbsp vanilla extract

DIRECTIONS

1. Preheat the sous vide water bath to 175°F.
2. Combine cream cheese, mascarpone and sugar. Mix well. Stir in the eggs. Add in lemon zest and vanilla extract. Mix well.
3. Pour the mixture in 6 mason jars. Seal and submerge in the water bath.
4. Cook for 90 minutes. Once the timer has stopped, remove the jars and allow chilling.
5. Top with fruit compote.

395. VANILLA APRICOT CRUMBLE

3 HOURS | 15 MIN | 6

NUTRITION:
CAL: 401 | FAT: 16 | PROTEIN: 4

INGREDIENTS

- 1 cup self-rising flour
- 1 cup granulated sugar
- 1 cup milk
- 1 tsp vanilla extract
- 8 tbsp melted butter
- 2 cups chopped apricots

DIRECTIONS

1. Preheat the sous vide water bath to 194°F. Grease 6 canning jars with butter.
2. Combine flour and sugar. Add in milk and vanilla. Mix in butter and apricots. Pour the mixture into the jars. Seal and submerge in the bath. Cook for 3 hours. Once done, remove the jars and allow cooling.

396. SAVORY BANANA & NUTS CUPS

2 HOURS | 15 MIN | 12

NUTRITION:
CAL: 284 | FAT: 13 | PROTEIN: 5

INGREDIENTS

- ½ cup butter
- ½ cup brown sugar
- ½ cup honey
- 2 eggs
- 1 tsp vanilla
- ½ tsp salt
- 3 tbsp milk
- 3 mashed bananas
- ½ tsp baking soda
- 2 cups all-purpose flour
- ½ cup nuts

DIRECTIONS

1. Preheat the sous vide water bath to 172°F.
2. Heat a pot over medium heat and cook the butter with the brown and white sugar. Remove from the heat and allow cooling.
3. Stir in the egg, vanilla, milk and honey. Cook until the sugar dissolved. Add the banana, flour, baking soda and salt. Mix well. Pour the mixture into mason jars.
4. Seal and submerge the jars in the water bath. Cook for 2 hours.
5. Once the timer has stopped, remove the jars and serve.

397. HOMEMADE COMPOTE OF STRAWBERRIES

75 MIN | 15 MIN | 8

NUTRITION:
CAL: 258 | FAT: 1 | PROTEIN: 1

INGREDIENTS

- ½ cup sugar
- 1 tbsp freshly squeezed lemon juice
- 1 tbsp lemon zest
- 1 tbsp cornstarch
- 1-lb strawberries

DIRECTIONS

1. Preheat the sous vide water bath to 181ºF. Combine well the sugar, lemon juice, lemon zest and cornstarch. Add strawberries and mix well. Place it in a vacuum-sealable bag. Release air by the water displacement method, seal and submerge the bag in the water bath. Cook for 60 minutes. Once the timer has stopped, remove the bag and transfer to a serving plate.
2. Serve warm.

398. ORANGE CHEESY MOUSSE

1 HOUR | 15 MIN | 8

NUTRITION:
CAL: 128 | FAT: 8 | PROTEIN: 4

INGREDIENTS

- 2 cups milk
- 6 tbsp white wine vinegar
- 4 oz chocolate chips
- ¼ cup powdered sugar
- Grand Marnier liquor
- 1 tbsp orange zest
- 2 oz goat cheese

DIRECTIONS

1. Preheat the sous vide water bath to 172ºF.
2. Place the milk and vinegar in a vacuum-sealable bag. Release air by the water displacement method, seal and submerge the bag in the water bath. Cook for 60 minutes.
3. Once the timer has stopped, remove the bag and reserve the curds. Discard the remaining liquid. Strain the curds for 10 minutes. Allow chilling for 1 hour.
4. Prepare a water bath to medium heat and add the chocolate chips. Cook until melted. Transfer to a blender and stir the sugar, orange zest, grand Marnier, goat cheese. Mix until smooth. Serve into individual bowls.

399. LEMON & BERRY MOUSSE

45 MIN | 15 MIN | 8

NUTRITION:
CAL: 194 | FAT: 14 | PROTEIN: 5

INGREDIENTS

- 1-lb raspberries, halved
- ¼ cup light brown sugar
- 3 tbsp freshly squeezed lemon juice
- ½ tsp salt
- ¼ tsp ground cinnamon
- 1 cup heavy cream
- 1 tsp vanilla extract
- 1 cup crème fraiche

DIRECTIONS

1. Preheat the sous vide water bath to 182ºF.
2. Place the raspberries, brown sugar, lemon juice, salt and cinnamon in a vacuum-sealable bag. Release air by water displacement method, seal and submerge the bag in the water bath. Cook for 45 minutes.
3. Once the timer has stopped, remove the bag and transfer the contents to a blender. Stir until smooth.
4. Whisk the heavy cream and vanilla. Pour in the raspberries mix with the créme fraiche and combine well. Transfer into 8 serving bowls. Allow chilling.

400. CREAMY BLUEBERRY MOUSSE

30 MIN | 5 MIN | 8

NUTRITION:
CAL: 144 | FAT: 11 | PROTEIN: 2

INGREDIENTS

- 1-lb blueberries
- ¼ cup sugar
- 3 tbsp lemon juice
- ¼ tsp ground cinnamon
- 1 cup heavy cream
- 1 tsp vanilla extract

DIRECTIONS

1. Preheat the sous vide water bath to 182°F.
2. Combine the blueberries, sugar, lemon juice and cinnamon and place in a vacuum-sealable bag. Release air by the water displacement method, seal and submerge the bag in the water bath. Cook for 30 minutes.
3. Once ready, remove the bag and transfer the contents to a blender. Stir until smooth. Whisk the cream and vanilla. Pour in the blueberries mix and combine well. Transfer into 8 serving bowls. Allow chilling.

401. FRUITY CHOCOLATE FLAN

45 MIN | 15 MIN | 12

NUTRITION:
CAL: 257 | FAT: 11 | PROTEIN: 3

INGREDIENTS

- 1 cup fruit-forward red wine
- ½ cup granulated sugar
- 12 oz white chocolate chips
- 8 oz white chocolate, chopped
- 1 cup milk
- ½ cup heavy cream
- 8 egg yolks

DIRECTIONS

1. Preheat the sous vide water bath to 182°F.
2. Heat a saucepan over medium heat and pour the wine and sugar. Stir for 20 minutes until reduced. Allow cooling for 10 minutes. Transfer to a blender and put the chocolate chips, milk, cream, and egg yolks. Mix until smooth.
3. Place the mixture in a vacuum-sealable bag. Release air by the water displacement method, seal and submerge the bag in the water bath.
4. Cook for 45 minutes. Once the timer has stopped, remove the bag and transfer the contents to a blender and mix for 2 minutes. Share into 12 ramekins and cover with plastic.
5. Allow chilling for 4 hours and serve.

402. MAPLE LEMON BRIOCHE PUDDING

2 HOURS | 5 MIN | 4

NUTRITION:
CAL: 743 | FAT: 36 | PROTEIN: 14

INGREDIENTS

- 1 cup whole milk
- 1 cup heavy cream
- ½ cup granulated sugar
- ¼ cup maple syrup
- 2 tbsp lemon juice
- 1 tbsp lemon zest
- 1 tsp vanilla bean paste
- 2 cups brioche, cubed

DIRECTIONS

1. Preheat the sous vide water bath to 172°F.
2. Combine well the milk, heavy cream, sugar, maple syrup, lemon zest, lemon juice, vanilla bean paste.
3. Put the brioche and mix together.
4. Pour the mixture into 4 mason jars.
5. Seal and submerge the jars in the water bath. Cook for 2 hours.
6. Once the timer has stopped, remove the jars and transfer to the broiler.
7. Bake for 2-3 minutes and serve

403. APPLE & CINNAMON PIE

2 HOURS | 10 MIN | 4

NUTRITION:
CAL: 276 | FAT: 6 | PROTEIN: 5

INGREDIENTS

- 2 lbs green, cored, peeled and sliced
- ¾ cup sugar
- 2 tbsp cornstarch
- 2 tbsp butter
- 2 tsp ground cinnamon
- 1 pack puff pastry
- 2 tbsp milk
- 2 tbsp sugar

DIRECTIONS

1. Preheat the sous vide water bath to 160ºF.
2. Put the sliced apples, cornstarch, sugar, cinnamon and butter in the vacuum bag and set the cooking time for 1 hour 30 minutes.
3. When the time is up, cool down the filling to the room temperature.
4. In the meantime, preheat the oven to 375ºF, grease a baking pan, and roll out 1 sheet of the pastry.
5. Pour the filling over the sheet, and cover it with another sheet, seal the sheets on the edges with your fingers.
6. Bake in the preheated oven for 35 minutes.

404. SPICY CUSTARD CRÈME

1.5 HOURS | 10 MIN | 4

NUTRITION:
CAL: 605 | FAT: 51 | PROTEIN: 8

INGREDIENTS

- 2 cups heavy cream
- 1 cup milk
- 3 tsp ginger root, sliced
- 4 fresh egg yolks
- ½ cup brown sugar
- A pinch of salt

DIRECTIONS

1. Before preheating the water bath, arrange the ramekins: install the rack half-inch below the water surface.
2. Place 4 ramekins on the rack. Make sure the water level is not higher than 2/3 of the ramekins. Remove the ramekins and set aside.
3. Combine the heavy cream, milk and sliced ginger in a small saucepan and heat the mixture but do not bring it to boil. Cover the pan and set aside for 30 minutes.
4. In 30 minutes, strain the liquid, return it to the pan, and reheat again.
5. Whisk the egg yolks with salt and sugar, and carefully pour the cream mixture into the yolk mixture. Whisk well until even.
6. Pour the custards into the 4 ramekins, wrap them with plastic and return back on the rack.
7. Set the timer for 50 minutes.
8. When the time is up, cool the ramekins to the room temperature then refrigerate until cold and serve.

405. APRICOT AND CRANBERRY PIE

2 HOURS | 10 MIN | 4

NUTRITION:
CAL: 336 | FAT: 6 | PROTEIN: 2

INGREDIENTS

- 2 lbs ripe apricots, bone removed, halved
- ½-lb cranberries
- ¾ cup sugar
- 2 tbsp cornstarch
- 2 tbsp butter
- 2 tsp ground cinnamon
- 1 pack puff pastry
- 2 tbsp milk
- 2 tbsp sugar

DIRECTIONS

1. Put the apricots, cornstarch, cranberries, sugar, cinnamon and butter in the vacuum bag and set the cooking time for 1 hour 30 minutes.
2. When the time is up, cool down the filling to the room temperature.
3. In the meantime, preheat the oven to 375ºF, grease a baking pan, and roll out 1 sheet of the pastry.
4. Pour the filling over the sheet, and cover it with another sheet, seal the sheets on the edges with your fingers.

406. CRÈME BRULÉE

2 HOURS | 10 MIN | 4

NUTRITION:
CAL: 568 | FAT: 48 | PROTEIN: 5

INGREDIENTS

- 2 cups heavy cream
- ½ tsp vanilla powder
- 1 cinnamon stick
- 4 fresh egg yolks
- ½ cup brown sugar
- A pinch of salt

DIRECTIONS

1. Install the rack in the water bath half-inch below the water surface.
2. Place 4 ramekins on the rack. Make sure the water level is not higher than 2/3 of the ramekins. Remove the ramekins and set aside.
3. Combine the heavy cream, vanilla powder and cinnamon stick in a small saucepan and heat the mixture but do not bring it to boil. Cover the pan and set aside for 10 minutes.
4. In 10 minutes, strain the cream and return it to the pan.
5. Whisk the egg yolks with salt and sugar, and carefully pour the cream mixture into the yolk mixture. Whisk well.
6. Pour the custards into the 4 ramekins, wrap them with plastic and return back to the rack.
7. Set the timer for 100 minutes.
8. When the time is up, cool the ramekins to the room temperature.

407. WHITE CHOCOLATE MOUSSE

6 HOURS | 10 MIN | 4

NUTRITION:
CAL: 337 | FAT: 25 | PROTEIN: 4

INGREDIENTS

- 2/3 cup white chocolate, chopped
- ½ cup milk
- ½ cup double cream
- ½ tsp gelatin powder
- 2 tbsp cold water

DIRECTIONS

1. Preheat the sous vide water bath to 194°F.
2. Place the chopped white chocolate in the vacuum bag.
3. Seal the bag, put it into the water bath and set the timer for 6 hours.
4. When the time is up, pour the chocolate into a bowl and stir with a spoon.
5. Pour the milk into a pan and warm it over medium heat.
6. Soak the gelatin powder in 2 tbsp cold water and dissolve it in the warm milk.
7. Carefully stir the milk-gelatin mixture into the chocolate paste until even and refrigerate for 25 minutes.
8. Remove from the fridge, stir again and refrigerate for 25 mins.
9. Beat the cream to peaks and combine with white chocolate mixture.
10. Pour into single serve cups and refrigerate for 24 hours before serving.

408. DARK CHOCOLATE MOUSSE

6 HOURS | 10 MIN | 4

NUTRITION:
CAL: 333 | FAT: 25 | PROTEIN: 6

INGREDIENTS

- 2/3 cup dark chocolate, chopped
- ½ cup milk
- ½ cup double cream
- ½ tsp gelatin powder
- 2 tbsp cold water

DIRECTIONS

1. Preheat the sous vide water bath to 194°F.
2. Place the chopped dark chocolate in the vacuum bag.
3. Seal the bag, put it into the water bath and set the timer for 6 hours.
4. When the time is up, pour the chocolate into a bowl and stir with a spoon.
5. Pour the milk into a pan and warm it over medium heat.

6. Soak the gelatin powder in 2 tbsp cold water and dissolve it in the warm milk.
7. Carefully stir the milk-gelatin mixture into the chocolate paste until even and refrigerate for 25 minutes.
8. Remove from the fridge, stir again and refrigerate for another 25 minutes.
9. Beat the cream to peaks and combine with white chocolate mixture.
10. Pour into single serve cups and refrigerate for 24 hours before serving.

409. SOUS VIDE CRÈME BRULEE

1 HOUR | 10 MIN | 4

NUTRITION:
CAL: 296 | FAT: 25 | PROTEIN: 5

INGREDIENTS

- ¼ cup sugar
- 1 pinch salt
- 1 cup heavy cream
- 3 large egg yolks
- Brown sugar, to sprinkle

DIRECTIONS

1. Preheat the sous vide water bath to 181ºF.
2. Combine all ingredients in a food blender.
3. Blend until smooth.
4. Transfer the content into Sous Vide bag.
5. Fold the edges, and remove as much as air possible.
6. Clip the bag to the side of your pot. Submerge the bag into a water bath and cook 60 minutes. Make sure you remove the bag after 30 minutes and shake gently.
7. Remove the bag from the cooker.
8. Divide the bag content between four ramekins. Sprinkle the egg custard with brown sugar.
9. Caramelize the sugar with a torch.
10. Serve.

410. CHOCOLATE CHILI CAKE

1 HOUR | 20 MIN | 6

NUTRITION:
CAL: 326 | FAT: 21 | PROTEIN: 7

INGREDIENTS

- 4 large eggs
- 4 oz. unsalted butter
- 2 tbsps cocoa powder
- ½ lb. chocolate chips
- ½ tsp chili powder
- ¼ cup brown sugar

DIRECTIONS

1. Preheat the sous vide water bath to 115ºF.
2. Place the chocolate chips, and butter in a sous vide bag.
3. Submerge in water and cook 15 minutes.
4. Remove the bag and set the sous vide to 170ºF.
5. Prepare 6 4oz. Mason jars by coating with cooking spray.
6. Beat the eggs with brown sugar until fluffy.
7. Stir in the chocolate, cocoa powder, and chili powder.
8. Divide the mixture between prepared mason jars and apply the lid on finger tight only.
9. Submerge the jars in a water bath for 1 hour.
10. Remove the jars and place onto wire rack to cool completely.
11. Invert the cake onto a plate.
12. Serve with raspberry ice cream.

411. CHOCOLATE CHIP COOKIES

30 MIN | 30 MIN | 12

NUTRITION:
CAL: 115 | FAT: 6 | PROTEIN: 2

INGREDIENTS

- ½ cup flour
- ½ tsp baking powder
- 1 pinch salt
- 3 tbsps unsalted softened butter
- 1/3 cup granulated sugar
- 1 small egg
- ½ cup mini chocolate chips
- 1 tsp vanilla paste

DIRECTIONS

1. Preheat the sous vide water bath to 195°F.
2. In a small bowl, combine flour, baking powder, and salt.
3. In a separate large bowl, cream butter and sugar until fluffy.
4. Fold in the egg and vanilla paste, and stir until smooth.
5. Mix in the flour mixture and stir until just combined. Fold in the chocolate chips.
6. Roll the dough between two pieces of baking paper and cut out the cookies using a cookie cutter.
7. Divide the cookies between two sous vide cooking bags.
8. Vacuum seal the cookies and submerge in a water bath.
9. Cook 30 minutes.
10. Remove the bag from the water bath.
11. Cool completely before opening.
12. Remove the cookies from the bag and serve.

412. COOKIE DOUGH

10 MIN | 10 MIN | 6

NUTRITION:
CAL: 384 | FAT: 27 | PROTEIN: 8

INGREDIENTS

- ½ cup softened butter
- ¾ cup brown sugar
- 1 tsp molasses
- 1 medium egg
- 1 ¼ cups almond flour
- ½ cup salted caramel chips

DIRECTIONS

1. Preheat the sous vide water bath to 171°F.
2. Cream the butter with sugar in a large bowl.
3. Fold in molasses and egg. Stir until smooth.
4. Fold in the almond flour and mix until just combined. Add caramel chips and mix until incorporated.
5. Refrigerate 1 hour.
6. Remove the dough from the fridge and shape into 12 balls.
7. Place the balls into sous vide bag and press each to ½-inch thick.
8. Vacuum seal the bag and submerge in water.
9. Cook the dough 10 minutes.
10. Remove the bag from the water bath and chill in a fridge 10 minutes.
11. Open the bag carefully and serve the cookie dough.

413. PISTACHIO ICE CREAM

1 HOUR | 20 MIN | 6

NUTRITION:
CAL: 341 | FAT: 24 | PROTEIN: 7

INGREDIENTS

- 1 cup shelled pistachios
- ½ cup brown sugar
- ¾ cup heavy cream

DIRECTIONS

1. Preheat the sous vide water bath to 180°F.
2. Process the pistachios and sugar in a food processor until you have a fine powder.
3. Combine the pistachio mixture with heavy cream, and milk in a saucepan.

- 1 cup almond milk
- 5 medium egg yolks
- ¼ tsp pistachio extract

4. Bring to a simmer and remove from the heat. Cover and let the milk infuse 1 hour.
5. Strain the milk and discard any solids.
6. Pour the milk into a food blender. Add eggs and pistachio extract. Blend until frothy.
7. Transfer the milk mixture into a Sous Vide bag. Seal the bag using water immersion technique.
8. Submerge the bag into a water bath and cook 1 hour. Make sure you shake the bag every 20 minutes.
9. Remove the bag from the water bath and transfer into the ice-cold water bath.
10. Once cooled churn into ice cream machine.
11. Serve

414. LEMON AND CRÈME BRULÉE

1 HOUR | 10 MIN | 4

NUTRITION:
CAL: 987 | FAT: 73 | PROTEIN: 8

INGREDIENTS

- 6 large egg yolks
- 1 and 1/3 cup, superfine sugar
- 3 cups heavy whipped cream
- 2 lemon zest
- 4 tbsps, freshly squeezed lemon juice
- 1 tsp, vanilla extract
- 1 cup, fresh blueberries

DIRECTIONS

1. Preheat the sous vide water bath to 195°F.
2. Take an electric mixer and whisk in egg yolks, sugar until you have a creamy mixture, keep it on the side
3. Take a medium saucepan and place it over medium heat, add cream and heat it up
4. Add lemon zest, lemon juice, vanilla and stir simmer for 4-5 minute over low heat
5. Remove the cream mixture from heat and allow it to cool, once cooled transfer a small amount into egg mix and whisk well
6. Add remaining cream mixture into the egg and stir
7. Divide the blueberries among six pieces of mini mason jars and pour the egg cream mix over the blueberries divide the mixture amongst the jars
8. Tightly seal the lid and submerge, cook for 45 Minutes. Remove the jars from water bath and chill for 5 hours
9. Caramelize a layer of sugar on top using a blowtorch and serve!

415. COCONUT MILK KHEER

3 HOURS | 10 MIN | 5

NUTRITION:
CAL: 295 | FAT: 29 | PROTEIN: 5

INGREDIENTS

- 5 heaping tbsp, basmati rice
- 2 cans, full-fat coconut milk
- 1 cup, water
- 3 tbsps, granulated sugar
- pinch, salt
- 10 green cardamom pods, crushed
- chopped shelled pistachios
- slivered almonds

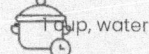

DIRECTIONS

1. Preheat the sous vide water bath to 180°F.
2. Divide the rice evenly amongst 5 half-pint jars
3. Take a large bowl and add coconut milk, sugar, water, salt and divide the mixture amongst the cans as well
4. Add 2 cardamom pods to each jar and seal lightly
5. Submerge and cook for 3 hours
6. Remove the jars from water bath and transfer to cooling rack
7. Remove the lids and stir the pudding
8. Allow them to cool and chill for 4 hours
9. Remove the lid and stir
10. Serve with a topping of pistachio or almonds

416. GENUINE CHEESECAKE FOR THE AGES

1.5 HOURS | 10 MIN | 6

NUTRITION:
CAL: 308 | FAT: 22 | PROTEIN: 7

INGREDIENTS

- 12-oz, cream cheese at room temperature
- ½ cup, sugar
- ¼ cup, creole cream cheese
- 2 eggs
- zest, 1 lemon
- ½ tbsp, vanilla extract

DIRECTIONS

1. Preheat the sous vide water bath to 180°F
2. Take a bowl and add cream cheese, sugar, yogurt and mix well
3. Gradually add the eggs one by one and keep beating until well combined
4. Add zest and vanilla and mix well
5. Pour the cheesecake mix into jars and distribute evenly
6. Seal the jars with lid and submerge them, cook for 1 hour and 30 minutes
7. Remove from water bath and chill for a while
8. Serve chilled with a topping of fresh fruit compote

417. MIND BOGGLING PEACH COBBLER

3 HOURS | 15 MIN | 6

NUTRITION:
CAL: 374 | FAT: 16 | PROTEIN: 4

INGREDIENTS

- 1 cup self-rising flour
- 1 cup granulated sugar
- 1 cup whole milk
- 1 tsp vanilla extract
- 8 tbsps unsalted melted butter
- 2 cups roughly chopped peaches

DIRECTIONS

1. Preheat the sous vide water bath to 195°F.
2. Prepare 6 half pint canning jars with butter
3. Whisk flour, sugar in a large bowl, whisk in milk and vanilla and mix
4. Stir in butter and peaches
5. Divide the batter between jars and wipe sides, seal gently
6. Cook for 3 hours
7. Remove the jars and place on cooling rack, rest for 10 minutes and enjoy!

418. MIND BOGGLING PEAR MANGO COBBLER

3 HOURS | 15 MIN | 6

NUTRITION:
CAL: 385 | FAT: 19 | PROTEIN: 5

INGREDIENTS

- 1 cup self-rising flour
- 1 cup granulated sugar
- 1 cup whole milk
- 1 tsp vanilla extract
- 8 tbsps unsalted melted butter
- 1 cup chopped pears
- 1 cup chopped mango

DIRECTIONS

1. Preheat the sous vide water bath to 195°F.
2. Prepare 6 half pint canning jars with butter
3. Whisk flour, sugar in a large bowl, whisk in milk and vanilla and mix
4. Stir in butter, pears and mango
5. Divide the batter between jars and wipe sides, seal gently
6. Cook for 3 hours
7. Remove the jars and place on cooling rack, rest for 10 minutes and enjoy!

419. RASPBERRY MOUSSE

45 MIN | 15 MIN | 8

NUTRITION:
CAL: 143 | FAT: 12 | PROTEIN: 2

INGREDIENTS

- 1 lb. raspberries
- ¼ cup ultrafine sugar
- 3 tbsps fresh squeezed lemon juice
- ½ tsp salt
- ¼ tsp ground cinnamon
- 1 cup heavy cream
- 1 tsp vanilla extract

DIRECTIONS

1. Preheat the sous vide water bath to 180ºF.
2. Add the raspberries, sugar, salt, lemon juice and cinnamon to a resealable bag and seal using the immersion method. Cook for 45 minutes.
3. Once done, take the bag out from the water bath and pour the contents into a blender.
4. Purée until it gets smooth.
5. Take a large mixing bowl and mix in cream, vanilla until stiff peaks form.
6. Fold in raspberry purée and mix.
7. Divide among 8 serving bowls, chill and serve!

420. STRAWBERRY MOUSSE

45 MIN | 45 MIN | 8

NUTRITION:
CAL: 195 | FAT: 16 | PROTEIN: 4

INGREDIENTS

- 1 lb. strawberries, stemmed, halved
- ¼ cup packed light brown sugar
- 3 tbsps freshly squeezed lemon juice
- ½ tsp salt
- ¼ tsp ground cinnamon
- 1 cup heavy cream
- 1 tsp vanilla extract
- 1 cup crème fraiche

DIRECTIONS

1. Preheat the sous vide water bath to 180ºF.
2. Add the strawberries, brown sugar, lemon juice, salt, and cinnamon to a large resealable zipper bag.
3. Seal using the immersion method and cook for 45 minutes.
4. Once done, remove the bag and pour the contents to a food processor.
5. Purée for a few seconds until you have a smooth mixture
6. Take a large chilled mixing bowl and add the heavy cream and vanilla, whisk well until stiff peaks form.
7. Fold in strawberry purée and crème fraiche.
8. Whisk them well and divide it among 8 serving bowls.
9. Serve chilled!

421. BLUEBERRY & LEMON COMPOTE

1 HOUR | 15 MIN | 6

NUTRITION:
CAL: 92 | FAT: 1 | PROTEIN: 1

INGREDIENTS

- ½ cup ultrafine sugar
- 1 tbsp freshly squeezed lemon juice
- 1 tbsp lemon zest
- 1 tbsp cornstarch
- 1 lb. blueberries

DIRECTIONS

1. Preheat the sous vide water bath to 180ºF.
2. Take a medium-sized bowl and mix in sugar, lemon juice, lemon zest, and cornstarch.
3. Add the blueberries and toss well to coat them.
4. Transfer the mixture to a resealable zip bag and seal using the immersion method.
5. Cook for 60 minutes.
6. Once done, remove the bag and transfer the contents to a serving dish.
7. Serve warm!

422. CHOCOLATE & RICOTTA MOUSSE

1 HOUR | 30 MIN | 8

NUTRITION:
CAL: 211 | FAT: 11 | PROTEIN: 6

INGREDIENTS

- 2 quarts' whole milk
- 6 tbsps white wine vinegar
- 4 oz. semisweet chocolate chips
- ¼ cup powdered sugar
- Grand Marnier liquor
- 1 tbsp orange zest
- 2 oz. ricotta

DIRECTIONS

1. Preheat the sous vide water bath to 172°F.
2. Put the milk and vinegar to a resealable zip bag.
3. Seal using the immersion method and cook for 1 hour.
4. Once done, remove the bag and skim the curds from top and transfer to a strainer lined with cheesecloth. Discard any remaining liquid.
5. Let it sit and drain the curd for about 10 minutes. Then chill for 1 hour.
6. Prepare your double broiler by setting a bowl over a small saucepan filled with 1 inch of water
7. Bring the water to a low simmer over medium heat.
8. Add the chocolate chips to a bowl of the double boiler and cook until it has melted.
9. Transfer to a food processor.
10. Add the sugar, orange zest, grand mariner, ricotta, and then process until smooth
11. Transfer to individual bowls and serve!

423. LEMON RASPBERRY RICOTTA CHEESECAKE

2 HOURS | 30 MIN | 12

NUTRITION:
CAL: 279 | FAT: 19 | PROTEIN: 4

INGREDIENTS

- 1 cup granulated sugar
- 7 oz. soft cream cheese
- ½ cup full-fat Greek yogurt
- ½ cup heavy cream
- 2 large eggs + 1 large egg yolk
- Finely grated zest one lemon + 2 tbsps freshly squeezed juice
- 2 tbsps all-purpose flour
- ¼ tsp vanilla extract
- Fine sea salt
- 1 ½ cup graham crackers
- 1/3 cup unsalted butter
- 2 pints' fresh raspberries

DIRECTIONS

1. Preheat the sous vide water bath to 170°F.
2. Preheat your oven to 375°F
3. Take a large bowl and mix in ricotta cheese, 2/3 cup of sugar, cream cheese, Greek yogurt, heavy cream, egg yolks, eggs, lemon zest, juice, 1 tbsp of flour, vanilla, and ½ a tsp of salt.
4. Transfer to a resealable bag and seal using the immersion method. Cook for 2 hours.
5. Make the crust by taking another medium bowl and add the graham cracker crumbs, butter, 1/3 cup of sugar, pinch of salt and 1 tbsp of flour.
6. Whisk well until fully combined and press the mixture into the bottom of a 9-inch springform pan.
7. Bake in your oven until the crust is browned, should take about 7-10 minutes.
8. Once cooked, remove the bag from the water bath and pat it dry.
9. Cut off one corner of the resealable bag. Pipe contents of bag carefully into the baked crust.
10. Press raspberries onto the surface and chill for 8 hours before serving.

424. DOCE DE BANANA

40 MIN | 10 MIN | 4

NUTRITION:
CAL: 338 | FAT: 1 | PROTEIN: 2

INGREDIENTS

- 5 small ripe bananas, firm, ripe, peeled and cut up into chunks
- 1 cup brown sugar
- 2 cinnamon sticks
- 6 whole cloves
- Whipped cream
- Vanilla ice-cream

DIRECTIONS

1. Preheat the sous vide water bath to 176ºF.
2. Put the bananas, brown sugar, cinnamon sticks, and cloves to a resealable bag.
3. Seal using the immersion method and cook for 30-40 minutes.
4. Remove the bag and allow the contents to cool.
5. Open the bag and remove the cinnamon sticks and cloves.
6. Serve warm in a bowl with a topping of whipped cream and vanilla ice cream.

425. CITRUS YOGURT

3 HOURS | 15 MIN | 4

NUTRITION:
CAL: 182 | FAT: 10 | PROTEIN: 8

INGREDIENTS

- ½ cup yogurt
- ½ tbsp orange zest
- ½ tbsp lemon zest
- ½ tbsp lime zest
- 4 cups full cream milk

DIRECTIONS

1. Preheat the sous vide water bath to 113ºF.
2. Heat the milk on stove top to a temperature of 180ºF
3. Transfer to an ice bath and allow it to cool down to 110ºF.
4. Stir in yogurt.
5. Fold in the citrus zest.
6. Pour the mixture into 4-oz canning jars and lightly close the lid.
7. Submerge underwater and cook for 3 hours.
8. Remove the jars and serve immediately!

426. SWEET CANDIED POTATOES

2 HOURS | 45 MIN | 8

NUTRITION:
CAL: 370 | FAT: 20 | PROTEIN: 6

INGREDIENTS

- 2 lbs. sweet potatoes, peeled up and cut into ¼ slices
- ½ cup unsalted butter
- ¼ cup maple syrup
- 2 oranges, juice and zest
- 1 tsp salt
- 1 cup chopped walnuts
- 1 cinnamon stick
- ¼ cup brown sugar

DIRECTIONS

1. Preheat the sous vide water bath to 155ºF.
2. Take a resealable bag and add the sweet potatoes and ¼ cup of butter.
3. Seal using the immersion method and cook for 2 hours.
4. Preheat your oven to 350ºF
5. Remove the potatoes from the bag and pat dry.
6. Arrange the potatoes evenly in a baking dish.
7. Take a medium saucepan and bring ¼ cup of butter, brown sugar, maple syrup, orange zest, juice, walnuts, salt, and cinnamon stick to a boil.
8. Remove from heat and pour over sweet potatoes, discard the cinnamon stick
9. Bake for 30 minutes and serve warm!

427. MOCHA POT DE CRÈME

40 MIN | 10 MIN | 4

NUTRITION:
CAL: 322 | FAT: 22 | PROTEIN: 6

INGREDIENTS

- 1/3 cup espresso
- ¾ cup milk
- 1 cup heavy cream
- 6 oz. chopped chocolate
- 1/3 cup sugar
- ¼ tsp fine salt
- Whipped cream
- Cinnamon powder
- 4 large egg yolks

DIRECTIONS

1. Preheat the sous vide water bath to 180°F.
2. Take a medium-sized saucepan and heat it up over medium heat.
3. Add the heavy cream, espresso, milk and bring to a boil.
4. Once done, turn-off the heat and stir in chocolate. Then, cook once again over medium heat and occasionally stir for 15 minutes.
5. Take a medium bowl and add in the egg yolks, salt, and sugar. Stir well and add the chocolate crème mixture.
6. Once mixed together, cool the mixture for 10-15 minutes.
7. Add the contents to a resealable zipper bag and seal using the immersion method.
8. Cook for 30 minutes.
9. Spoon the mixture into small ramekins and garnish with cinnamon powder or whipped cream.
10. Chill for 2 hours and serve!

428. BAKED RICOTTA

1 HOUR | 50 MIN | 6

NUTRITION:
CAL: 148 | FAT: 10 | PROTEIN: 8

INGREDIENTS

- 2 quarts whole milk
- 6 tbsps white wine vinegar
- 2 large eggs
- 2 tbsps olive oil
- 1 ½ tsp smoked salt
- 1 tsp fresh ground smoked black pepper

DIRECTIONS

1. Preheat the sous vide water bath to 172°F.
2. Add the milk and vinegar to a resealable zip bag.
3. Seal using the immersion method and cook for 1 hour.
4. Preheat your oven to 350°F
5. Remove the bag and skim the curd off the top.
6. Then, pass the mixture through a strainer lined with a cheesecloth and discard any remaining liquid.
7. Drain the curd for 10 minutes.
8. Transfer drained curds to food processor alongside the eggs, salt, olive oil, and pepper.
9. Process for 20 seconds.
10. Divide the ricotta mixture between 6 oven proof ramekins and bake for 30 minutes until golden brown.
11. Serve!

429. SWEET BASIL SYRUP

1 HOUR | 5 MIN | 4

NUTRITION:
CAL: 414 | FAT: 1 | PROTEIN: 1

INGREDIENTS

- 2 cups water
- 2 cups basil
- 2 cups sugar
- 1 lime, use the rind only

DIRECTIONS

1. Preheat the sous vide water bath to 180°F.
2. Combine all the ingredients into sous vide bag and seal using a water immersion technique.
3. Cook the syrup 1 hour.
4. Prepare ice-cold water bath.
5. Remove the bag from the cooker and place into ice-cold water bath 30 minutes.
6. Strain the syrup into a clean glass jar.
7. Serve or store in a fridge.

430. GINGER SYRUP

55 MIN | 15 MIN | 8

NUTRITION:
CAL: 111 | FAT: 7 | PROTEIN: 6

INGREDIENTS

- 2 quarts whole milk
- 6 tbsps white wine vinegar
- 2 large eggs
- 2 tbsps olive oil
- 1 ½ tsp smoked salt
- 1 tsp fresh ground smoked black pepper

DIRECTIONS

1. Preheat the sous vide water bath to 185°F. Place the onion in a vacuum-sealable bag.
2. Release air by the water displacement method, seal and submerge the bag in the water bath. Set the timer for 40 minutes.
3. Once the timer has stopped, remove and unseal the bag.
4. Transfer the onion with 4 tbsps of water to a blender and puree to smooth.
5. Place a pot over medium heat, add the onion puree and the remaining listed ingredients. Bring to a boil for 15 minutes.
6. Turn off heat, cool, and strain through a fine sieve.
7. Store in a jar, refrigerate, and use for up to 14 days. Use it as a spice in other foods

431. HONEY LEMON THYME INFUSION

1.5 HOURS | 5 MIN | 10

NUTRITION:
CAL: 204 | FAT: 0.2 | PROTEIN: 0.2

INGREDIENTS

- 2 cups water
- 2 organic lemons, sliced
- 2 cups honey
- 2 bunches lemon thyme

DIRECTIONS

1. Preheat the sous vide water bath to 135°F.
2. Combine all ingredients in a sous vide bag.
3. Seal the bag using water immersion technique.
4. Cook the syrup 1 ½ hours.
5. Prepare ice-cold water bath.
6. Remove the bag from the cooker and place into the water bath.
7. Chill the syrup 30 minutes.
8. Strain into a clean glass jar and serve.

432. TOM COLLINS COCKTAIL

1 HOUR | 10 MIN | 10

NUTRITION:
CAL: 302 | FAT: 0.4 | PROTEIN: 0.2

INGREDIENTS

- 3 cups gin
- ½ cup lemon juice
- 1 cup lemon rind
- 1 cups granulated sugar
- Soda water, to serve with

DIRECTIONS

1. Preheat the sous vide water bath to 131ºF.
2. In a large sous vide bag, combine gin, lemon juice, lemon rind, and sugar.
3. Fold the edges of the bag few times and clip to the side of your pot.
4. Cook the cocktail 1 hour.
5. Strain the cocktail into a large glass jug.
6. Place aside to cool completely before use.
7. Serve over ice and finish off with a soda water.
8. Garnish the cocktail with lemon rind or fresh thyme.

433. CHERRY MANHATTAN

1 HOUR | 10 MIN | 8

NUTRITION:
CAL: 426 | FAT: 3 | PROTEIN: 1

INGREDIENTS

- Bourbon infusion:
- 1 cup bourbon
- ¼ cup raw cocoa nibs
- 1 cup dried cherries
- To finish:
- 4 oz. sweet vermouth
- Chocolate bitters, as desired

DIRECTIONS

1. Make the infusion; Preheat the sous vide water bath to 122ºF.
2. In a Sous Vide bag combine bourbon, cacao nibs, and cherries.
3. Seal the bag, and cook 1 hour
4. Remove the bag from the water bath and let cool. Strain the content into a jar.
5. Fill the tall glasses with ice.
6. Add chocolate bitters (3 dashes per serving) and 1/8 of the infused bourbon.
7. Skewer the Sous vide cherries and garnish.

434. LAVENDER SYRUP

1 HOUR | 5 MIN | 4

NUTRITION:
CAL: 206 | FAT: 0.4 | PROTEIN: 0.2

INGREDIENTS

- 1 cup water
- 1 cup sugar
- 1 tbsp culinary grade dried lavender

DIRECTIONS

1. Preheat the sous vide water bath to 135ºF
2. Take a heavy-duty resealable zipper bag and add the water, lavender, and sugar.
3. Seal it using the immersion method.
4. Submerge it underwater and cook for about 1 hour.
5. Once done, let it cool down to room temperature and strain through a metal mesh.
6. Serve chilled!

435. THYME LIQUEUR

1.5 HOUR | 15 MIN | 12

NUTRITION:
CAL: 115 | FAT: 0.4 | PROTEIN: 0.2

INGREDIENTS
- Zest, 8 large oranges
- 4 sprigs fresh thyme
- 1 cup ultrafine sugar
- 1 cup water
- 1 cup vodka

DIRECTIONS
1. Preheat the sous vide water bath to 180ºF.
2. Add all the listed ingredients to a heavy-duty resealable zip bag and seal using the immersion method.
3. Cook for 90 minutes.
4. Strain the mixture and serve chilled!

436. VODKA LEMON MEYER

2 HOURS | 15 MIN | 6

NUTRITION:
CAL: 145 | FAT: 0.3 | PROTEIN: 0.2

INGREDIENTS
- 1 cup granulated sugar
- 1 cup freshly squeezed Meyer lemon
- Zest, 3 Meyer lemons

DIRECTIONS
1. Preheat the sous vide water bath to 135ºF.
2. Take a resealable zip bag and add all the ingredients.
3. Seal the bag using the immersion method. Submerge and cook for about 2 hours.
4. Once done, strain the mixture through a fine metal mesh strainer into a medium bowl.
5. Chill the mixture overnight and serve!

437. BLOODY MARY VODKA

3 HOURS | 20 MIN | 10

NUTRITION:
CAL: 95 | FAT: 0.3 | PROTEIN: 0.2

INGREDIENTS
- 1 bottle vodka
- 6 quartered Roma tomatoes
- 1 Anaheim pepper, stemmed, seeds removed, sliced into ½ inch pieces
- ¼ onion, peeled, sliced into ½-inch pieces
- 6 whole garlic cloves, peeled
- 1 thinly sliced jalapeno pepper
- 1 tbsp whole black peppercorns
- Zest of 3 large limes

DIRECTIONS
1. Preheat the sous vide water bath to 145ºF.
2. Add all the listed ingredients to your resealable zipper bag.
3. Seal using the immersion method.
4. Cook for about 3 hours and transfer the contents through a mesh strainer.
5. Serve!

438. HONEY GINGER SHRUB

2 HOURS | 10 MIN | 6

NUTRITION:
CAL: 103 | FAT: 0 | PROTEIN: 0.2

INGREDIENTS
- 1 cup water
- 1 cup honey

DIRECTIONS
1. Preheat the sous vide water bath to 134ºF.
2. Take a resealable zipper bag and add water, vinegar, honey, ginger, and seal it using the immersion method.

- ½ cup balsamic vinegar
- 1 tbsp freshly grated ginger
- Bourbon whiskey
- Club soda
- Lemon wedges

3. Submerge and cook for about 2 hours.
4. Once cooked, strain the mixture through a fine metal mesh strainer into a medium bowl.
5. Chill the mixture overnight.
6. Serve with one-part whiskey and one-part club soda in a glass over ice. Garnish with a lemon wedge and serve!

439. CHERRY BOURBON

2 HOURS | 20 MIN | 8

NUTRITION:
CAL: 220 | FAT:0 | PROTEIN: 0.2

INGREDIENTS
- 1 lb. fresh cherries
- 1 cup bourbon

DIRECTIONS
1. Preheat the sous vide water bath to 135°F.
2. Then, pit the cherries using a cherry pitter.
3. Add the cherries and bourbon to a resealable zipper bag.
4. Seal using the immersion method and mash the cherries. Cook for 2 hours.
5. Let the mixture cool and strain it to a bowl through a fine metal mesh
6. Pour in the bottles and serve chilled!

440. RASPBERRY CORDIAL

2 HOURS | 15 MIN | 14

NUTRITION:
CAL: 238 | FAT:0 | PROTEIN: 0.2

INGREDIENTS
- 2 cups fresh raspberries
- 2 cups sugar
- 3 cups vodka

DIRECTIONS
1. Preheat the sous vide water bath to 135°F.
2. Add the raspberries and sugar to a resealable zip bag.
3. Mash the berries by hand.
4. Open the bag and add the vodka.
5. Seal using the immersion method.
6. Cook for 2 hours and allow it to come to room temperature.
7. Pour into bottles and serve chilled!

441. SPICED RUM

2 HOURS | 5 MIN | 10

NUTRITION:
CAL: 89 | FAT:0 | PROTEIN: 0.2

INGREDIENTS
- 1 bottle rum
- 1 vanilla bean, split lengthwise
- 2 whole cloves
- ½ cinnamon stick
- 2 whole black peppercorns
- ½ piece star anise
- 2 pieces of 3-inch fresh orange zest

DIRECTIONS
1. Preheat the sous vide water bath to 153°F.
2. Add all the listed ingredients to a resealable zipper bag.
3. Seal using the immersion method and cook for 2 hours.
4. Once cooked, transfer it to an ice bath and chill.
5. Strain to bottle and serve the drink!

442. BACON VODKA

🍲 45 MIN　⏱ 20 MIN　🍴 10

NUTRITION:
CAL: 125| FAT:4| PROTEIN: 2

INGREDIENTS

- 2 cups vodka
- 8 oz. bacon
- 3 tbsps reserved bacon grease

DIRECTIONS

1. Preheat the sous vide water bath to 150ºF.
2. Bake the bacon for 16 minutes at 400ºF.
3. Allow the mixture to cool.
4. Add all the ingredients to a resealable bag and seal using the immersion method.
5. Cook for 45 minutes.
6. Strain the liquid into bowl and chill until a fat layer form.
7. Remove and skim off the fat layer, strain using a cheesecloth once again.
8. Serve Chilled.

443. MULLED WINE

🍲 1 HOUR　⏱ 15 MIN　🍴 2

NUTRITION:
CAL: 155 | FAT: 0.5| PROTEIN: 0.6

INGREDIENTS

- ½ bottle red wine
- Juice, 2 oranges, peel of 1
- 1 cinnamon stick
- 1 bay leaf
- 1 vanilla pod, sliced in half lengthways
- 1-star anise
- 2 oz. caster sugar

DIRECTIONS

1. Preheat the sous vide water bath to 140ºF.
2. Add all the listed ingredients to a large bowl.
3. Divide the mixture across two resealable zip bags and seal using the immersion method. Cook for 1 hour.
4. Serve chilled!

444. TOMATO SHRUB

🍲 1.5 HOUR　⏱ 15 MIN　🍴 12

NUTRITION:
CAL: 174 | FAT:0 | PROTEIN: 0.2

INGREDIENTS

- 2 cups diced tomatoes
- 2 cups granulated sugar
- 2 cups red wine vinegar
- 1 cup water

DIRECTIONS

1. Preheat the sous vide water bath to 180ºF.
2. Add all the listed ingredients to a resealable zip bag and seal using the immersion method.
3. Cook for 1 ½ hour.
4. Once done, remove and strain the contents into a bowl.
5. Discard any solids and transfer to storing jar.
6. Serve as needed!

445. STRAWBERRY & RHUBARB SHRUB

1.5 HOURS | 15 MIN | 12

NUTRITION:
CAL: 195 | FAT: 1| PROTEIN: 4

INGREDIENTS

- 2 cups granulated sugar
- 2 cups balsamic vinegar
- 1 cup diced rhubarb
- 1 cup strawberries, diced
- 1 cup water

DIRECTIONS

1. Preheat the sous vide water bath to 180°F.
2. Add all the listed ingredients to a large-sized heavy-duty zip bag
3. Seal using the immersion method and cook for 1 ½ hour.
4. Remove the bag and strain the contents to a bowl.
5. Save the fruit for later.
6. Transfer to liquid storage, chill and serve!

446. RHUBARB & THYME SYRUP

1.5 HOURS | 15 MIN | 12

NUTRITION:
CAL: 74 | FAT:0 | PROTEIN: 0.2

INGREDIENTS

- 2 cups diced rhubarb
- 1 cup ultrafine sugar
- 1 cup water
- 5 sprigs thyme

DIRECTIONS

1. Preheat the sous vide water bath to 180°F.
2. Add all the listed ingredients to a heavy-duty zip bag
3. Seal using the immersion method
4. Submerge underwater and cook for 1 ½ hour.
5. Remove the bag and strain the contents to a bowl.
6. Transfer to liquid storage, chill and serve!

447. CHILI AGAVE LIQUEUR

45 MIN | 10 MIN | 8

NUTRITION:
CAL: 135 | FAT: 1| PROTEIN: 4

INGREDIENTS

- 2 cups vodka
- ½ cup water
- ½ cup light agave nectar
- 3 dried Guajillo chili peppers
- 1-piece Serrano pepper, sliced in half, seeded
- 1 Fresno pepper, sliced in half, seeded
- Zest, 1 lemon
- 1 cinnamon stick
- 1 tsp black peppercorns

DIRECTIONS

1. Preheat the sous vide water bath to 180°F.
2. Add all the listed ingredients to a heavy-duty zip bag.
3. Seal using the immersion method and cook for 45 minutes.
4. Once done, remove the bag and strain the contents to a bowl.
5. Transfer to liquid storage, chill and serve!

448. BOURBON GRAPE & GINGER BEER COCKTAIL

2 HOURS | 30 MIN | 8

NUTRITION:
CAL: 234 | FAT: 0 | PROTEIN: 0.2

INGREDIENTS

- 2-3 cups sliced seedless red grapes
- 1 ¼ cups vanilla sugar
- ½ cup bourbon
- ½ vanilla bean, split
- 1 lemon, peeled
- 1-star anise pod
- 1 cardamom pod
- ½ cup ginger beer
- Fresh mint leaves
- Lemon twists
- Sliced grapes for garnishing

DIRECTIONS

1. Preheat the sous vide water bath to 167ºF.
2. Add the grapes, sugar, vanilla, bourbon, star anise, lemon peel, and cardamom to a large resealable zip bag.
3. Seal using the immersion method and cook for 2 hours.
4. Once done, remove the bag and transfer to an ice bath, once the grape mix is cool, transfer to the refrigerator and chill.
5. Strain the grape mixture through a metal mesh strainer over a bowl and reserve the fruit for later use.
6. Then, fill a rocks glass with ice and add ½ cup ginger beer, 1 ½ oz of infused bourbon.
7. Garnish with mint and lemon twist.
8. Serve with a garnish of sliced grapes.

449. SOUS VIDE GIN

2 HOURS | 10 MIN | 1

NUTRITION:
CAL: 198 | FAT: 0 | PROTEIN: 0.5

INGREDIENTS

- 3 oz. vodka
- Zest, small orange
- 8 juniper berries
- 10-12 coriander seeds
- 2 cardamom pods
- 8-10 grains of paradise
- 1 Tasmanian pepper berry

DIRECTIONS

1. Preheat the sous vide water bath to 176ºF.
2. Add all the listed ingredients to a resealable bag and seal using the immersion method.
3. Cook for 90 seconds.
4. Once done, take the bag out from the water bath and transfer it to an ice bath.
5. Massage the bag to infuse the gin carefully.
6. Cool down the mixture and strain the mixture through a metal mesh strainer and pour it to a medium-sized bowl
7. Serve!

450. LIMONCELLO VODKA COCKTAIL

3 HOURS | 20 MIN | 5

NUTRITION:
CAL: 328 | FAT: 0 | PROTEIN: 0.2

INGREDIENTS

- 1 bottle vodka
- Grated zest/peel, 10-15 thoroughly washed lemons
- 1 cup granulated sugar
- 1 cup water

DIRECTIONS

1. Preheat the sous vide water bath to 135ºF.
2. Add the vodka and lemon zest to a large zip bag and seal using the immersion method. Cook for 2-3 hours.
3. Take a saucepan and put it over medium-high heat
4. Add the sugar and water and stir until the sugar dissolves to prepare the syrup
5. Once done, take the bag out from the water bath and strain through metal mesh into a bowl.
6. Stir in syrup.
7. Pour Limoncello into bottles and serve!

451. SWEDISH ROSEMARY SNAPS

2 HOURS | 10 MIN | 10

NUTRITION:
CAL: 83 | FAT: 0 | PROTEIN: 0.5

INGREDIENTS

- 1 bottle vodka
- 3 sprigs fresh rosemary + plus extra for storage
- 4 strips, fresh orange peel

DIRECTIONS

1. Preheat the sous vide water bath to 135°F.
2. Add the vodka, 3 sprigs rosemary, and 3 strips of orange peel to a resealable zip bag.
3. Seal using the immersion method. Cook for 2 hours.
4. Once done, take the bag out from the water bath and pass-through metal mesh strainer into large bowl.
5. Put one fresh sprig of rosemary and one strip of orange peel into bottle.
6. Pour the prepared snaps into bottle.
7. Chill and serve!

452. STRAWBERRY BASIL SHRUB

2 HOURS | 10 MIN | 12

NUTRITION:
CAL: 208 | FAT: 0 | PROTEIN: 1

INGREDIENTS

- 1 lb. fresh strawberries, trimmed
- 1 lb. ultrafine sugar
- 2 cups balsamic vinegar
- 1 cup water
- 1 cup fresh basil leaves

DIRECTIONS

1. Preheat the sous vide water bath to 135°F.
2. Add all the listed ingredients to a resealable zip bag.
3. Seal using the immersion method. Cook for 2 hours.
4. Once cooked, take the bag out from the water bath and pass-through metal mesh strainer into large bowl.
5. Chill and serve!

453. DRAMBUIE

30 MIN | 15 MIN | 8

NUTRITION:
CAL: 146 | FAT: 3 | PROTEIN: 3

INGREDIENTS

- 1 cup scotch
- ½ cup water
- ½ cup honey
- 2 tsps fresh rosemary
- 2 tsps whole fennel seeds

DIRECTIONS

1. Preheat the sous vide water bath to 180°F.
2. Add all the above ingredients to a resealable zip bag.
3. Seal using the immersion method.
4. Cook for 30 minutes.
5. Once done, take the bag out from the water bath and pass-through metal mesh strainer into a large bowl.
6. Chill and serve!

454. BACON INFUSED BOURBON

1 HOUR | 20 MIN | 8

NUTRITION:
CAL: 346 | FAT: 0| PROTEIN: 0.5

INGREDIENTS

- 2 cups bourbon
- 8 oz. smoked bacon, cooked until crisp
- 3 tbsp bacon fat reserved from cooking
- 3 tbsps light brown sugar

DIRECTIONS

1. Preheat the sous vide water bath to 150°F.
2. Add all the listed ingredients to a resealable zip bag.
3. Seal using the immersion method. Cook for 1 hour.
4. Once done, take the bag out from the water bath and strain the contents through a fine-mesh strainer into a large bowl
5. Transfer the bourbon to the refrigerator and chill until the pork fat solidifies on top. Skim off the fat
6. Then, strain the bourbon a second time through a cheesecloth-lined strainer.
7. Pass it to a storage container and store in the refrigerator

455. LEMONGRASS SYRUP

1 HOUR | 15 MIN | 4

NUTRITION:
CAL: 160 | FAT: 0| PROTEIN:1

INGREDIENTS

- 4 stalks lemongrass, cut into 1-inch pieces
- 1 cup water
- 1 cup ultrafine sugar

DIRECTIONS

1. Preheat the sous vide water bath to 180°F.
2. Add all the above ingredients to a resealable zip bag.
3. Seal using the immersion method.
4. Cook for about 1 hour.
5. Once cooked, remove the bag from the water bath and transfer it to an ice-cold bath.
6. Strain into a large bowl and transfer to a container
7. Serve chilled!

456. THAI BASIL DRINK

1 HOUR | 15 MIN | 4

NUTRITION:
CAL: 176 | FAT:3 | PROTEIN:3

INGREDIENTS

- 1 bunch, Thai basil rinsed
- 1 cup water
- 1 cup ultrafine sugar

DIRECTIONS

1. Preheat the sous vide water bath to 180°F.
2. Add all the listed ingredients to a resealable zipper bag.
3. Seal using the immersion method.
4. Submerge underwater and cook for 1 hour.
5. Once done, take the bag out from the water bath and transfer to an ice bath.
6. Strain into a large bowl and transfer to a container
7. Serve chilled!

457. JALAPENO VODKA

2 HOURS | 10 MIN | 5

NUTRITION:
CAL: 173 | FAT: 0 | PROTEIN: 0.5

INGREDIENTS

- 2 jalapeno peppers
- 1 bottle vodka

DIRECTIONS

1. Preheat the sous vide water bath to 147°F.
2. Cut the peppers and remove the stem, veins and seeds.
3. Add the ingredients to a resealable zipper bag.
4. Seal using the immersion method. Cook for 2 hours.
5. Once done, take the bag out from the water bath and transfer to an ice bath.
6. Strain into a large bowl and transfer to a container
7. Serve chilled!

458. APPLE & CARDAMOM GIN

2 HOURS | 10 MIN | 4

NUTRITION:
CAL: 186 | FAT: 0 | PROTEIN:1

INGREDIENTS

- 1 cup Gin
- 1 pink lady apple cored, sliced into rings
- 1 green cardamom pod

DIRECTIONS

1. Preheat the sous vide water bath to 136.4°F.
2. Add all the above ingredients to a resealable zip bag.
3. Seal using the immersion method. Cook for 2 hours.
4. Once done, take the bag out from the water bath and transfer to an ice bath.
5. Strain into a large bowl and transfer to a container
6. Serve chilled!

459. GINGER BRANDY

2 HOURS | 10 MIN | 4

NUTRITION:
CAL: 207 | FAT:0 | PROTEIN:0.3

INGREDIENTS

- 4 ½ oz. fresh ginger
- 1 ½ cup brandy
- 5 oz. sugar
- 1 cup water

DIRECTIONS

1. Preheat the sous vide water bath to 135°F.
2. Peel and grate the ginger.
3. Add the ginger and brandy to a resealable zip bag and seal using the immersion method. Cook for 2 hours.
4. Then, take a saucepan and place it over medium heat. Add the water and sugar and allow the sugar to dissolve.
5. Strain the brandy and ginger mixture into a clean bottle and add all the sugar syrup.
6. Serve!

9. RUBS, SAUCES AND SEASONINGS

460. SWEET AND SOUR SAUCE

2 HOURS | 10 MIN | 6

NUTRITION:
CAL: 118| FAT: 2| PROTEIN: 2

INGREDIENTS

- 1/3 cup olive oil
- 1 shallot, chopped
- 1 cup fresh pineapple chunks
- ¼ cup rice vinegar
- Salt and pepper, to taste

DIRECTIONS

1. Preheat the sous vide water bath to 130ºF.
2. Combine all ingredients in a Sous Vide bag.
3. Seal the bag using immersion water technique.
4. Cook the pineapple 2 hours.
5. Finishing steps:
6. Remove the bag from the cooker.
7. Open the bag and allow to cool 10 minutes.
8. Transfer the pineapple, and cooking juices into a food blender.
9. Blend until smooth.
10. Serve.

461. BEARNAISE SAUCE

1 HOUR | 20 MIN | 2

NUTRITION:
CAL: 288 | FAT: 27| PROTEIN:4

INGREDIENTS

- ¼ cup white wine
- 2 sprigs fresh tarragon
- 1 shallot, minced
- 2 egg yolks
- ¼ cup butter
- ½ tsp salt
- ½ tsp pepper

DIRECTIONS

1. Preheat the sous vide water bath to 170ºF.
2. Combine all ingredients in a bag and seal. Place in water bath and cook 1 hour.
3. Remove tarragon sprigs. Blend until smooth.

462. BALSAMIC TOMATO AND PINEAPPLE MIX

1 HOUR | 5 MIN | 4

NUTRITION:
CAL: 100 | FAT:5 | PROTEIN: 3

INGREDIENTS

- 1-lb tomatoes, cut into wedges
- 1 cup pineapple, peeled and cubed
- 2 tbsps olive oil
- 2 tbsps balsamic vinegar
- 1 tbsp chives, chopped
- Salt and black pepper to the taste

DIRECTIONS

1. In a sous vide bag, combine the tomatoes with the pineapple and the other ingredients, seal the bag, submerge in the preheated water bath and cook at 140 ºF for 1 hour.
2. Divide between plates and serve as a side dish

463. SPROUTS SALAD

40 MIN | 10 MIN | 4

NUTRITION:
CAL: 100 | FAT: 5 | PROTEIN: 6

INGREDIENTS

- 1 green apple, cored and cubed
- 1 cup cherry tomatoes, halved
- 1 cup shallots, chopped
- 1 lb Brussels sprouts, trimmed and halved
- 2 tbsps olive oil
- Juice of ½ lemon
- ½ tsp chili powder
- 1 tbsp balsamic vinegar
- Salt and black pepper to the taste

DIRECTIONS

1. In a sous vide bag, mix the sprouts with the shallots, tomatoes and the other ingredients, seal the bag, submerge in the preheated water bath and cook at 183 °F for 40 minutes.
2. Divide between plates and serve as a side dish.

464. DILL EGGPLANT

30 MIN | 5 MIN | 4

NUTRITION:
CAL: 57 | FAT: 4 | PROTEIN: 3

INGREDIENTS

- 1 lb eggplant, roughly cubed
- 1 tbsp dill, chopped
- 1 tbsp olive oil
- 1 red onion, chopped
- Juice of 1 lime
- ½ tsp coriander, ground
- ½ tsp rosemary, dried
- A pinch of salt and black pepper

DIRECTIONS

1. In a sous vide bag, mix the eggplant with the dill, oil and the other ingredients, seal the bag and cook in the water bath at 170 °F for 30 minutes.
2. Divide the mix between plates and serve.

465. CREME ANGLAISE

20 MIN | 20 MIN | 2

NUTRITION:
CAL: 319 | FAT: 19 | PROTEIN: 7

INGREDIENTS

- 3 egg yolks
- ½ cup milk
- ¼ cup heavy cream
- ¼ cup sugar
- 1 tsp vanilla

DIRECTIONS

1. Preheat the sous vide water bath to 170ºF.
2. Combine all ingredients in a bag. Seal and cook 20 minutes.
3. Blend sauce until smooth. Transfer to refrigerator and cool completely before serving.

466. APPLESAUCE

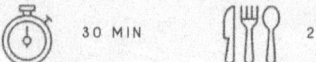

3 HOURS | 30 MIN | 2

NUTRITION:
CAL: 108 | FAT: 0 | PROTEIN: 0

INGREDIENTS
- 3 apples, coarsely chopped
- 1 cinnamon stick

DIRECTIONS
1. Preheat the sous vide water bath to 170°F.
2. Seal all ingredients in the bag. Cook 3 hours.
3. Transfer apples to a bowl. Remove cinnamon stick. Mash to your desired consistency.

467. BASIL TOMATO SAUCE

1 HOUR | 20 MIN | 4

NUTRITION:
CAL: 319 | FAT: 2 | PROTEIN: 5

INGREDIENTS
- 1 can (28-oz) whole tomatoes, crushed
- 1 onion, diced
- 2 cloves garlic, minced
- 1 tbsp olive oil
- 1 bay leaf
- 1 sprig rosemary
- ½ tsp salt
- ½ tsp pepper
- 1 cup fresh basil, chopped
- Cooked pasta for serving

DIRECTIONS
1. Preheat the sous vide water bath to 185°F.
2. Combine all ingredients in a bag. Seal and place in water bath. Cook 1 hour.
3. Remove bay leaves and rosemary sprig. Serve with cooked pasta.

468. SOY CHILI SAUCE

30 MIN | 5 MIN | 6

NUTRITION:
CAL: 67 | FAT: 1 | PROTEIN: 2.5

INGREDIENTS
- 1 cup light soy sauce
- 2 green chilies, chopped, seeded
- ¼ cup honey
- 1 tsp cumin

DIRECTIONS
1. Preheat the sous vide water bath to 160°F.
2. Combine all ingredients in sous vide bag.
3. Seal using water immersion technique.
4. Submerge the bag into the water bath.
5. Cook 30 minutes.
6. Remove the bag from cooker and serve sauce in a bowl.

469. CHEDDAR CHEESE SAUCE

20 MIN | 10 MIN | 6

NUTRITION:
CAL: 48 | FAT: 5 | PROTEIN: 3

INGREDIENTS
- 5 oz Cheddar cheese, sliced
- 1/5 tsp sodium citrate
- 1/3 cup water

DIRECTIONS
1. Preheat the sous vide water bath to 167 °F.
2. Carefully place the ingredients into the vacuum bag, seal the bag and cook in the preheated water bath for 20 minutes.
3. When the time is up, pour the sauce into a bowl and blend with an immersion blender until even.

470. BLUE CHEESE SAUCE

20 MIN | 10 MIN | 5

NUTRITION:
CAL: 56 | FAT:5 | PROTEIN: 3

INGREDIENTS

- 5 oz blue cheese, crumbled
- 1/5 tsp sodium citrate
- 1/3 cup water

DIRECTIONS

1. Preheat the sous vide water bath to 167 °F.
2. Carefully place the ingredients into the vacuum bag, seal the bag and cook in the preheated water bath for 20 minutes.
3. When the time is up, pour the sauce into a bowl and blend with an immersion blender until even.

471. CORIANDER TOMATO AND SPINACH MIX

1 HOUR | 10 MIN | 4

NUTRITION:
CAL: 42 | FAT:2 | PROTEIN: 1

INGREDIENTS

- ½ lb tomatoes, halved
- ½ lb baby spinach
- Juice of 1 lime
- 1 tsp coriander, ground
- ½ tsp chili powder
- 1 tbsp olive oil
- 3 garlic cloves, minced
- 1 tbsp basil, chopped

DIRECTIONS

1. In a sous vide bag, combine the tomatoes with the spinach and the other ingredients, seal the bag, submerge in the preheated water bath and cook at 180 °F for 1 hour.
2. Divide between plates and serve as a side dish.

472. TOMATO AND MANGO SALSA

1 HOUR | 10 MIN | 4

NUTRITION:
CAL: 145 | FAT:7 | PROTEIN: 3

INGREDIENTS

- 1 lb cherry tomatoes, halved
- 1 cup mango, peeled and cubed
- ½ cup black olives, pitted and halved
- 1 tbsp olive oil
- 1 tbsp balsamic vinegar
- Salt and black pepper to the taste
- 1/3 cup red onion, cut into wedges
- ¼ cup cilantro, finely chopped
- 3 tbsps lemon juice

DIRECTIONS

1. In a sous vide bag, mix the tomatoes with the mango, olives and the other ingredients, seal the bag, submerge in the preheated water bath and cook at 140 °F for 1 hour.
2. Divide the mix between plates and serve as a side dish.

473. CRANBERRY SAUCE

2 HOURS | 10 MIN | 4

NUTRITION:
CAL: 36 | FAT: 0.5 | PROTEIN: 0.3

INGREDIENTS
- 1 cup fresh cranberries
- Zest of 1/2 orange
- 7 tbsp white sugar

DIRECTIONS
1. Preheat the sous vide water bath to 194 °F.
2. Carefully place the ingredients into the vacuum bag, seal the bag and cook in the preheated water bath for 2 hours.
3. When the time is up, pour the sauce to a sauceboat and serve with lamb or beef.

474. THYME GARLIC AND LEMON SOUS VIDE RUB

5 MIN | 10 MIN | 2

NUTRITION:
CAL: 80 | FAT: 9 | PROTEIN: 1

INGREDIENTS
- 1 garlic clove
- 2 tbsp olive oil
- 1 tsp dried thyme
- 1 tbsp lemon juice
- Salt and pepper to taste

DIRECTIONS
1. Whisk all the ingredients in a small bowl.
2. Rub the mixture into the lamb leg or ribs and cook according to the instructions.
3. This rub is ideal for cooking lamb but can also be used for fish.
4. You can scale the amount of ingredients depending on the number of meats you are going to cook Sous Vide.

475. CARAMEL SAUCE

2 HOURS | 15 MIN | 4

NUTRITION:
CAL: 120 | FAT: 5 | PROTEIN: 3

INGREDIENTS
- 1/3 cup sugar
- 4 large egg yolks
- ½ tsp vanilla extract
- ¼ tsp fine sea salt

DIRECTIONS
1. Preheat the sous vide water bath to 179°F.
2. In a bowl, add all ingredients and beat until well combined.
3. Place sugar mixture in a cooking pouch. Seal pouch tightly after squeezing out the excess air. Place pouch in sous vide bath and set the cooking time for about 2 hours.
4. Remove pouch from the sous vide bath and carefully open it. Transfer into a bowl and keep aside to cool slightly. Transfer sauce into a jar and refrigerate until cold before serving.

476. CAULIFLOWER ALFREDO

2 HOURS | 15 MIN | 4

NUTRITION:
CAL: 76 | FAT: 6 | PROTEIN: 0

INGREDIENTS
- 2 cups cauliflower florets, chopped
- 2 garlic cloves, crushed
- ½ cup chicken or vegetable broth
- 2 tbsps milk
- 2 tbsps butter
- salt and freshly ground black pepper, to taste

DIRECTIONS
1. Preheat the sous vide water bath to 181°F.
2. Place all ingredients in a cooking pouch. Seal pouch tightly after squeezing out the excess air. Place pouch in the sous vide bath and set the cooking time for about 2 hours.
3. Remove pouch from the sous vide bath and carefully open it.
4. Pour pouch mixture into a blender and pulse until smooth.

477. HERB INFUSED OLIVE OIL

3 HOURS | 10 MIN | 16

NUTRITION:
CAL: 238 | FAT: 27 | PROTEIN: 1

INGREDIENTS

- 2 cups mild olive oil
- 5 fresh herb sprigs (of your choice)

DIRECTIONS

1. Preheat the sous vide water bath to 131°F.
2. Place all ingredients in a cooking pouch. Seal pouch tightly after squeezing out the excess air. Place pouch in sous vide bath and set the cooking time for about 3 hours.
3. Remove pouch from the sous vide bath and carefully open it.
4. Discard herb sprigs from oil. Store oil in a glass bottle or jar.

478. LEMON OLIVE OIL

1 HOUR | 10 MIN | 16

NUTRITION:
CAL: 230 | FAT: 27 | PROTEIN: 2

INGREDIENTS

- 2 cups olive oil
- peel of 1 Meyer lemon
- 1 large bunch lemon thyme

DIRECTIONS

1. Preheat the sous vide water bath to 131°F.
2. Place all ingredients in a cooking pouch. Seal pouch tightly after squeezing out the excess air. Place pouch in sous vide bath and set the cooking time for about 1 hour.
3. Remove pouch from the sous vide bath and carefully open it. Strain oil through a fine-mesh strainer into a bowl.
4. Store oil in a glass bottle or jar. Oil can be refrigerated for up to 2 months.

479. COFFEE BUTTER

3 HOURS | 15 MIN | 8

NUTRITION:
CAL: 407 | FAT: 45 | PROTEIN: 0

INGREDIENTS

- 2 cups salted butter (17.6 oz)
- 1 cup coffee beans (8.8 oz)

DIRECTIONS

1. Preheat the sous vide water bath to 194°F.
2. In a cooking pouch, place butter and coffee beans. Seal pouch tightly after squeezing out the excess air. Place pouch in sous vide bath and set the cooking time for about 3 hours.
3. Remove pouch from the sous vide bath and carefully open it. With a sieve, strain the butter into a bowl. Discard coffee beans.
4. Place butter into sealed bag and refrigerate until serving

480. GARLIC CONFIT

7 HOURS | 15 MIN | 4

NUTRITION:
CAL: 59 | FAT: 3 | PROTEIN: 1

INGREDIENTS

- 2 jars peeled garlic
- 2 tbsps apple cider vinegar or sherry vinegar
- 1 tbsp dried thyme
- olive oil, as required

DIRECTIONS

1. Preheat the sous vide water bath to 180°F.
2. In 2 mason jars, divide garlic, vinegar, and thyme. Fill jars with olive oil to the brim and cover with the lid tightly. Place jars in sous vide bath and set the cooking time for about 7 hours.
3. Remove the jars from the sous vide bath and place onto a wire rack to cool completely.
4. Store in the refrigerator for no more than a week.

481. RASPBERRY INFUSED VINAIGRETTE

2 HOURS | 25 MIN | 4

NUTRITION:
CAL: 193 | FAT:11 | PROTEIN: 1

INGREDIENTS

- 1 cup fresh raspberries
- 1 cup white wine or champagne vinegar
- For Raspberry Vinaigrette:
- 3 tbsps infused raspberry vinegar
- 1 tbsp honey
- 1 tbsp orange juice
- 1 shallot, finely chopped
- 5 tbsps olive oil
- salt and freshly ground black pepper, to taste

DIRECTIONS

1. Preheat the sous vide water bath to 140ºF.
2. Place raspberries and vinegar in a cooking pouch. Seal pouch tightly after squeezing out the excess air. Place pouch in sous vide bath and set the cooking time for 1-2 hours.
3. Remove pouch from the sous vide bath and immediately plunge into a bowl of ice water for about 15-20 minutes. Strain vinegar and transfer into an airtight container.
4. For raspberry vinaigrette: in a bowl, add infused vinegar, honey, and orange juice and beat until well combined. Stir in the shallots and let sit for about 10 minutes.
5. Slowly add olive oil, beating continuously until well combined. Stir in salt and black pepper and serve.

482. INFUSED RASPBERRY SYRUP

2 HOURS | 5 MIN | 4

NUTRITION:
CAL: 63 | FAT:1 | PROTEIN: 1

INGREDIENTS

- 1-2/3 cups white wine or champagne vinegar
- 1 cup raspberries

DIRECTIONS

1. Preheat the sous vide water bath to 140ºF.
2. Place vinegar and raspberries in a cooking pouch. Seal pouch tightly after squeezing out the excess air. Place pouch in sous vide bath and set the cooking time for about 1-2 hours.
3. Remove pouch from the sous vide bath and immediately immerse in a large bowl of ice water for about 15-20 minutes. Strain the vinegar. Store in a sealed container.

483. BLACKBERRY VINEGAR

3 HOURS | 5 MIN | 4

NUTRITION:
CAL: 129 | FAT:3 | PROTEIN: 1

INGREDIENTS

- 4 cups white balsamic vinegar
- 3 cups blackberries

DIRECTIONS

1. Preheat the sous vide water bath to 153ºF.
2. Place vinegar and blackberries in a cooking pouch. Seal pouch tightly after squeezing out the excess air. Place pouch in sous vide bath and set the cooking time for about 2-3 hours.
3. Remove pouch from the sous vide bath and immediately immerse in a large bowl of ice water for about 15-20 minutes. Strain the vinegar. Place in a sealed container and store in refrigerator for up to 6 weeks.

484. BLACKBERRY BASIL VINEGAR

3 HOURS | 15 MIN | 4

NUTRITION:
CAL: 365 | FAT: 0 | PROTEIN: 1

INGREDIENTS

- 4 cups white balsamic vinegar
- 3 cups blackberries
- ½ cup basil leaves

DIRECTIONS

1. Preheat the sous vide water bath to 153°F.
2. Place all ingredients in a cooking pouch. Seal pouch tightly after squeezing out the excess air. Place pouch in sous vide bath and set the cooking time for about 2-3 hours.
3. Remove pouch from sous vide bath occasionally and with your fingers, massage the mixture to mix.
4. Remove pouch from the sous vide bath and carefully open it.
5. Strain vinegar through a fine mesh strainer into a container. Discard the solids.
6. Keep in refrigerator for up to six weeks.

485. RICOTTA CHEESE

40 MIN | 10 MIN | 6

NUTRITION:
CAL: 331 | FAT: 25 | PROTEIN: 11

INGREDIENTS

- 8 cups whole milk
- 1 cup heavy cream
- 1 tsp sea salt
- 1 tsp citric acid

DIRECTIONS

1. Preheat the sous vide water bath to 195°F.
2. Add all ingredients to a bowl that fits into a cooking pouch. Arrange bowl inside cooking pouch and seal tightly after squeezing out the excess air. Place pouch in sous vide bath and set the cooking time for about 35-40 minutes.
3. Remove pouch from the sous vide bath and carefully open it. Remove bowl from cooking pouch.
4. With a slotted spoon, gently scoop out curd from top and transfer into straining vessel.
5. Strain ricotta until desired consistency of cheese is achieved.

486. CRÈME FRAICHE

12 HOURS | 10 MIN | 4

NUTRITION:
CAL: 205 | FAT: 22 | PROTEIN: 1

INGREDIENTS

- 1 cup heavy whipping cream
- 2 tbsps low-Fat buttermilk

DIRECTIONS

1. Preheat the sous vide water bath to 149°F.
2. Place all ingredients in a mason jar. Cover with cap tightly. Place jar in sous vide bath and set the cooking time for about 8 and no more than 12 hours.
3. Carefully remove jar from sous vide bath and open it.
4. Transfer mixture into an airtight container. Seal tightly and refrigerate for up to 3 weeks.

487. PERSIMMON BUTTER

1.5 HOURS | 10 MIN | 4

NUTRITION:
CAL: 157 | FAT: 2 | PROTEIN: 1

INGREDIENTS

- 2 lbs ripe Fuyu persimmons, peeled, hulled and cut into ¼-inch thick wedges
- ¼ cup apple juice
- 1 tsp lemon juice
- 1 cinnamon stick
- 1 tsp vanilla
- ¼ tsp salt

DIRECTIONS

1. Preheat the sous vide water bath to 185ºF.
2. Place all ingredients in a cooking pouch. Seal pouch tightly after squeezing out the excess air. Place pouch in sous vide bath and set the cooking time for about 1½ hours.
3. Remove pouch from the sous vide bath and set aside to cool slightly.
4. In a food processor, add mixture and pulse until smooth.

488. STRAWBERRY & GRAPEFRUIT COMPOTE

30 MIN | 10 MIN | 4

NUTRITION:
CAL: 69 | FAT: 1 | PROTEIN: 1

INGREDIENTS

- juice grapefruit
- 1 tbsp honey
- ½ tsp vanilla extract
- 1-lb fresh strawberries, hulled

DIRECTIONS

1. Preheat the sous vide water bath to 180ºF.
2. In a bowl, add grapefruit juice, honey, and vanilla extract and beat until well combined.
3. Place strawberries and honey mixture in a cooking pouch. Seal pouch tightly after squeezing out the excess air. Place pouch in sous vide bath and set the cooking time for about 30 minutes.
4. Remove pouch from the sous vide bath and carefully open it. Keep aside to cool slightly.
5. In a blender, pulse strawberry mixture until desired consistency is achieved.
6. Serve immediately.

489. HOLLANDAISE

55 MIN | 15 MIN | 4

NUTRITION:
CAL: 244 | FAT: 26 | PROTEIN: 2

INGREDIENTS

- 3 large egg yolks, beaten well
- ½ cup butter
- 1 tbsp fresh lemon juice
- ½ tsp salt
- pinch of dry mustard

DIRECTIONS

1. Preheat the sous vide water bath to 149ºF.
2. Place all ingredients in a wide mouth glass jar. Cover with cap tightly. Place jar in sous vide bath and set the cooking time for about 45-55 minutes, shaking the jar once after 20-25 minutes.
3. Carefully remove jar from sous vide bath and open it.
4. With a stick blender, blend mixture until smooth.

490. PEACH CHUTNEY

5 HOURS | 15 MIN | 4

NUTRITION:
CAL: 109 | FAT: 4 | PROTEIN: 1

INGREDIENTS

For Pickling Spice:

- 1 tbsp whole mustard seeds
- 2 tsps ground cinnamon
- 1½ tsps whole allspice berries
- 1 tsp whole coriander seeds
- ½ tsp red pepper flakes
- 6 whole cloves
- 1 bay leaf, crumbled finely

For Chutney:

- 1/8 cup apple cider vinegar
- 1 tbsp olive oil
- ¼ cup packed brown sugar
- 1 tbsp pickling spice
- 1 tsp chili powder
- ¾ tsp mustard seeds
- ¼ tsp curry powder
- ½ lb peaches, peeled, pitted, and chopped
- ½ yellow onion, chopped
- 1 garlic clove, minced
- 1/8 cup preserved ginger, chopped
- ½ cup raisins, chopped roughly

DIRECTIONS

1. Preheat the sous vide water bath to 182ºF.
2. For pickling spice: in a spice grinder, add all spices and grind until powdered finely.
3. Keep in an airtight container.
4. In a small bowl, add vinegar, oil, brown sugar, pickling spice, chili powder, mustard seeds, and curry powder and mix until a paste is formed.
5. In a cooking pouch, place remaining ingredients and spice paste. Seal pouch tightly after squeezing out the excess air. Place pouch in sous vide bath and set the cooking time for about 5 hours.
6. Remove pouch from the sous vide bath and set aside to cool slightly. Mash pouch mixture roughly.
7. Transfer into an airtight container and keep in refrigerator.

491. HOT SAUCE

20 MIN | 15 MIN | 4

NUTRITION:
CAL: 61 | FAT: 2 | PROTEIN: 1

INGREDIENTS

- 1½ lb fresh red jalapeño peppers, stemmed, seeded, and chopped roughly
- 9 garlic cloves, smashed
- 1 tsp sea salt
- 3 tbsps simple syrup
- 1/3 cup rice vinegar

DIRECTIONS

1. Preheat the sous vide water bath to 210ºF.
2. In a food processor, pulse peppers, garlic, and salt until puréed.
3. In a cooking pouch, place puréed mixture. Seal pouch tightly after squeezing out the excess air. Place pouch in sous vide bath and set the cooking time for about 20 minutes.
4. Remove pouch from the sous vide bath and carefully open. Transfer mixture into a bowl. Add simple syrup and vinegar and stir to combine.
5. Transfer into an airtight container and keep in refrigerator for up to 2 weeks.

492. ORANGE ROSEMARY VINEGAR

3 HOURS | 15 MIN | 16

NUTRITION:
CAL: 89 | FAT: 0 | PROTEIN: 0

INGREDIENTS

- 4 cups balsamic vinegar
- zest of 10 blood oranges
- 10 fresh rosemary springs

DIRECTIONS

1. Preheat the sous vide water bath to 153°F.
2. Place all ingredients in a cooking pouch. Seal pouch tightly after squeezing out the excess air. Place pouch in sous vide bath and set the cooking time for about 2-3 hours.
3. Remove pouch from sous vide bath occasionally and with your fingers, massage the mixture to mix.
4. Remove pouch from the sous vide bath and carefully open it.
5. Strain vinegar through a fine mesh strainer into a container. Discard the solids.
6. Keep in refrigerator for up to six weeks.

493. LEMON GINGER VINEGAR

3 HOURS | 10 MIN | 16

NUTRITION:
CAL: 19 | FAT: 0 | PROTEIN: 1

INGREDIENTS

- 2 cups white wine vinegar
- peel of 1 lemon
- 1 - 1-inch piece of fresh ginger root, peeled, and cut into ¼-inch-thick rounds
- 1 thick lemon slice
- 1 tbsp granulated sugar

DIRECTIONS

1. Preheat the sous vide water bath to 153°F.
2. Place all ingredients in a cooking pouch. Seal pouch tightly after squeezing out the excess air. Place pouch in sous vide bath and set the cooking time for about 3 hours.
3. Remove pouch from the sous vide bath and carefully open it. Strain the mixture through a cheesecloth-lined fine-mesh strainer into a jar.
4. Keep in refrigerator for up to six weeks.

494. SPICY BBQ SAUCE

40 MIN | 25 MIN | 8

NUTRITION:
CAL: 38 | FAT: 2 | PROTEIN: 3

INGREDIENTS

- 1 ½ lb. small tomatoes
- ¼ cup apple cider vinegar
- ¼ tsp sugar
- 1 tbsp Worcestershire sauce
- ½ tbsp liquid hickory smoke
- 2 tsp smoked paprika
- 2 tsp garlic powder
- 1 tsp onion powder
- Salt to taste
- ½ tsp chili powder
- ½ tsp cayenne pepper
- 4 tbsp water

DIRECTIONS

1. Preheat the sous vide water bath to 185°F.
2. Separate the tomatoes into two vacuum-sealable bags. Release air by the water displacement method, seal and submerge the bags in the water bath. Set the timer for 40 minutes.
3. Once the timer has stopped, remove and unseal the bag. Transfer the tomatoes to a blender and puree until smooth and thick. Do not add water.
4. Put a pot over medium heat, add the tomato puree and the remaining listed ingredients. Bring to a boil, stirring continuously for 20 minutes. A thick consistency should be achieved.

495. PERI PERI SAUCE

30 MIN | 45 MIN | 16

NUTRITION:
CAL: 129 | FAT: 14 | PROTEIN: 2

INGREDIENTS

- 2 lb. red chili peppers
- 4 cloves garlic, crushed
- 2 tsp smoked paprika
- 1 cup cilantro leaves, chopped
- ½ cup basil leaves, chopped
- 1 cup olive oil
- 2 lemons' juice

DIRECTIONS

1. Preheat the sous vide water bath to 185°F.
2. Place the peppers in a vacuum-sealable bag. Release air by the water displacement method, seal and submerge the bag in the water bath. Set the timer for 30 minutes.
3. Once the timer has stopped, remove and unseal the bag. Transfer the pepper and the remaining listed ingredients to a blender and puree to smooth.
4. Store in an airtight container, refrigerate, and use for up to 7 days.

496. CHICKEN STOCK

12 HOURS | 15 MIN | 10

NUTRITION:
CAL: 220 | FAT: 15 | PROTEIN: 22

INGREDIENTS

- 2 lb. chicken, any parts – thighs, breasts
- 5 cups water
- 2 celery sticks, chopped
- 2 white onions, chopped

DIRECTIONS

1. Preheat the sous vide water bath to 194°F. Separate all the ingredients in 2 vacuum bags, fold the top of the bags 2–3 times. Place in the water bath. Set the timer for 12 hours.
2. Once the timer has stopped, remove the bag and transfer the ingredients to a pot. Boil the ingredients over high heat for 10 minutes. Turn off heat and strain. Use the stock as a soup base.

497. ONION POMODORO SAUCE

15 MIN | 20 MIN | 4

NUTRITION:
CAL: 190 | FAT: 11 | PROTEIN: 4

INGREDIENTS

- 4 cups tomatoes, halved and cored
- ½ onion, chopped
- ½ tsp sugar
- ¼ cup fresh oregano
- 2 garlic cloves, minced
- Salt and black pepper to taste
- 5 tbsp olive oil

DIRECTIONS

1. Preheat the sous vide water bath to 175°F. Place the tomatoes, oregano, garlic, onion and sugar in a vacuum-sealable bag.
2. Release air by the water displacement method, seal and submerge the bag in the water bath.
3. Cook for 15 minutes.
4. Once the timer has stopped, remove the bag and transfer the content into a blender and mix for 1 minute until smooth. Top with black pepper.

498. BELL PEPPER PUREE

25 MIN | 15 MIN | 4

NUTRITION:
CAL: 220 | FAT: 19 | PROTEIN: 3

INGREDIENTS

- 8 red bell peppers, cored
- 1/3 cup olive oil
- 2 tbsp lemon juice
- 3 cloves garlic, crushed
- 2 tsp sweet paprika

DIRECTIONS

1. Preheat the sous vide water bath to 183°F. Put the bell peppers, garlic, and olive oil in a vacuum-sealable bag.
2. Release air by the water displacement method, seal and submerge the bags in the water bath.
3. Set the timer for 20 minutes and cook.
4. Once the timer has stopped, remove the bag and unseal it.
5. Transfer the bell pepper and garlic to a blender and puree to smooth.
6. Place a pan over medium heat; add bell pepper puree and the remaining listed ingredients.
7. Cook for 3 minutes. Serve warm or cold as a dip

499. JALAPENO SEASONING

45 MIN | 7 MIN | 4

NUTRITION:
CAL: 20 | FAT: 2 | PROTEIN: 1.8

INGREDIENTS

- 2 jalapeno peppers
- 2 green chili peppers
- 2 cloves garlic, crushed
- 1 onion, peeled only
- 3 tsp oregano powder
- 3 tsp black pepper powder
- 2 tsp rosemary powder
- 10 tsp aniseed powder

DIRECTIONS

1. Preheat the sous vide water bath to 185°F.
2. Place the peppers and onion in a vacuum-sealable bag.
3. Release air by the water displacement method, seal and submerge the bag in the water bath.
4. Set the timer for 40 minutes.
5. Once the timer has stopped, remove and unseal the bag.
6. Transfer the pepper and onion with 2 tbsps of water to a blender and puree to smooth.
7. Place a pot over low heat, add the pepper puree and the remaining listed ingredients.
8. Simmer for 15 minutes.
9. Turn off heat and cool. Store in a spice jar, refrigerate, and use for up to 7 days.
10. Use it as a spice in other foods.

500. BEEF BROTH

13 HOURS | 15 MIN | 15

NUTRITION:
CAL: 184 | FAT:14 | PROTEIN:16

INGREDIENTS

- 3 lb. beef feet
- 1 ½ lb. beef bones
- 5 cups tomato paste
- 6 sweet onions
- 3 heads garlic
- 6 tbsp black pepper
- 5 sprigs thyme
- 4 bay leaves
- 10 cups water

DIRECTIONS

1. Preheat an oven to 425°F.
2. Place beef bones and beef feet in a roasting pan and rub them with the tomato paste.
3. Add garlic and onion. Place aside.
4. Place and crumble ground beef in another roasting pan.
5. Place the roasting pans in the oven and roast until dark brown.
6. Once done, drain Fat from the roasting pans.
7. Preheat the sous vide water bath to 195°F. Separate the ground beef, roasted vegetables, black pepper, thyme, and bay leaves in 3 vacuum bags.
8. Deglaze the roasting pans with water and add it to the bags.
9. Fold the top of the bags 2 to 3 times.
10. Place the bags in the water bath and clip it to the Sous Vide container. Set the timer for 13 hours.
11. Once the timer has stopped, remove the bags and transfer the ingredients to a pot.
12. Bring the ingredients to a boil over high heat.
13. Cook for 15 minutes. Turn off heat and strain.
14. Use the stock as a soup base.

COOKING CHARTS

MEAT	TEMPERATURE (°F)	TIME
Beef Steak, rare	129	1 h 30 min
Beef Steak, medium-rare	136	1 h 30 min
Beef Steak, well done	158	1 h 30 min
Beef Roast, rare	133	7 h
Beef Roast, medium-rare	140	6 h
Beef Roast, well done	158	5 h
Beef Tough Cuts, rare	136	24 h
Beef Tough Cuts, medium-rare	149	16 h
Beef Tough Cuts, well done	185	8 h
Lamb Tenderloin, Rib eye, T-bone, Cutlets	134	4 h
Lamb Roast, Leg	134	10 h
Lamb Flank Steak, Brisket	134	12 h
Pork Chop, rare	136	1 h
Pork Chop, medium-rare	144	1 h
Pork Chop, well done	158	1 h
Pork Roast, rare	136	3 h
Pork Roast, medium-rare	144	3 h
Pork Roast, well done	158	3 h
Pork Tough Cuts, rare	144	16 h
Pork Tough Cuts, medium-rare	154	12 h
Pork Tough Cuts, well done	154	8 h
Pork Tenderloin	134	1 h 30 min
Pork Baby Back Ribs	165	6 h
Pork Cutlets	134	5 h
Pork Spare Ribs	160	12 h
Pork Belly (quick)	185	5 h
Pork Belly (slow)	167	24 h
POULTRY		
Chicken White Meat, super-supple	140	2 h
Chicken White Meat, tender and juicy	149	1 h
Chicken White Meat, well done	167	1 h
Chicken Breast, bone-in	146	2 h 30 min
Chicken Breast, boneless	146	1 h
Turkey Breast, bone-in	146	4 h
Turkey Breast, boneless	146	2 h 30 min
Duck Breast	134	1 h 30 min
Chicken Dark Meat, tender	149	1 h 30 min
Chicken Dark Meat, falling off the bone	167	1 h 30 min
Chicken Leg or Thigh, bone-in	165	4 h
Chicken Thigh, boneless	165	1 h
Turkey Leg or Thigh	165	2 h

Duck Leg	165	8 h
Split Game Hen	150	6 h
FISH AND SEAFOOD		
Fish, tender	104	40 min
Fish, tender and flaky	122	40 min
Fish, well done	140	40 min
Salmon, Tuna, Trout, Mackerel, Halibut, Snapper, Sole	126	30 min
Lobster	140	50 min
Scallops	140	50 min
Shrimp	140	35 min
VEGETABLES		
Vegetables, root (carrots, potato, parsnips, beets, celery root, turnips)	183	3 h
Vegetables, tender (asparagus, broccoli, cauliflower, fennel, onions, pumpkin, eggplant, green beans, corn)	183	1 h
Vegetables, greens (kale, spinach, collard greens, Swiss chard)	183	5 min
FRUITS		
Fruit, firm (apple, pear)	183	45 min
Fruit, for puree	185	30 min
Fruit, berries for topping desserts (blueberries, blackberries, raspberries, strawberries, cranberries)	154	30 min

What Temperature Should Be Used? The rule of thumb is that the thicker the piece, the longer it should cook. Higher temperatures shorten the cooking time. Lower temperatures may take longer.

	TEMPERATURE	MIN COOKING TIME	MAX COOKING TIME
Chicken			
Rare	140°F (60°C)	1 hour	3 hours
Medium	150°F (65°C)	1 hour	3 hours
Well Done	167°F (75°C)	1 hour	3 hours
Beef Steak			
Rare	130°F (54°C)	1½ hours	3 hours
Medium	140°F (60°C)	1½ hours	3 hours
Well Done	145°F (63°C)	1½ hours	3 hours

	Roast Beef		
Rare	133°F (56°C)	7 hours	16 hours
Medium	140°F (60°C)	6 hours	14 hours
Well Done	158°F (70°C)	5 hours	11 hours
	Pork Chop Bone-In		
Rare	136°F (58°C)	1 hour	4 hours
Medium	144°F (62°C)	1 hour	4 hours
Well Done	158°F (70°C)	1 hour	4 hours
	Pork Loin		
Rare	136°F (58°C)	3 hours	5½ hours
Medium	144°F (62°C)	3 hours	5 hours
Well Done	158°F (70°C)	3 hours	3½ hours
	Fish		
Tender	104°F (40°C)	½ hour	½ hour
Medium	124°F (51°C)	½ hour	1 hour
Well Done	131°F (55°C)	½ hour	1½ hours
	Eggs		
Soft Yolk	140°F (60°C)	1 hour	1 hour
Creamy Yolk	145°F (63°C)	¾ hour	1 hour
	Green Vegetables		
	183°F (84°C)	¼ hour	¾ hour
	Roots		
	183°F (84°C)	1 hour	3 hours
	Fruits		
Warm	154°F (68°C)	1¾ hour	2½ hour
Soft Fruits	185°F (85°C)	½ hour	1½ hour

MEASUREMENT CONVERSIONS

VOLUME EQUIVALENTS (LIQUID)

US STANDARD	US STD (OZ)	METRIC (approx)
2 tbsps	1 fl.oz.	30 ml
¼ cup	2 fl.oz.	60 ml
½ cup	4 fl.oz.	120 ml
1 cup	8 fl.oz.	240 ml
1 ½ cup	12 fl.oz.	355 ml
2 cup or 1 pint	16 fl.oz.	475 ml
4 cup or 1 quart	32 fl.oz.	1 L
1 gallon	128 fl.oz.	4 L

OVEN TEMPERATURES

FAHRENHEIT (F)	CELSIUS (approx)
250° F	120° C
300° F	150° C
325° F	165° C
350° F	180° C
375° F	190° C
400° F	200° C
425° F	220° C
450° F	230° C

WEIGHT EQUIVALENTS

US STANDARD	METRIC (approx)
½ oz	15 g
1 oz	30 g
2 oz	60 g
4 oz	115 g
8 oz	225 g
12 oz	340 g
16 oz or 1 lb	455 g

VOLUME EQUIVALENTS (DRY)

US STANDARD	METRIC (approx)
¼ tsp	1 ml
½ tsp	2 ml
¾ tsp	4 ml
1 tsp	5 ml
1 tbsp	15 ml
¼ cup	60 ml
1/3 cup	80 ml
½ cup	120 ml
1 cup	240 ml
2 cup or 1 pint	475 ml
3 cup	700 ml
4 cup or 1 quart	1 L